Net trading

ft.com

There is a new world which we can look at but we cannot see. Yet within it, the forces of technology and imagination are overturning the way we work and the way we do business.

ft.com is both gateway and guide to this world.

We understand it because we are part of it. But we also understand the needs of businesses which are taking their first steps into it, and those still standing hesitantly on the threshold. Above all, we understand that, as with all business challenges, the key to success lies not with the technology itself, but with the people who must use it and manage it. People like you.

See the world.
Visit us at www.ft.com today.

Net trading

get online with the new trading strategies

Alpesh B. Patel

ft.com, an imprint of

PEARSON EDUCATION LIMITED

Head Office:
Edinburgh Gate
Harlow CM20 2JE
Tel: +44 (0)1279 623623
Fax: +44 (0)1279 431059

London Office:
128 Long Acre
London WC2E 9AN
Tel: +44 (0)207 447 2000
Fax: +44 (0)207 240 5771
Website: www.ft.com

First published in Great Britain in 2000

ISBN 0 273 64502 1

British Library Cataloguing in Publication Data
A catalogue record for this book is available from the British Library.

10 9 8 7 6 5 4 3 2 1

Typeset by M Rules.
Printed and bound by Redwood Books, Trowbridge, Wiltshire.

The Publishers' policy is to use paper manufactured from sustainable forests.

Alpesh B. Patel is a barrister who now trades and invests for a living. As a barrister, Alpesh was involved in advising banks, building societies, and pension funds on financial services. He started buying stocks sixteen years ago at the age of twelve, moving on from privatization stocks to penny shares. Today he concentrates on futures, options, and stock trading, making extensive use of the internet for research and combining this with his own technical analysis systems. Alpesh also owns stocks in US, UK, French and Indian companies. Alpesh is a non-executive director and founder of several internet start-ups.

Alpesh is the author of *Trading Online: A Step-by-Step Guide to CyberProfits* (FT Pitman 1999), *The Mind of a Trader: Lessons in Trading Strategy from the World's Leading Traders* (FT Pitman 1998), and *Your Questions Answered: Money, Savings and Financial Planning* (Rushmere Wynne 1997). *Trading Online* was the Number 1 best-selling investment book on Amazon UK, and reached Number 2 on the overall best-seller list – even out-selling the *Star Wars: Episode 1* book for a long while.

Alpesh has appeared on Sky Business News, CNBC Europe Squawk Box, BBC TV and Radio, as well as numerous US radio shows, to discuss trading, and has provided evidence to the UK Parliamentary Select Committee on Trade and Industry's Report on E-Commerce. He writes a column for the *Financial Times* and is the presenter of Money on the Net on Bloomberg TV.

Alpesh lectures on online trading, trading psychology, and technical analysis around the world and in the latter half of 1999 and the first half of 2000 had thirteen speaking engagements, including Central America, the Middle East and Australasia, and a six-city tour of the UK. He also acts as consultant up to CEO level of multi-billion dollar internet content and online trading companies advising on market entry and expansion strategy, providing site content.

He is an Associate of the Society of Technical Analysts, a Colleague of the International Federation of Technical Analysts, a Member of the Global Association of Risk Professionals and a Member of the Bar Association of Commerce, Finance and Industry, and has a degree in Law from King's College, London and a degree in Philosophy, Politics and Economics from St Anne's College, Oxford University.

You can find out more about Alpesh's courses at www.tradermind.com

Contents

This book is for my wife, Selina Patel:
my greatest publicist.

ॐ

Without beginning, middle or end, of infinite power,
of infinite arms, whose eyes are the moon and sun,
I see thee, whose face is flaming fire,
Burning this whole universe with Thy radiance.
Bhagavad Gita xi.19

You are what your deep driving desire is.
As your desire is, so is your will.
As your will is, so is your deed.
As your deed is, so is your destiny.
Upanishads

Acknowledgments

I am most grateful to Richard Stagg for yet another excellent opportunity to pursue a very enjoyable project indeed. I must also thank him for the ideas which helped shape and steer the book's direction as it was being constructed in the dryport of my wordprocessor, before sailing off the print machines into the open oceans of the world's bookstores.

Selina, my wife, who was as worried about deadlines as my editor. How foolish was I to embark on a book during a summer when she bought a soft-top sportscar? Oh no, I would *much* rather sit for hours day and night in front of a computer, curtains closed to stop the sun's glare entering my office, than speed down the highways and byways in a sleek red two-seater, with the warm evening air blowing through what is left of my hair.

The team at Pearson Education has done yet another magnificent job. Especial thanks to Kate Jenkins, who truly appreciates the importance of publicity to the world of publishing and has been an excellent sounding board on ideas about book promotion.

Thank you Claudia Orrell for great ideas on title and for searching the thesaurus for just the right combination of words to capture in eight words what took me 80,000 to say. I agree with you, 'Murderously exotic online trading tactics of the globe's numero uno mercantiles' was, in hindsight, not the best of subtitles.

Then there will be people I will probably not meet who are no less a part of the successful castlist. Those who will edit, proof, design, print, sell, promote and do just about everything to make sure this book hits the Number 1 slot in its category as surely as its predecessor did. Thank you all. I especially want to thank Penelope Allport and Helen Baxter. As I read all the amendments to my manuscript, I feel they should be co-authors!

No one should believe that producing a successful finance book is a solitary one-man affair. It is undoubtedly teamwork at its best.

Preface

Even Polynesians do it

E-trading is fast becoming as mainstream as owning stocks. And owning and trading stocks is becoming as essential to making money as having a job. By 2002 one in three investors will have an online account; there will be 25 million online accounts in the US alone. In 1996 there were a mere 1.6m. Whoever you are, whatever you do, if you want a piece of the action, you need to know the leading profit strategies of online traders. That is the aim of this book.

Whoever you are, whatever you do, if you want a piece of the action, you need to know the leading profit strategies of online traders.

The popularity of online trading is not a purely American phenomenon. You know you are on to a winner when someone opens an online trading account from Easter Island, a Chilean territory in Polynesia. What's more, by 2002 there will be an estimated 8 million online accounts in Europe, a collection of independent countries located several thousand miles to the east of New York State.

Not just your average run-of-the-mill book

This is your book. It is written for online traders by an online trader, with the best tips and strategies from other online traders; people who do well, for those who want to do better. Each strategy is given in detail so you know the level of risk, what to look for before executing it, the precise entry point with examples, and the exit point.

What this book covers:

- day trading (with ample warnings) as well as other short- to medium-term trading
- trading of stocks and also futures and options. All three have similar risk profiles and attract similar audiences and technology, meaning that all three are possible for the average investor, yet no one book combines all three for an online day trading audience

■ topics never before seen in one volume, that logically belong together: online trading; psychology; systems; money and risk management; strategy; advice from both online traders and leading institutional traders.

What is in the book

Trading time frame	Medium	Reader experience level	Product	Strategy coverage
Day trading ✔	Thru Direct Access ✔	Beginner ✔	Stocks ✔	Superficial
Short- to medium-term ✔	Trading online ✔	Intermediate ✔	Options ✔	Detailed ✔
Medium- to long-term	Off-line software ✔	Rocket scientist level	Futures ✔	Expert comment ✔

No book is enough to make you a good trader. This is especially true of short-term trading. Just as clothes do not maketh the man, nor do computers, software, modem, and books maketh the trader. What a book can do, however, is teach you so much that you can avoid every mistake possible just by reading. From a book you can learn enough to make as much profit as possible from reading books alone.

Why we trade online: masters of the universe and barbarians at the gates

We online traders trade online to save commissions, to be in charge of our investments, to be more in control of our futures, to keep more of the profits, because we refuse to pay underworked, overpaid, underperforming, overeducated, talentless fund managers.

No longer are we obliged to hand our cash over to the institutions because they hold all the information. They can strive to be masters of the universe all they want, but know this: we barbarians are at their gates. Their palaces, paid for by our toils, will stand no more. The internet has further democratized capitalism. The right to own property is a fundamental human right. We vigorously exercise our right to trade property in the form of securities.

We trade online because we refuse to pay underworked, overpaid, underperforming, overeducated, talentless fund managers.

We hold these truths to be self-evident, that all traders are created equal, that they are endowed by the internet with certain inalienable rights, that among these are inexpensive trading in the pursuit of wealth. That to secure these rights, brokers are instituted among men and women, deriving their income from the commission from traders. That whenever any form of brokerage becomes destructive of this end, it is the right of traders to abandon such form of brokerage, and to institute new forms of brokerage, laying their foundation on such principles and organizing their facilities in such form as to them shall seem most likely to affect their e-trading's best interests and wealth.

Is it safe?

I cannot highlight often enough, and believe me I repeat the warnings many, many times throughout the book, online trading can be risky – like any trading. Popular perception has it that online trading is some secret possessed by the few who are in the know and who therefore make a fortune, while the rest of us can merely look in from the outside. The truth is that online trading is like most activities that carry some degree of risk, be it exercise, driving, drinking, smoking – they can be dangerous and highly risky depending on YOU.

You will undoubtedly have met the two stereotypes of e-trading. They appear in every one of the thousands of articles written in near-identical fashion. You know the ones. They begin: "Jason used to work as a dentist, now he only has to walk from the bedroom to the living room to get to work. He dons a baseball cap, jeans and sneakers, and stares hypnotized at the screen for hours each day . . ."

So, in the same fashion, let me reacquaint you with our stereotypes. First, meet Richard Traderman, his friends call him "Rich." Rich is 25 years old. He used to wait tables in a rough neighborhood in the Bronx, New York. His other job was as a cleaner at JFK. He worked on minimum wage. Last year he left his job, borrowed $2000, and decided to day trade. In little over six months he had turned $2000 into $300,000 and moved to a studio flat in Manhattan. By the end of next year he aims to have made his first million.

Now meet Lucy Spinster. Her friends call her "Loser" for short. A Harvard graduate, she practised in a prominent New York international law firm. The pay was excellent, she lived in a penthouse apartment in Manhattan but she dreamed of taking charge of her destiny, living an entrepreneurial dream. Last year she scraped together her savings of $100,000 and started online treading. She would monitor her positions at work and do research at night.

After three months she felt confident enough to leave her high-powered job to trade full time. But losses mounted. It was not as easy as it first seemed. It was as if having more time to focus on her trading led her to chase the markets and overtrade.

She sold her apartment last week to pay off outstanding credit card debts. The buyer was a certain Richard Traderman.

There are many more Lucy Spinsters than Richard Tradermans. Short-term online trading is not for everyone. Some would be better off buying and holding. Some would be better off giving their money to a fund manager. This book is also aimed at helping you to determine if online trading is for you. Unlike other books there is no promise of guaranteed wealth for all. Some people should not trade online. Inside you will discover if you are one of them. If you are, then at least you will know.

> **Unlike other books there is no promise of guaranteed wealth for all. Some people should not trade online. Inside you will discover if you are one of them. If you are, then at least you will know.**

The vast amount of information on the internet has the ability to create the illusion among traders that they are experts. But they are no more expert for having access to information than a law librarian would be as a law professor. Trading is difficult, it requires far more skill than knowing where the books are. This book tries to help you to avoid the potholes, and takes you through what experienced online traders know about:

- creating systems
- strategies online to extract market profit
- best web-sites
- using technical indicators
- the importance of trading psychology.

If you ignore these things, then, yes, online trading can be risky. Just as risky as driving without having taken any driving lessons.

Why is online trading so popular?

In the USA 15,000 new online accounts are opened daily. Why? The answer does not lie in trite, well-trodden statements about technological advances, the internet, ECNs and the desire to save commissions. The answer lies in history, in culture, and in character. If James Bryce were writing *The American Commonwealth* today instead of in 1888 he might have written:

How does [online trading] tell on the character of the people? They are naturally inclined to be speculative. The pursuit of wealth is nowhere so eager as on the [internet], the opportunities for acquiring it nowhere so numerous ... It can hardly be doubted that the pre-existing tendency to encounter risks and "back one's opinion," inborn in the Americans, and fostered by the circumstances of their country, is further stimulated by the existence of so vast a number of stocks ... Similar facilities exist in the Old World; but few of the inhabitants of the Old World have yet learned how to use and abuse them. The Americans, quick at everything, have learned long ago. The habit of speculation is now a part of their character, and it increases that constitutional excitability and high nervous tension of which they are proud.

It was the observers of an America early in the twentieth century who unknowingly provided the truth behind the popularity of this activity long after their deaths:

What prevails, what sets the tune, is the American scale of gain, more magnificent than any other, and the fact that the whole assumption, the whole theory of life, is that of the individual's participation in it, that of his being more or less punctually and more or less effectually "squared." To make so much money that you won't, that you don't "mind," don't mind anything – that is absolutely, I think, the main American formula.

The American Scene, Henry James, 1907

Alpesh B. Patel
alpesh-patel@msn.com

Reader experience key

The degree of experience required by the reader to appreciate each chapter is indicated by the tinted chevrons at the end of the chapter title, thus:

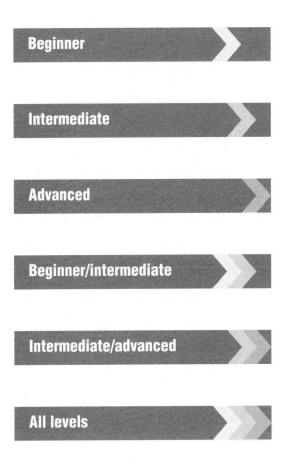

Beginner

Intermediate

Advanced

Beginner/intermediate

Intermediate/advanced

All levels

Who are the online traders?

1

Who is doing it?

If we are going to trade online, we will, of course, want to know more about our community. In this introductory chapter we have a quick sketch of who online traders are.

Cue online traders

They are everyone

Online traders do not appear to be a special breed apart. Assuming that they are proportionate part of the general internet audience then they are from a broad cross-section of society generally (see Fig 1.1).

They trade quite small online

The results of one particular survey by TheStreet.Com reveals relatively small online trades (see Fig 1.2). That is not to say they are not wealthy.

Most are active traders rather than long-term investors

According to TheStreet.Com most online traders do not do so in the long term (see Table 1.1).

Online traders are a growing force

Fig 1.3 reveals the rising proportion of trades being placed online. This is clearly the way to go for more and more people. As more trades occur online, the daily average number of trades through online brokerages has been increasing (see Fig 1.4). The result being more investors are becoming online investors.

	All US adults	Web users*	
Total	196.4 million	55.9 million	Index
Sex			
Male	48%	52%	109**
Female	52%	48%	92
Age			
18–24	13%	16%	126
25–34	21%	26%	125
35–44	22%	28%	124
45–54	17%	21%	125
55–64	11%	6%	61
65+	16%	3%	17
Household income			
$150 000 or more	3%	7%	217
$100 000 to $149 999	8%	15%	207
$75 000 to $99 999	10%	17%	173
$50 000 to $74 999	21%	29%	137
$35 000 to $49 999	17%	16%	90
$20 000 to $34 999	20%	11%	56
Less than $20 000	21%	5%	24
Education			
Post-graduate	7%	16%	228
Bachelor's degree	15%	28%	190
Attended college	26%	35%	135
High school graduate	33%	18%	53
Did not graduate high school	19%	3%	18
Occupation			
Professional, manager	20%	40%	205
Technical, clerical, sales	19%	28%	148
Craft, precision production	7%	5%	70
Other	19%	13%	64
Not employed, retired	35%	14%	41
Race			
White	84%	88%	104
Black	12%	7%	57
Asian	2%	4%	149
Other	2%	2%	132
Speak Spanish at home	10%	8%	74
Marital status			
Single	23%	28%	121
Married	57%	62%	108
Divorced, other	20%	10%	51

* Accessed the Web the past 30 days
** That is, Web surfers are 9 percent more likely to be male compared to US adults overall

Source: Mediamark Research, 1999

Fig 1.1 Web users are an upscale group

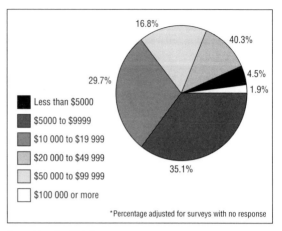

- Less than $5000
- $5000 to $9999
- $10 000 to $19 999
- $20 000 to $49 999
- $50 000 to $99 999
- $100 000 or more

16.8%
40.3%
29.7%
4.5%
1.9%
35.1%

*Percentage adjusted for surveys with no response

Source: International Data Corp.

Fig 1.2 What size is your average trade?

Brokerage commissions to top $5.3 billion		
Online trading forecast		
	1998	**2002**
Commission revenues	$1.3 billion	$5.3 billion
Accounts	6.4 million	24.7 million
Individual investors	5.6 million	22.7 million
Percent of total investors	8%	30%

Source: Credit Suisse First Boston

Fig 1.3 Increase in online trading activity

Average trades/day			
	Q3 '98	**Q4 '98**	**%increase**
Schwab	76 635	93 000	21.4%
E-Trade	27 450	39 992	45.7%
Fidelity	24 190	31 900	31.9%
Waterhouse	26 500	42 000	58.5%
Datek	21 272	33 965	59.7%
Ameritrade	17 881	25 787	44.2%
DLIdirect	10 111	12 656	25.2%
Quick & Reilly	9 500	11 500	21.1%
Discover	9 500	11 250	25.0%
Total	**253 000**	**340 000**	**34.4%**

Source: Credit Suisse First Boston

Fig 1.4 Growth in online trading

Investor type	Description	%
Active investor	Five or more trades a month, usually held for less than six months	51.3%
Day trader	Trades held for less than a day	9.4%
Long-term investor	Fewer than five trades a month usually held for one year or longer	2.1%
None of the above		2.1%

Table 1.1 Type of investor

Most trade stocks

Quite expectedly, most online traders are traders of stock, but nearly one in three also trades options (see Fig 1.5).

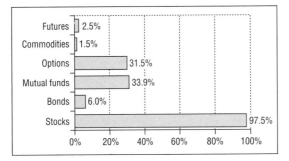

Source: TheStreet.Com

Fig 1.5 Products traded online in past year

Summary

As you can see we online traders keep mixed company. Perhaps the sterotype would be a white married man in a profession, 35–44 years old, with a household income of $50,000–$74,999, who trades with his $5000 more than five times a month and holds his positions for a few months. Not you? Don't worry, I don't fall into that category, either. But what this chapter shows is that online traders are diverse in background, and whoever you are, whatever you do, there is an online trade waiting for you. Cheesy, but true.

Short-term trading vs. longer term investing: Who wins in a street fight?

Online trader problems

- Isn't short-term trading just gambling?
- Isn't Warren Buffett the second richest man in the world?
- Don't 95 percent of futures traders lose money and 90 percent of day traders too?
- Why are online traders doing it?
- Should I be a short-term trader?

You mean everyone isn't doing it?

I do not want my readers to be under any misapprehension about the risks of short-term trading and the difficulties you need to overcome. I want you to have an appreciation for why your successful short-term online trading compatriots have chosen the time frame they have. This should avoid any superficial and misleading attractions to this form of trading, which can lead to substantial losses. I care. Excuse me while I wipe away a tear.

Just to reinforce the point, check out chat boxes 2.1 and 2.2, two online investors discussing the benefits of longer term investing over shorter term trading.

The charges being leveled against those seeking a path down the road of short-term trading can usually be summarized as follows: "You are a set of greedy gamblers who inevitably lose." How do we respond?

Day trade or invest

Posted on Yahoo!Finance on 7.10.1999

There are far too many losers in the field of day trading to sufficiently overcast the few winners and their gains.

My "old" tactics are the same as those followed by fund managers both now and in the past; these fund managers are professionals; what makes you think most day traders know more than professional fund managers?

I take it you place yourself above other novice day traders? If so, why the superiority complex?

Another investor

Posted on Yahoo!Finance on 7.10.1999

We'll see how many of these day traders will be retired with us in 3–5 years, eh, Zorba?

They're nothing more than compulsive gamblers, constantly doubling down and getting in and out of stocks for that occasional adrenaline rush they get when they make a big hit. If they actually took the time to see how much money they actually make, they'd be surprised to find they're squandering the greatest bull market in history.

Why 90 percent of day traders and futures traders fail

A figure often passed around is the level of failure among short-term traders in stocks and futures. It is enough to make you think twice. There are essentially five key reasons why the level of failure is so high. If you are considering short-term trading then you should be aware of these:

- trading system issues
- trading psychology issues
- commission issues
- skills issues
- money and risk management issues.

Trading system issues

If you buy and hold your system is relatively simple – buy and hold. Of course, you need to research companies and if you are particularly good at research you may have bought Coca-Cola in 1960, Microsoft in 1988, and Yahoo! in 1997. If you were more mediocre in research you may have bought Pepsi in 1960, Apple in 1987, and Infoseek in 1997 (although these are still not bad results). The point is that buy and hold on the whole produces good results over long periods of time, especially if you reinvest your dividends.

Short-term trading by its active nature requires a more developed trading system. That is why we spend several chapters of this book looking at system design and construction, to help avoid your becoming a statistic. Many of the 90 percent of short-term losers simply do not adequately understand trading system issues.

Trading psychology issues

In discussing the strategies in this book and system design, one point is emphasized. If you can't beat a buy and hold strategy, then you should just buy and hold. Short-term strategies can beat buy and hold, but because you are actively trading you do need a disciplined approach to your trading. It is these "psychological" elements that can let the short-term trader down.

Because you are trading very regularly you are called on to make decisions far more regularly than a buy and holder. Each decision, whether you are deciding what to do when sitting on a profit or a loss or wondering whether to get in at all, is an issue of trading psychology. Many traders simply have not mastered the issues surrounding trading psychology and that contributes to the 90 percent of short-term trading losers. We discuss the trading psychology issues towards the end of the book.

expert advice ✓ **The one thing to be good at trading**

Paul RT Johnson Jr, Senior Vice President, ING Barings Futures and Options comments: "You should probably study psychology rather than math to trade . . . that is why Tom Baldwin is so good – he's a psychology major, he knows when and why people are sweating and how they are likely to behave."

Commission issues

Commission costs are another factor that weigh more heavily on short-term trading relative to longer term trading and we later reinforce the point that testing a system requires an examination of post-commission cost profits vs. buy and hold results. Many short-term traders have successful systems or can make money until commission costs are factored in. Some just assume commissions are too small a factor to make a difference between profit and loss. They're not.

Skills issues

Compare a buy and hold strategy against being an electronic day trader. The latter is pitting his wits against the market makers from Lehman Brothers. It is going to take a lot more than reading books to succeed at short-term trading, even if the book is as good as this one.

With a buy and hold strategy you may be able to get away with reading a few books about Buffet and go out and buy some blue-chip stocks and do okay in 30 years. But short-term trading relies far more on experience to succeed. Please remember, this book, and all the books in the world on trading, will not be worth a month's trading experience. But if you do not read them then that first month of experience is going to be far more expensive than the cost of the books. Ninety percent of short-term traders fail and most of them do so in the first year of trading – when they have the least experience. Of course, experience is not enough – ask Victor Niederhoffer and John Merriwether.

Money and risk management issues

When you are short-term trading compared to long-term you are of course "churning" or turning over your capital very frequently. For that reason, it is very important to have calculated your reward:risk levels very carefully and to work out how much of your total funds you should risk on any one trade. This is a key reason for the failure of many short-term traders. We cover this issue in some detail in this book to make sure you are well-equipped to side step failure.

Just because you short-term trade does not mean you can long-term trade as well

We all know the importance of diversification to superior trading performance. There is nothing wrong with placing a part of your funds in long-term trades.

Long-term traders can have a hellish time of it

Consider Fig 2.1. Not exactly great for a buy and hold trader is it? Moreover there can be prolonged times when buying and holding can leave you with mediocre performance.

In the 16 years between 1966 and 1982 the US stock market actually lost money when adjusted for inflation. I guess to a buy and holder 16 years is no time at all. Bill Lipschutz, former global head of forex trading for Salomon Brothers, made on average $250,000 profits each trading day for his employer over an eight-year period. But then again, he is half as old as Buffet. Soros trades short term, too, you know.

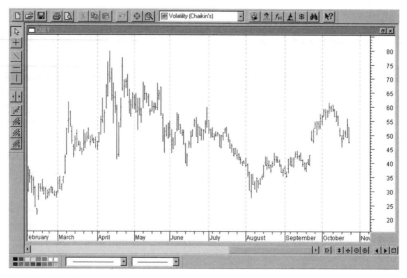

Fig 2.1 Volatility

We are young, we are free

It is all very well the buy and holders telling us that $1 invested in the age of the dinosaurs would be worth a guzzillion dollars today, but who the heck wants to wait that long to get at their money?! The problem with buy and hold is that you are encouraged to reinvest for 30 years or so. Great! I can have a whale of a time in my Ferrari – when I have lost all my hair, and incontinence and impotence are a nightly fear. And what if you are worm bait in 29 years? Doh! Have you seen how gray and old Warren Buffet is?

Short-term traders are looking to make enough to take out some of their winnings and enjoy life a little each month. Buy and holders can't do that.

Summary

So, just to make it clear:

■ Just because you day trade does not mean you have a passport to "Richesville."

■ The shorter the time frame the more intense and stressful the trading.

■ There are many, many people who believe day traders are on a "hiding to nothing."

■ You can make money day trading and short-term trading, but it takes effort – lots of effort – and a mastery of certain key issues which we cover in this book, including commission, risk and money management, experience, trading system, and trading psychology.

3

Choice of time frame: Day trader or days trader?

Online trader problems

- Just what type of short-term trading should I do, and what affects online traders' choices?
- What do other experienced online traders have to say about the choices available?

Rather like a presidential definition of "sexual relations," short-term trading, too, encapsulates a lot of different meanings and activities. You need to be absolutely clear you understand what is involved and that your personality, abilities, and other commitments are suited to it.

Day trading and short-term trading:
The choices we make, and the lives we lead

It is a very important aspect of trading success that we online traders understand whether we want to trade short term (for a few days at a time), or day trade, and why. The most frightening phenomenon of recent times is the rise of day trading in the press and the inevitable interest among people thinking this is a "get rich quick scheme." It is almost as if they think the shorter the time frame they trade the more money they can make. It is a recipe for disaster if ignorance and greed overcome diligent hard work (see Table 3.1).

You *can* make money trading short term, not because it is a "secret" short-cut to riches, but because you have applied a special set of difficult-to-learn skills.

	Day trading (stocks, futures, options)	Days trading (stocks, futures, options)
Holding period	Intra-day. No overnight positions	Typically a few days to a couple of weeks
How profits made	Stocks: A large sum of money trading on a small price move Futures and options: Leverage to produce gain from a relatively small price move	A medium sum of money making a gain from a medium-sized price move
Monitoring time commitment	Trader in front of screen taking advantage of quick price moves	Since price move typically develops over a number of days, can check up on position every few hours
Research time commitment (i.e. after market hours)	Nightly research not strictly necessary	Nightly updating of price charts and analysis to find new trading opportunity
Particular trader characteristics	Ability to think fast Intense concentration Decisiveness Calmness under pressure	More premeditated, thoughtful and relaxed
Examples	Level II Nasdaq trader Trader on earnings "pops"	Swing trader, momentum trader

Table 3.1 Characteristics of day trading and days trading

What an online trader needs to know when deciding how short a time frame to trade

So, now that we have put the longer term traders behind us, we need to be aware of some factors in deciding exactly how short our short-term trading is going to be. For instance, is it going to be trading online by the minute or holding a position for a few days? These are the considerations to bear in mind when making the choice.

Analysis methods you prefer

One of the factors affecting your choice of time frame should be the form of analysis you would have to conduct in order to be profitable trading that time frame. You must ensure you are comfortable with it. For most online traders this means trying out the different ways and seeing which fits best, or reading about them and taking a calculated guess at which they think, given what they know about themselves, they will like best.

Fig 3.1 shows the type of analysis undertaken by people trading different time frames.

Intra-day	2 weeks	3 weeks		12 months+
◄───►				
Technical analysts mainly (and tape readers and Level II screen traders)	- ►			Fundamental mainly
Few fundamental				Few technical
Breakdown by analysis method (FA is fundamental analysis and TA is technical analysis)				
◄───►				
Pure TA	TA with FA supplementing	Techno-fundamental	TA with FA supplementing	Pure TA

Fig 3.1 Analysis by trading time frame

Techno-fundamentalists

Profile: Combine TA and fundamental analysis. These types of traders want the best of both worlds.

Requirements: They usually pay equal attention to both types of analysis and are usually short- to medium-term traders (two weeks up to nine months between buying and selling). As well as examining what fundamental traders do (see Appendix 1) they will also examine what technicians do.

Short-cutters and pure TAs

Profile: "I can't be bothered reading all this fundamental analysis." This type of trader uses technical analysis solely. He may have rationalized why or may just be lazy.

Technical analysis, being graphical, is easier to grasp and assimilate than fundamental analysis, which requires some understanding of company accounts at least.

Requirements: Sometimes these traders' time frames can be over one year, but it is generally rare to be a long-term investor based solely on technicals because the general perception is that technical systems work best over shorter periods and fundamentals over longer, although the interaction between the two can be subtle and complex.

Day traders/frequent traders

Profile: Almost certainly technicians, including those who just look at price moves and order-flow. A few look to buy on the release of fundamental data (e.g. profits greater than expected) to sell a few days later.

Requirements: Need live streaming quotes and real-time charting facilities because they should be watching every price move.

Fundamental investor

Profile: The pure fundamental trader will hold charts as nonsense. Most are willing to examine them and may supplement their fundamental analysis with some technical analysis. Intermittent use of charting interest in charting fundamental data (P/E ratios, news flow). Charting of fundamental data, i.e. a graphical depiction of information, is innovative. I have yet to see it even on the best US sites. I think most site designers have simply not considered the potential of providing traditionally textual material in a visually appealing and readily digestible format because they do not yet understand the mind of a trader/investor.

Requirements: Fundamental traders will often have a medium- to long-term (buy and hold) interest. However, although most long-term investors find technical analysis of little use, it can be used in the short term by them to determine the precise entry point. That is something few realize because they lack professional training or experience.

Novice investor

Profile: New to trading. Tend to know more about fundamentals than technicals simply because more people talk about it.

Requirements: Technical analysis because of its potential simplicity, i.e. finding correlation between prices and other indicators and trading off that can seduce more new traders and investors than can fundamentals with its focus on heavy reading, accounts, and the like.

Most successful short-term online traders are not doing it simply for the money. They are doing it because they believe in the method of analysis they are using. For instance, if they are using technical analysis, they do believe in it. If you think trading short term is some short-cut to riches, and have no interest in analysis or belief in the theory, you could stand to lose a lot of money. You cannot deceive the market, it will see through you.

So if you are going to trade short term you must note that the types of strategies in this book involve either technical analysis of charts, tape reading, or monitoring quotes, occasionally you may be buying on a news item such as analysts' downgrade or earnings surprise. Whichever of the strategies take your fancy, you must make sure you look upon them in rational terms as to whether they make sense to you, and not as some secret formula or recipe.

Additionally, you will have to satisfy yourself that you can skilfully practice the skills needed to execute the strategies. For instance, day trading futures using real-time tick-by-tick data requires quickness of mind, intense concentration, and a decisive mind. That comes with the territory. Only you can answer which strategies apply or whether a slightly longer time frame may be better for you.

Daily data requirements

Trading is all about price. So you need price data for the markets you are trading. The cost and availability of these can be a determining influence on the trading method you choose.

For intra-day trading you need real-time tick-by-tick data. Don't even think about following positions using delayed quotes or the occasional call to your broker. You would lose too much if the market went against you while you were not watching it. Trust me, the market always goes *against* you when you are not watching it. There speaks a man from bitter experience.

Real-time tick-by-tick data are more expensive than end-of-day data. Indeed, end-of-day charts are available free on many web-sites which also permit you to do technical analysis. (Some of the best sites are listed later.)

Historical data requirements

With end-of-day data you need not only the daily updates of course but price history with which to test your trading system ideas. These also are available relatively inexpensively from specialist web-sites. Again the best ones compatible with most top software are listed in a later chapter. The technical analysis web-sites listed later also provide historical price charts on their web-sites, for free of course.

With real-time data it is either often impossible or prohibitively expensive to obtain historical tick-by-tick data. The usual practice is to build a historical database as you go along by collecting and storing your real-time data.

Software requirements

Having data is one thing, you also need some way of displaying them. Here you have two choices. You can either view it on a web-site itself (more of these in a later chapter) or you view it on your PC using specialist software (again, the top providers are reviewed and listed later). I prefer viewing things on the PC using software, rather than a web-site, because web-site charts are always more limited in what they can do. Although they can be a cheap alternative to software. Both are considered later.

The longer the time frame you trade the cheaper it will be in software terms because you will have slightly less need for specialist software, and therefore your costs may be lower. That is one reason why short-term online traders start out days trading not day trading. If you are placing trades you expect to hold for several days, you could get by with using the online charts available on sites such as www.equis.com (see Fig 3.2).

Fig 3.2 MetaStock Online

Day job

This is simple. If you have a day job, you cannot day trade. Day trading requires your total attention in front of a PC. There are those who may start work late or finish early who may be able to squeeze in some trading, but I do not recommend such an approach. Your best option is the short-term trade where you can hold a position for a few days and monitor it occasionally with a call to your broker or a quick illicit view of the web.

The lifestyle you want to lead

If you are day trading then the chances are you are going to spend at least a couple of exhausting hours in front of the PC daily. Some days you may be there from before the markets open until they close.

By the same token, if you are trading so as to make your profits from holding positions for a few days, then you will do most of your analysis each night after the close of trading and after you have updated that day's end-of-day price data.

I trade both intra-day (futures) and short term (in stocks and options). I trade a couple of hours in the morning or afternoon (rarely both, because I just get too exhausted) and then for my trading where I would be looking to hold positions for a few days I will do the analysis in the evening. That leaves me time to do other things in the day (such as writing, TV appearances, etc.). It is simply a matter of personal choice. Your personal choice may be to day trade all day then analyze all evening. I prefer a more balanced life with different activities – even if they are trading related.

So these types of lifestyle issues will also have to be added to the cauldron in which your choices are stewing when you decide what time frame you want to trade.

A day in the life of . . .

To give you an even better idea of how short-term traders' days may be spent consider the following scenarios.

The day trader in FTSE futures (times are local)

0800 At desk, make sure computer up and running, data being collected

0805 Go through latest headlines on financial web-sites (www.yahoo!finance.com etc.) to check what has happened overnight

0820 Make a note of likely pivot points and supports and resistances for the day based on past week's action and yesterday's action

0830 Monitor market but as per system do not enter before 0900

0900 View momentum indicators on three-minute and five-minute bar charts of likely buy or short signals

0915 Possible buy signal. Call broker, wait. No, false alarm

0930 Still no signal, continue watching

0940 Possible signal to short. Confirmed. Call broker and enter order

0941 Still on line awaiting fill. Five sold at 5995. Make note of stop-loss (and print out price chart)

0942 While monitoring prices, draw possible target levels, supports, and resistances on price chart

0945 Price rises to 6000. Doubts creep in

0950 Price hits 6006, within 4 points of stop-loss. Indicators still suggest holding position

1000 Position still open, price at 5982

1002 Price now running up quickly, indicators not showing sell, price 5990, with paper profits eroded. Trailing stop at 5991, get ready to call broker

1003 Price hits 5991, then drops to 5989

1005 Price continues dropping. Reaches 5979

1015 Price starts rising 5984. Momentum on three-minute chart suggests exit

1016 Price at 5987. Momentum on three- and five-minute charts suggest exit, moving average convergence divergence indicator (MACD) still suggests in

1017 Price at 5988, trailing stop-hit. Exit

1018 Call broker, wait for fill price: five bought at 5989. Disappointment

1019 Reconfigure for next trade. Return to screen

An options trader holding positions for a few days

7.7

2000 Download end-of-day data for all stocks

2010 Screen stocks according to system looking for signals

2100 Rank buy signals for three of the best opportunities

2115 Evaluate probable reward:risk ratio based on anticipated price moves

2120 Evaluate option chain for most profitable strategy

2150 Make note of strategy, anticipated exits, stop-losses

7.8

1030 Check to make sure price confirms previous day's analysis and place trade through online broker

Hourly monitor price just to make sure no disasters

2000 Download end-of-day data for all stocks

2010 Screen stocks according to system looking for signals

2100 Rank buy signals for three of the best opportunities

2115 Evaluate probable reward:risk ratio based on anticipated price moves

2120 Evaluate option chain for most profitable strategy

2150 Make note of strategy, anticipated exits, stop-losses

2200 Re-analyze open position in light of today's updated prices

7.9

Same as yesterday

Summary

Not all short-term trading is the same. Many people who want to trade do not realize this. They think they can do it on the side with 30 minutes' analysis on the weekends. If you want to do it that way, then consider a buy and hold strategy.

For short-term trading you must accommodate everything else going on in your life and what you *want* going on in your life. Think ahead. Choose the type of trading you think you will be most suited to, otherwise, like a round peg in a square hole, you just won't fit.

4

Overview: Getting trading ideas on your radar screen

Online trader problems

- What are the various online trading options open to me?
- Where can I get trading ideas from and how do I know what to look for?
- How can I scan lots of stocks based on various conditions I want them to meet?

This is an overview chapter. How and where you get your trading ideas determines whether or not you can place a trade or not. Tarot cards, sun spots, black magic, and crystal balls are not the usual methods for making good-quality trading decisions. But they have their uses. Anyway, here we overview the various (mainstream) methods online traders use to set the scene for the rest of the book.

Types of trading

As a trader you are looking for securities to trade in. There are several ways to trade.

Single security trading

You can select one security and trade that based on certain criteria, e.g. intra-day trade stocks or futures based on a system. You may use online sites to plot the price chart and monitor news items. Most intermediate and advanced level traders so this.

Multiple security single system trading

You can have your system and go through a list of securities, e.g. all the stocks in the S&P 500, periodically (e.g. daily), and see if your system signals buy or sell. Software, which we review in Chapter 9, can actually scan a database of securities for you automatically, based on your system. However, if you have a discretionary system, or have not programmed one, you would have to scan by eye. Most intermediate and advanced level traders so this.

Black box and newsletter trading

You may simply follow someone else's recommendations blindly, e.g. a newsletter or a black box trading system you have purchased. This is not recommended since your fate lies in the hands of another. Another version of this is to foolishly follow chat room recommendations. Very few traders do this other than the naïve, although it can be legitimate to use newsletters' recommendations as something on your radar to look more deeply into.

Black box system

Software which is designed by traders to produce buy and sell signal, but which does not reveal the rules by which the signals are generated.

Online screen trading

You can scan securities by certain criteria, e.g. those with recent earning upgrades, and then examine them more closely to see if they are worth trading. Some specialist software can do this, but the best way to do it is using web-sites that provide screening facilities. Beginner and often intermediate level traders may do this.

Multiple security system-based scanning

As an online trader you can develop your own trading system on software and scan for stocks based on your system using the software. Most advanced level traders do this.

Combo

You can combine one or more of these types. For instance, you may have your own trading system but instead of searching lots of stocks to see if your system signals a buy on any of them, you only search those that are listed, based on an online stock screening. Intermediate and advanced level traders do this.

For example, imagine I have a very simple trading system to be long the market if the stock closes above the 50-day moving average, and be out of the market otherwise. Instead of scanning all the stocks in the, say, S&P 500, I may just search those that on an online stock screen have P/E ratios less than 10 and a market capitalization above $100m. That way you save time in scanning.

Summary

In this chapter we have seen that there are many ways in which to get stock ideas. The choice of traders depends on their experience and what they feel makes sense. Some will choose a system based on the amount of time they wish to spend researching, others will experience all the methods and settle on one based on results, while others will go for one method straight from the start, and stick with it.

I mostly use the multiple security system–based scanning, but will use a combo. You pays your money and you takes your choice.

5

Board advice: Success tips before you begin from our esteemed peers

Online trader problem

■ Are boards yada, yada, yada, or are you going to prove they are not?

In recent years I have changed my mind about boards (for those not in the loop, a board is an online bulletin board – more of these in a later chapter). Popular opinion has it that only the naïve would be so foolish as to heed the views of an anonymous windbag with little better to do than write on boards, inevitably with a hidden agenda. Yet closer inspection reveals there may be gems in dung. To prove the point, and because they provide advice as good as any experienced trader could, I have taken a few from the excellent Silicon Investor (www.siliconinvestor.com), relating to trading success. You may want to dog-ear this page and come back to it later as well.

The very unboring boardsters

This first posting (chat box 5.1) is an excellent tip from someone who has been to the battlefront and come back alive.

The next posting (chat box 5.2) succinctly advises on the winning traits of winning traders.

chat box 5.1

Trading keys – for me – fwiw [for what it's worth]

1 Limit your stocks for a particular day to one, or two, if possible. And learn their chart action like the back of your hand. Know where support and resistance levels are.

2 Get a sense of the general market's movement for the day. Watch the bond yield and the foreign markets and get a good read on the "perception" of the market in general, as well as the perception towards your stocks and their sector. Often stocks follow a daily pattern in a particular market environment (i.e. gap and trap, etc. . . .). Don't fight the pattern. No one wants to sit on a losing position all day long.

3 Be as up to the minute as possible on any news items that may affect your stocks' (or their industry or even sector's) movement. Know how seemingly unrelated news may affect your stocks. Economic news. Fed news. Legal news. SEC filings. Insider action. Institutional buying. Rumors. CNBC or CNNF plug.

4 Know which stocks in the industry trade along with your stocks. Which lead the group. And which lag. This is often a vital tool.

5 Watch the specific trading patterns of your stocks (on Level II if Nasdaq issue). Which banks seem to buy the rallies. Which sell into them. Note how the day traders are playing it. They can often be found on Island . . . and they often trade on perception.

6 Be ready to move in a millisecond.

7 Sell losers fast. Losers can rack up larger than winners. That's because you'll tend to wait them out longer. Don't do it. Sometimes there's a reason a stock is dropping . . . and others aren't. Punt it fast. You don't ever want to get caught in a plunge and be forced to sell into it with a market order.

8 Never look back with regret. After a losing trade (or a winning trade you sold too early), move on to the next trade. Don't be tempted to jump back in because you think you are "missing the big run." There will be others. There always are.

9 Which brings me to the most important rule: BE PATIENT.

These are all off the top of my head. I'm sure there are many others, too.

What winning traders have in common

1   All those interviewed had a driving desire to become successful traders – in many cases, overcoming significant obstacles to reach their goal.

2   All reflected confidence that they could continue to win over the long run. Almost invariably, they considered their own trading as the best and safest investment for their money.

3   Each trader had found a methodology that worked for him and remained true to that approach. It is significant that discipline was the word most frequently mentioned.

4   The top traders take their trading very seriously; most devote a substantial amount of their waking hours to market analysis and trading strategy.

5   Rigid risk control is one of the key elements in the trading strategy of virtually all those interviewed.

6   In a variety of ways, many of the traders stressed the importance of having the patience to wait for the right trading opportunity to present itself.

7   The importance of acting independent of the crowd was a frequently emphasized point.

8   All the top traders understand that losing is part of the game.

9   They all love what they are doing.

This next posting (chat box 5.3) not only reflects some of the gems you can find on boards but also the quality of this particular site. Of course, there will still be those miserable bleeders who complain that all such tips are too general. If it appears too general then you may just not "get trading."

chat
box 5.3   **Time-tested tips**

This is a list of classic trading rules that was given to me while on the trading floor in 1984. A senior trader collected these rules from classic trading literature throughout the 20th century. They obviously withstand the age-old test of time.

I'm sure most everybody knows these truisms in their hearts, but the list is nicely edited and makes a good read.

1   Plan your trades. Trade your plan.

2   Keep records of your trading results.

3   Keep a positive attitude, no matter how much you lose.

4   Don't take the market home.

5   Continually set higher trading goals.

6   Successful traders buy into bad news and sell into good news.

7   Successful traders are not afraid to buy high and sell low.

8   Successful traders have a well-scheduled and planned time for studying the markets.

9   Successful traders isolate themselves from the opinions of others.

10 Continually strive for patience, perseverance, determination, and rational action.

11 Limit your losses – use stops!

12 Never cancel a stop-loss order after you have placed it!

13 Place the stop at the time you make your trade.

14 Never get into the market because you are anxious of waiting.

15 Avoid getting in or out of the market too often.

16 Losses make the trader studious – not profits. Take advantage of every loss to improve your knowledge of market action.

17 The most difficult task in speculation is not prediction but self-control. Successful trading is difficult and frustrating. You are the most important element in the equation for success.

18 Always discipline yourself by following a pre-determined set of rules.

19 Remember that a bear market will give back in one month what a bull market has taken three months to build.

20 Don't ever allow a big winning trade to turn into a loser. Stop yourself out if the market moves against you 20 percent from your peak profit point.

21 You must have a program, you must know your program, and you must follow your program.

22 Expect and accept losses gracefully. Those who brood over losses always miss the next opportunity, which more than likely will be profitable.

23 Split your profits right down the middle and never risk more than 50 percent of them again in the market.

24 The key to successful trading is knowing yourself, and your stress point.

25 The difference between winners and losers isn't so much native ability as it is discipline exercised in avoiding mistakes.

26 In trading as in fencing there are the quick and the dead.

27 Speech may be silver but silence is golden. Traders with the golden touch do not talk about their success.

28 Dream big dreams and think tall. Very few people set goals too high. A man becomes what he thinks about all day long.

29 Accept failure as a step towards victory.

30 Have you taken a loss? Forget it quickly. Have you taken a profit? Forget it even quicker! Don't let ego and greed inhibit clear thinking and hard work.

31 You cannot do anything about yesterday. When one door closes, another door opens. The greater opportunity always lies through the open door.

32 The deepest secret for the trader is to subordinate his will to the will of the market. The market is truth as it reflects all forces that bear upon it. As long as he recognizes this he is safe. When he ignores this, he is lost and doomed.

33 It's much easier to put on a trade than to take it off.

34 If a market doesn't do what you think it should do, get out.

35 Beware of large positions that can control your emotions. Don't be overly aggressive with the market. Treat it gently by allowing your equity to grow steadily rather than in bursts.

36 Never add to a losing position.

37 Beware of trying to pick tops or bottoms.

38 You must believe in yourself and your judgment if you expect to make a living at this game.

39 In a narrow market there is no sense in trying to anticipate what the next big movement is going to be – up or down.

40 A loss never bothers me after I take it. I forget it overnight. But being wrong and not taking the loss – that is what does the damage to the pocket book and to the soul.

41 Never volunteer advice and never brag of your winnings.

42 Of all speculative blunders, there are few greater than selling what shows a profit and keeping what shows a loss.

43 Standing aside is a position.

44 It is better to be more interested in the market's reaction to new information than in the piece of news itself.

45 If you don't know who you are, the markets are an expensive place in which to find out.

46 In the world of money, which is a world shaped by human behavior, nobody has the foggiest notion of what will happen in the future. Mark that word – nobody! Thus the successful trader does not base moves on what may happen but reacts instead to what does happen.

47 Except in unusual circumstances, get in the habit of taking your profit too soon. Don't torment yourself if a trade continues winning without you. Chances are it won't continue long. If it does, console yourself by thinking of all the times when liquidating early reserved gains that you would otherwise have lost.

48 When the ship starts to sink, don't pray – jump!

49 Lose your opinion, not your money.

50 Assimilate into your very bones a set of trading rules that works for you.

This next posting (chat box 5.4) reveals the correct perspective for trading and systems.

chat box 5.4

Execute the plan

Many people think that a winning trade is a good trade, and a losing trade is a bad trade. This can be a very unprofitable and naïve view.

A more successful way to look at your trades (IMHO [**i**n **m**y **h**umble **o**pinion]) is to view a good trade as *any* trade in which you followed your trading plan precisely. Of course, you must also have confidence that your trading plan is sound, and will be profitable over the long term.

A bad trade is *any* trade in which you did not follow your trading plan, regardless of whether the trade was profitable or not. This is a very important point. The most dangerous trades are trades in which you did not follow your trading plan, but managed to close out profitably. Why are these dangerous? They reinforce the idea that you can "wing it," or ignore your stop-loss limit, or wait a little longer for the market to turn when *your* system tells you to GET OUT! By ignoring your system, you have failed. By ignoring your system, you have lost your structured plan which ensures that you can trade reproducibly, day after day, without emotion. In short, by not following your well-thought-out trading plan, you have given into the emotion of the moment. This is a dangerous and losing path to follow.

Conversely, by following your plan, you have eliminated emotion from your trading. Over time, you can *modify* your trading approach to reflect your increased understanding of the market and to build in the lessons you have learned from your previous winning and losing trades. However, you will modify your trading plan when the market is *closed* after carefully reviewing your reasons for the change. You will not be giving into emotion by changing your trading plan "on-the-fly" during the trading day on a whim.

I hope this concept is clear. A "losing" trade can be a "good" trade. Simply follow your plan. Assume you enter a long position in WXYZ at a price of 90 5/8 and subsequently exit your position when your stop-loss is hit at 90 1/8. Immediately thereafter, the stock reverses and goes directly to 93 without even hesitating. Unfortunate? Yes. Annoying? Yes. But did you make a mistake by exiting? Absolutely not. The trade was exited per your trading plan. The stop-loss in your trading plan was design to protect your account balance against a devastating loss, and you followed your plan. It was a successful trade, a good trade. Pat yourself on the back for doing the right thing.

During the trading day, don't focus on whether individual trades are profitable or not. Instead, focus on making "good" trades, i.e. always follow your plan. After the market is closed, you can work to refine or modify your trading plan as needed. But during the day, follow your rules!

Summary

I hope the examples of top-quality postings in this chapter reveal the goodness out there. It is not entirely a dark and selfish world. Luke felt the good in Mr Vader, and now I feel the good in the boards. The usual cautions remain as to not taking stock tips from strangers, and don't take sweets, either, while you are at it.

6

Trading online is easy and trading online is difficult: Know what you are getting into

Online trader problems

- Should I increase my involvement in online trading?
- Exactly what are the pitfalls that never seem to be discussed?
- How can I go in, eyes wide open?

Online trading is too often portrayed as a very simple way to make money. It is not. I know from experience that what the market gives easily with one hand, it takes away with both hands, twice as much, and a lot more readily.

I know from experience, and from the ample e-mails I receive each week of online trading newbies who double their money in a week or a month, only to lose five times as much in a year, that online trading is a difficult but rewarding skill. In this chapter I want to get across the pitfalls as well as the joys, so that everyone enters the online trading revolution fully aware of and equipped to face both the difficulties and the joys.

Online trading is easy

Do not fall foul of any of the following assertions. They may come from an advertisement, or a friend or even an overheard conversation.

- **False:** Online trading is the way the few who dare make a fortune.
- **True:** There is no more a secret to online trading than there is in buying books from Amazon or buying a second-hand kidney from Ebay. The mechanics are relatively easy, the skill of knowing what to buy and when, and then when to sell is where the skill lies. Whether you are an online trader or not, you will need to master the skills of investment and this book tries to teach you those.

■ **False:** The costs you save in placing an order online make it far easier to come out ahead at the end of the year.

■ **True:** Discount online brokers do offer very low brokerage rates, saving you a lot of money compared to placing trades with a full-fee broker. But you still need to be good at picking stocks.

■ **False:** Online trading allows rapid short-term gains.

■ **True:** While with online trading you can trade relatively short term because orders are transmitted electronically, most online brokers are not intended to be used as a substitute to your being a floor trader. They confirm your orders as quickly as possible, but day trading, where you are looking to buy and sell in a few seconds, is not appropriate through online brokers, because by the time you get a price, place the order, get a confirmation, review the new price, place a new order, get another confirmation, the market could have moved away from what you thought it was.

That small move matters to day trader because even 1/32 of a dollar is a big hit to them. Online brokers are not for that type of trading. However, if you are looking to hold for at least a day or longer they are ideal.

■ **False:** Online trading offers an instant daily income from a small capital start-up.

■ **True:** We have all heard stories of the online trader who makes $150 daily and therefore a comfortable living over a year. The more you want to make, the more capital you need. If you are looking to make money every day, then you will have to trade every day. That will be expensive in commissions, let alone time, and soon you may find yourself without any trading capital. That is why most short-term traders look to place say two trades a week instead.

■ **False:** There is so much free information about stocks on the internet that you have an advantage over everyone else in making profitable trades.

■ **True:** Information without an understanding of how to use it, or what it means, is useless. There is a lot of information in a law library, yet the librarian is not a lawyer, let alone a good one. Again, I want to provide, with the help of other online traders who have placed comments on bulletin boards, more than just information, but knowledge, and wisdom too. I will show you what I consider the best places to get information, but that is just the starting point. We must then know what to do with it to make money, and that is where I have tried to cram in the pages of this book the accumulated knowledge of many profitable strategies of our fellow online traders.

■ **False:** You can make profits off the back of more knowledgeable traders' postings on chat sites and bulletin boards.

■ **True:** The best places for research are reputable sources of company information such as Hoovers (US) or Hemmington Scott (UK). Chat rooms are a great place to ask questions, double-check your own views, but they are not a place to form opinions about a stock, because any old anonymous Joe or Josephine can type away at the keyboard promoting stocks only of interest to them. For more details on chat rooms and bulletin boards see the chapter on them later in the book.

expert advice ✓ **Arthur Levitt, Chairman SEC**

From a statement of 27.2.1999

While the manner in which orders are executed may be changing, the time-honored principles of evaluating a stock have not. An investor's consideration of the fundamentals of a company – net earnings, P/E ratios, the products or services offered by the company – should never lose their underlying importance.

Investing in the stock market – however you do it and however easy it may be – will always entail risk. I would be very concerned if investors allow the ease with which they can make trades to short-cut or bypass the three golden rules for all investors:

1   know what you are buying
2   know the ground rules for all investors under which you buy and sell a stock or bond
3   know the level of risk you are undertaking.

Online investors should remember that it is just as easy to lose money through the click of a button as it is to make it, if not easier.

- **False:** You can give up your day job and work from home.
- **True:** While some people have given up careers to pursue online trading (myself included) it requires capital and experience. Without capital you will not earn enough to pay the bills, and without the experience, you will make mistakes that the pressure to perform intensifies.

    Also, giving up the day job is a risky proposition for anyone. Do you really want to sit all day in front of the computer, by yourself? Even if you make money, how fulfilling would a 20 percent pay rise be, if the quality of life is tedious? So, be mentally prepared if you do want to go down that route, and do not start online trading with a view to leaving full-time employment – that may not be the right thing to do.

Customer best practice

There are key things every online trader should do to avoid the problems of trading on the internet.

Keep accounts

The more often you trade, the more confirmations you will receive. You must keep all these in a safe place, and I recommend keeping a file on a spreadsheet which provides a running list of purchases, sales, profits, losses, commissions paid. This way, you should know immediately how much you are paying in commissions, and what kinds of profits or losses you are making. If you also note how many days you are keeping your positions open, you may notice, for instance, that there is a link between how long you keep a position open and the profit or loss from it. I found, years ago, that on one system, the longer I kept a position open the less I was making on it. That suggested to me that I may not have been cutting my losses short, or my system may lose its predictive power after a short time from a buy signal, or any other number of reasons. But I knew to investigate further.

All this may seem a far cry from the "making money hand over fist" visions you may have had, but while online trading is fun, it is also hard work if you want to do it seriously.

Question, question, and then, question some more

Always question advice, and try to find independent corroborating advice. If there is someone talking up a stock, only ever use that to start your own research, and discount the advice itself.

Contingency plans

You should be fully aware of your options for placing a trade if you cannot gain access to your account online. A good major reputable broker will always be able to offer telephone back-up in case of a failure of technology. They may also have a fax number, or touch-tone phone trading. It may be that you only need to access this once a year, if at all, but do make a note of the methods. There is no point planning to go online to find the appropriate information, if it is not available because the site is "down."

Canceled?

If you cancel an online trade, you must make sure you get confirmation of the cancellation, before assuming it was canceled. (Almost sounds like a country and western song – maybe not then.) Otherwise, you may place other orders in the erroneous belief that your previous trade was canceled. Sometimes it is too late to cancel a trade because it is impossible to get to the floor broker in time.

Take care with your clicking ways

When executing the order you must always be careful not to click away like crazy on the "place order" button just because you do not get instantaneous feedback. Otherwise, you may well end up owning more of Microsoft than Bill Gates does.

Trading on margin

Some brokers allow trading on margin through margin accounts. This is where they borrow money from the broker to trade. The amount they can borrow depends on the firm itself. The loan is secured on the securities and cash belonging to the client held with the broker.

example

If a customer has $50 000 cash in an account, the firm requires deposit margin of 50 percent, in which case the customer may borrow $50 000 and so buy $100 000 of stock. If the price of the security falls so that the next day it is worth only $60 000, then since the customer still, of course, owes $50 000, his equity is only $10 000.

If the maintenance margin for the account is 25 percent then the client has to maintain $15 000 in equity (if he has $60 000 in stock) and the client here only has $10 000, so he will get a *margin call* of $5000, in which case, if he did not meet the call, the broker could liquidate stock to meet that margin call without requiring additional authority from the customer.

When trading on margin do not forget you are increasing the risk you face, because you could end up having to pay back more than you have in assets. Always remember you are borrowing money to buy stocks and remember you do not have to trade on margin.

Summary

Online trading deserves our respect or it will have our money. Frankly, I will give it respect – it's a lot cheaper. You cannot appreciate enough that there is more to online trading than placing an order. It is a mechanism. You still need to do your homework – albeit with the quantity and quality of information on the internet, doing your homework is easier than ever, and can possibly even be fun. You need, too, to be aware of boring things like margin requirements, broker back-up phone numbers, record keeping – dull but essential.

What you must know about trading systems

7

On trading systems: Online traders do it in front of a PC

With proper strategy the strongest enemy may be overcome.

The Mahabharat

The general who wins a battle makes calculations in his temple before the battle is fought. The general who loses a battle makes but few calculations beforehand. Thus, do many calculations lead to victory, and few calculations to defeat.

The Art of War, Sun Tzu (edited by James Clavell)

Online trader problems

- Why exactly are online traders using systems and what do they mean by "system"?
- Should I create my own or take someone else's?
- How do I choose between the wealth of ideas to trade by?
- What am I going to put in my system?
- How do I select the right time frame?
- What do professional traders and private online traders have to advise about systems?
- What are the problems of over-optimization?

Having a trading system is as essential to profitable trading as having a steering wheel is to driving around a corner. Yet you would be surprised by the number of people who try to undertake trading without a detailed understanding of systems. In this chapter we examine some of the issues every good trader faces when making choices about trading systems.

Trading systems 101: Watchya doing here then?

Most online traders, and certainly the good ones, do not trade by the seat of their pants. They do not get their ideas by telepathy about when to buy and when to sell. Instead, they have a "system." Many people bandy the word "system" about without truly having a trading system, or without having one as good as it could be. They just do not actually understand what a trading system really is. So, I thought I would spell it out:

1   A trading system tends to be mechanical in nature in that you input price data, and it outputs buy and sell signals, based on rules, although there are good discretionary systems whereby an ultimate decision is made by the trader. For example: "Buy if today's high price is greater than yesterday's high price by 2 percent on 10 percent greater volume."

2   A system is built up of an indicator or indicators, such as the relative strength index (RSI). It can have one indicator or a multitude overlaid. For example: "Buy if the RSI, MACD, and momentum indicators all move above 30."

3   A good system should be as clear as possible in telling you when to enter and when to exit the market. Otherwise, the mind being as it is, you will seize on any ambiguity and fail to act according to your trading system.

4   A good system will also incorporate entry and exit strategies (such as using stop-losses, limit orders).

5   A good system will also cover issues of risk and money management, such as the amount of total equity to be placed on any one trade, under what circumstances scaling back will occur, etc.

6   A system is not a system until it is back-tested for profitability, and then refined and optimized. Until then it is just a speculation.

7   A mechanical, as opposed to discretionary, system is one that is always followed and not overridden on whim. Later, we will compare the two types and examine why online traders prefer each type.

8   Creating a system should be fun, otherwise you should question whether you will enjoy any aspect of trading (or question whether you are congenitally miserable).

System and strategy

A trading system is a complete set of rules relating to every aspect of your trading from entry, position, size, to exit. A strategy is part of a system. For instance, you may have a strategy whereby you only exit on a sell signal from the RSI signal if the price makes a lower low relative to the preceding day. Strategies are part of a system. I thought I would clear that up because we are going to use those two words a lot in this book.

My place or yours?

A common problem online traders face, one they share with other traders, is whether to even bother trying to develop their own trading systems, use someone else's, or buy one for several thousand dollars.

There are several key reasons why you should try to develop your own trading system:

- When you go through all the steps of trying to build your own trading system, even a very simple one, you will learn a lot about trading, such as why it is difficult to make money in the markets, how the market changes over time, how the line between profit and loss can be very fine. Plus a lot more. Education about how prices and indicators interact, and how prices move adds to your databank of experience. Of course, you can just give up, go for a drink instead, and forget the markets.

- If you follow someone else's system you are likely never to truly believe in it, especially if it starts making losses. Then you may dump it and waste your money.

- Another way to lose your money is to buy a system that promises eternal profits, especially on historical tests. Yes, it may be the bee's knees of systems, but what do *you* think?

- You will gain an insight into trading which should result in a perception shift and an understanding that trading is about probabilities not certainties.

Mechanical or discretionary?

Many online traders ask if they should have a purely mechanical trading system, or a discretionary one. A mechanical system is one in which, by a strict set of rules, for every market eventuality you know whether to be in or out of the market. For instance, a very simple system may involve being long if the price is above the 50-day moving average and being out if it is not.

Discretionary system	Mechanical system
No amount of programming can incorporate human experience into a mechanical system	No emotions involved in decision making. Should lead to a less stressful life
Can never be as thoroughly back-tested because the trader himself cannot put himself back in time to decide how he would have felt about a particular trade and whether he would have placed it	Since it can be mathematically back-tested you can have a fairly good idea, albeit inconclusive, about future performance
Do not need to know how to program trading software	No constant decision making. Relatively stress free

Table 7.1 Discretionary system or mechanical system?

With a discretionary system the ultimate decision is down to the trader who may consider all the facts before him plus gut instinct and try to incorporate experience, etc. So, which should you go for? (See Table 7.1.)

There are certain personality-related issues to resolve too, before you decide the type of strategy you should go for. Here is a simple test. It meets the highest standards in psychometric testing and has been designed with cunning subtlety – so you should take it very seriously.

- How disciplined are you when it comes to executing trades?
    1 My name is General Colin Powell ❑
    2 Very disciplined, always take a signal, no problems ❑
    3 Sometimes disciplined, but occasionally go for a wild shot ❑
    4 Not very disciplined at all, trade on whim ❑
    5 My name is Homer Simpson ❑

- Are you mathematical in nature?
    1 I've lost count of my age ❑
    2 Hate math ❑
    3 Intermediate, competent ❑
    4 Very good ❑
    5 I work for NASA ❑

- Do you like programming computers?
    1 I can't program the microwave ❑
    2 I could probably learn but wouldn't really enjoy it ❑
    3 I wouldn't be bad ❑
    4 I could do it and would enjoy it ❑
    5 I taught Bill Gates all he knows ❑

- Are you more logical or more emotional?
    1 I cried through *Star Wars* ❑
    2 Pretty emotional and feeling-based rather than strictly rational ❑
    3 Probably a bit of both most of the time ❑
    4 I think things through clearly and methodically, logic is my light ❑
    5 My name is Spock, I work on the Starship *Enterprise* ❑

- What do you enjoy about trading?
    1. Soros comes to me for my opinion on the markets ❏
    2. I like being involved, part of the game, plus want to profit, too ❏
    3. I want to make money, but want to enjoy trading, too ❏
    4. I want to make lots of money. Period. I don't care too much about the trading ❏
    5. Greed ❏

- What type of trader do you admire most?
    1. George Soros ❏
    2. The type that has to make choices and work hard ❏
    3. I don't know ❏
    4. The type that can put his feet up ❏
    5. John Merriwether ❏

- How good are you at decision making?
    1. I told you, my name is General Colin Powell ❏
    2. Quite good. I like to make them, stick by them and watch them succeed or fail ❏
    3. Alright most of the time. Have difficulties occasionally ❏
    4. Pretty indecisive ❏
    5. I have just spent an hour on this question ❏

- How lazy are you?
    1. I don't do sleep ❏
    2. Not very, I like to work hard, play hard ❏
    3. As much as the next guy. I like my short-cuts ❏
    4. If there is a quicker way of doing something I would like to know it ❏
    5. I am answering this in bed. It is 4pm ❏

- How do you handle stress?
    1. I am a space shuttle commander when I am not sailing naked down the Amazon coated in honey ❏
    2. Quite well. It gives me a buzz ❏
    3. Sometimes I dislike it ❏
    4. Hate it ❏
    5. On my wedding night I had to use Viagra. I was 22 ❏

Now tot up your scores and use the following guidelines to determine whether you are more suited to a mechanical system or a discretionary one:

9–23: You would handle a discretionary system well given your personality, and would probably enjoy it too.

24–36: You could probably handle both quite well. You may want a very mechanical system with occasional override discretion.

37+: Better do it by the book. Mechanisation for you, my friend, is the best option.

Smart, new, and sexy – your very own system: You just gotta have one

Since this is a book about trading systems, I feel obliged to give you a few reasons why you should have one. Although it is arguable that if you have bought the book, you do not need converting.

Trading Valium: A stress reliever

Trading gets frustrating. Whoever you are. It gets stressful if you have had a string of losses. It can consume your waking hours, and your sleeping ones. You can get to a stage where you think of nothing but how you have been trading. With a trading system some of that stress can be alleviated, if not avoided altogether, if you have the knowledge that your system was tested for profits and that despite some losses you will make money by following it.

Much anxiety in trading, as in life, stems from uncertainty about the future. It is when we do not know what the future holds that we become anxious. Man, and woman, desires certainty. While a plan cannot predict the future, it can lay down how you will react to the possible outcomes. This is why a plan is essential. It is a list of strategic responses to events beyond your control. You control the only thing you can control – yourself.

Consequently, a system removes much uncertainty, which itself is the cause of anxiety, confusion, anger, and frustration. A good plan should therefore release psychological energy that is unnecessarily being expended on uncertainties. The flip side is that trading should become effortless, you should be more relaxed and possibly even enjoy your trading more!

expert ✓ advice **Pat Arbor, former Chairman, Chicago Board of Trade**

As a trader you must decide what you are. You are either a speculator, spreader, or local scalper. You have to fit into one of those categories. Me, I am suited to spreading. To find what suits his personality, he just has to see whether or not he makes money at what he's doing. I have had people come into the office, saying, "I am a great trader." I say, "You're right," they say, "Know how to trade." I say again, "You're right" and they say, "I predicted that the market was going to go up or down," and I say again, "You are right. But the bottom line is whether you make any money."

Don't chase me

Strategically, too, a good plan improves trading. It assists in identifying opportunities and so stops you from chasing the market. It tells you when to exit, so you are not left clinging to the mast of a sinking ship. You gain some control instead of being swept and buffeted around.

Save me from temptation

A system makes it easier for you to resist the temptation of doing what is comfortable, because in trading, doing what is comfortable is often the wrong thing. Think of how many times you have let a loss run or cut a profit short because it was the comfortable thing to do. Eventually, as you get used to following your system, it will become second nature. So, too, a plan is a means of changing your trading behavior for the better. A kind of trading straitjacket, protecting you against your wilder emotions.

expert ✓ advice **Phil Flynn, Vice President, Alaron Trading**

"If you go into a trade with a wishy-washy attitude, then you are going to be wishy-washy in execution. That is why some plan is better than no plan. You have to look at it like this: win or lose this is a good trade, because if I was stopped out then I was wrong, then this is still a good trade. You never make a bad trade. The only bad trade is when you do not follow your rules and you get yourself into trouble. If you look at it from a longer term viewpoint it makes it a lot easier."

I am in charge

Your own trading strategy is going to give you the independence to test your own ideas, and not to have to wait for a particular market guru to give you his opinion. The buck can stop with you, for profits and losses.

Pick and choose

When you are building your own trading system, you can pick and choose which fits your trading personality and preferences instead of choosing someone else's system, designed for their particular foibles. For example, you may want a profitable system, but with very few losing trades. You may be happier with such a system than one which is 10 percent more profitable but has double the number of losing trades.

Confidence

With your own creation, you know you have tested it for profitability. That can mean a lot when it comes to actually "pulling the trigger," when you are unsure whether or not to place a particular trade. Good traders have confidence in their abilities to the point they know they are destined to make money. Part of this confidence comes from having spent hours developing their own systems. Once they execute the trade, confident in the system, they can focus on the trade itself, and not have to waste time on whether it was a mistake, or whether "expert" Joe Shmoe in the newspaper was right in his opinion about the trade.

Emotions are out, certainty is in

For many online traders deciding when to place a trade and when to get out can be an agonizing time. With a system, you can almost automate the process. The additional benefit of this is that you can remove the fear of cutting a loss and the hope that comes from hanging onto losers when you should have cut them.

System is friend, me is enemy

You are your own worst enemy when it comes to trading. You are human, and inevitably make irrational decisions based on tips, fear, greed. The system is like a port in a storm. It keeps you safe and makes sure you remain on track and do not get side-tracked.

---

key points

The benefits of a trading system:

- a stress reliever
- prevents market chasing
- controls inappropriate, ill-planned trades
- control over your own trading
- having a made-to-measure system suited to your preferences
- gives you confidence in your trading future
- more certainty, less emotion.

The role of "you" in system choice: Let my personality be my light

Trading with a system that does not suit your personality inevitably results in fighting both the system and yourself. Without an appropriate system you will wear yourself and your finances down. It is a little like playing football with someone else's gear on, or playing tennis with someone else's racket. It is self-evident that even if the football gear belongs to Joe Montana and the racket to Steffi Graf, you will not perform as they did.

expert advice ✔ **Martin Burton, Managing Director, Monument Derivatives**

"The key thing is that you have to trade within your personality. If you are a certain type of a person you have to identify what you are. Come to terms with yourself as a personality, genuinely and without lying, and not something you would like to be. Trade with what you are. That to me is a really big key issue with traders. I am what I am and I have no pretensions as to what I am and I am happy to trade within my own personality. That is a very important point for me."

Your system must play to your personality strengths and mitigate the influences of your personality weaknesses. You first need to ask yourself what your personality strengths and weaknesses are, and what you like and dislike about trading. For instance are you patient or impatient, do you believe in technical analysis, do you enjoy plotting charts, do you prefer a diverse or concentrated portfolio?

Next, decide if your system plays to your attributes. For instance, if you are impatient, then when devising your system, you would obviously not be looking at long-term investments. You would want a system, probably based upon technical analysis, that indicates imminent price movements. A system based on projections of likely long-term demand for a company's products is hardly likely to suit your personality, and would probably lead to frustration.

A further example of harmonizing your personality to your trading system is, if you dislike examining graphs and do not believe in technical analysis, you should not be spending much time on the rate of change (ROC) indicator as a predictor of price. Or, to take another example, if your personality is very risk-averse you may consider options a better instrument than futures. If you are indecisive you may want a system which spells out in detail when exactly you ought to enter and exit. If you are not a very quick thinker, you should probably not to be an intra-day trader. Finally, if you find you are overstressed when managing more than, say, three open positions at a time, you would want a system whereby each week you select only the very best trade that is available to you and open no new positions once you reach your limit of three open positions.

Before considering an actual system it helps to think about the kinds of results you want it to produce. If you consider what you want it to do, you will have a better idea of how it should be built. An analogy that comes to mind is making a car; if you know you want a fast red Italian two-seater, then you know you need some red paint and don't need four seats. Okay, so it's a dumb analogy, but it works for me. Come to answers for the following issues. We will discuss these issues in more detail later and how you can affect this various issues in designing your system.

Phil Flynn, Vice President, Alaron Trading

"Probably the biggest downfall traders have is that once they have found success they change their trading rules from what gave them success in the first place. A perfect example is a trader who was a day trader. He started with 50 point stops. These turned to 100 point stops. These then become 200 point stops. I have said to him many times, 'I can take any 5 days of your trading and if you had put on a stop you could have made tremendous money.' He had no control over his risk. All he could think was, 'I have to be right, I have to be right.'"

Why are you trading?

The answer is clear. Ultimately, you are trading in order to make money. Sure, you want to have a little fun along the way, perhaps laugh a little, cry a little, maybe even fall in love. But the bottom line is you are trading to make money. That being the case your trading system profits need to beat two benchmarks.

First, your profits have to beat a buy and hold strategy. Otherwise what are you sweating in front of a PC for? You may as well, um, buy and hold. Second, your profits using the system you design should beat the S&P 500. Again, if you can't beat the index, then why not just give your money to a mutual fund?

But it is not enough to just beat these benchmarks, you have to beat them by a sufficient margin to make all this effort worthwhile. In my opinion, that means a system producing at the very least 50 percent returns per annum.

David Kyte, Chairman, Kyte Group

"I don't come [to the trading floor] to earn a living, I come to make money."

How much risk?

When testing your system you will have to input how much initial equity you are starting with and how much you want to risk on any one trade. The risk issue will also determine the markets you can trade. Obviously, futures and options trading is not for the very low risk traders. I would recommend starting out in equities trading with a minimum of $10,000 and placing only $1000 on any one trade, with a stop-loss of $300 (i.e. maximum loss of 3 percent of your total equity on any one trade).

How long to be in the fire?

The length of time you want your trades to last is a major factor in system construction. There is little point perfecting a system which keeps you in the market on average for a week if you are more comfortable being in and out in a couple of days. (By the way, we will go through how you can vary your system parameters to achieve all these goals later.) The usual way to alter the time you are in the market is to select short periods for your indicators, e.g. using a five-day RSI instead of a 18-day one. Experimentation is the best way to see how long signals are taking between buy and sell. Remember, the shorter the period between entry and exit, the more of your time will be consumed in monitoring the markets, and therefore the greater the returns you should be looking for.

I tend to find also that the shorter the time you are in the market, the more intense and stressful trading can be. See Fig 7.1, which is a five-minute chart of the S&P 500 futures contract. Observe by how many points the contract has moved in the space of a few minutes. Now consider that each point is worth $xx per contract. As you can see, blink and you could be down a small fortune.

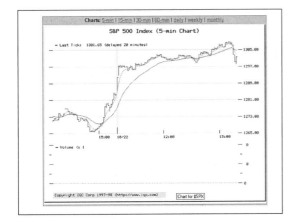

Fig 7.1 S&P 500 futures contract

Win-loss ratios: Pleasure to pain

Imagine you create two systems that produce the same profits (see Table 7.2). You would obviously go for the one which gives more wins than losses. Why, when the overall profit is the same? Because we all like taking winning trades to losing ones, even if we end up with the same bottom-line profit.

The more complicated thing you have to ask yourself, however, when designing a system is how much lower overall profit are you willing to accept to increase your wins to losses (see Table 7.3). What if the only choices you had were between System 1 and System 2. Which system would you prefer? This is a personality issue, because the answer will depend on how many losses you can take.

Imagine, for instance, a system that produces 55 percent return per annum. What if it had 98 losing trades and two profitable ones? Could your personality take that?

Another reason to have a high win to loss ratio is that it is all very well making a net profit, but it would be quite disturbing if it were done on just one or two trades. So, beware if your system is producing most of its profits from just a few winning trades.

System 1		System 2	
Profit	Wins to losses	Profit	Wins to losses
55% p.a.	15 to 85	55% p.a.	85 to 15

Table 7.2 Two systems, same profit

System 1		System 2	
Profit	Wins to losses	Profit	Wins to losses
55% p.a.	15 to 85	45% p.a.	40 to 60

Table 7.3 Two systems, two scenarios

example ## Winner sometimes take less than all

A few years ago I had a momentum-based trading system which produced healthy profits overall but would often have up to three consecutive losses. I had a strategy which required me to paper trade for a while if I ever had three consecutive losses.

Now, the three consecutive losses affected me in several ways. I would end up having to paper trade and be out of the market. Also, these losses were affecting me emotionally. I would have a lousy day, and spend hours going over both the trades and my system. Eventually, I realized I would rather sacrifice a little profit to have a "tighter, stricter" system which gave fewer signals, but more correct ones. In other words, I had a slightly less profitable system which had a higher win to loss ratio, but overall was in phase with my personality more. Just don't like losing, you see.

Most consecutive losses

What if your system reports 10 consecutive losses – can you handle such a string of losses? What kind of effect would it have on your faith in your system? You want this number to be as low as possible. It is also preferable to have the ratio of most consecutive wins to losses as large as possible. Otherwise you may have an "unbalanced" system whereby your net profit is being earned from a few winners with many losers. The danger of that is that you could get a string of losses which wipe you out either financially or emotionally.

Longest period out

A system which leaves you out of the market for very long periods of time may suggest there are better systems out there that have you more in the market extracting profits. While it is sometimes good to "be in cash," you have to play the game to win too. My own personality dictates that I am not out of the markets for too long at a time, otherwise I start thinking I am missing out on the action, and potential profits.

Maximum open trade drawdown

This figure represents the largest "paper" loss below the initial investment equity, i.e. a loss while the trade was still "open." Can you handle such a drawdown? If it more than 20 percent of your initial trade equity then it is too great.

Amount of losing trades

This sum represents the cumulative value of losses you have suffered. In the unlikely event that all your losing trades occurred consecutively, this is the amount you would be losing by. If it is greater than your equity, beware, because one day you may just suffer all your losses consecutively, and run out of capital.

Can personality be that important?

A question many traders pose when the issue of personality arises is whether it can really be *that* important. After all, if you are following buy and sell decisions then is not emotion and, hence, personality excluded?

Nevertheless, there are two reasons why personality is intertwined with system design. First, if you are unhappy with the system, for instance, maybe it is profitable but producing a lot of consecutive losses, then you are more likely to ditch the system you

check-list Personality issues affecting system design:

- profit levels per annum
- risk tolerance
- time in the market
- most consecutive losses
- longest time out of the market
- maximum drawdown while in a trade
- amount lost on losing trades.

have designed. Second, if you have the type of personality that hates the intense pressure and concentration of, say, intra-day trading, then it may be a miserable existence you will be leading, and, boy, the profits are going to have to be high to compensate for that.

Optimization: Eureka! The best system in the world

Sooner or later, all online traders developing their own systems think they have found that one treasure the Crusaders of centuries past searched for: the Holy Grail. They create a system and the results seem too good to be true. The only problem is that they *are* too good to be true. So what does the experience of other traders reveal who have been down this path, only to find that instead of being paved with gold (actually, better make that paved with platinum, given the price of gold) it is a dead end? How can we save our time and without bitter experience avoid the same mistakes?

The optimum problem

■ Take a price chart, maybe a stock like Walt Disney (DIS (see Fig 7.2)), or the S&P 500 futures contract.

■ Next, take a system. It could be your own, someone else's, but for the purposes of this chapter we will take a simple RSI trading system. The rules for the system are:

 – Buy: the system buys long when the relative strength index crosses above 30.

 – Exit: It closes the position when the relative strength index crosses below 70.

 – Stops: There is a stop-loss preventing losses greater than 10 percent.

 – Starting equity is $1000.

 – Commissions are $8 to buy and $8 to sell.

■ As you will know (he says, optimistically: see Chapter 35 if you need a refresher on the RSI), the RSI graph varies according to the periods it looks back over. This indicator therefore has one "optimizable variable." This variable is the "periods." (It may sometimes sound close to rocket science, but trust me, it isn't.) Therefore we next test the system for each period value/parameter of the RSI from 1 to 24 and see which parameter produces the best result.

■ Indulge me by assuming it is May 1998.

Fig 7.3 plots the buy and sell signals for the seven-period RSI. Computer testing revealed that the seven-period RSI was the most profitable signal generator. The upper part of the chart plots the equity graph. As you can see it reveals an approximately 42 percent return. Table 7.4 shows the optimization results.

Not bad, eh? With a more complex system we could probably have got even more

Fig 7.2 Disney

Fig 7.3 Buy and sell signals

Fig 7.4 Optimization equity

superior results. But that is just the beginning. Two common problems we traders now face are that we could suffer a loss, and, therefore, we need to undertake out-of-sample tests.

We next try the seven-period RSI from June 1988 to the present day. As you can see from the equity line in Fig 7.4, we suffer a big loss. A 41 percent loss, in fact. Yet this is still Disney, and still with an indicator which just produced a 42 percent return using the same parameter.

Out-of-sample tests

So where we may have thought we had arrived at a great profitable system, we have, in fact, arrived back at the drawing board. Sure, you could say I could have used a more complex system, or that only one security for a small period is not sufficient time to test a system. Well, you would be right, but the principle is the same: you need to test the same system across different securities, time frames and datasets (out-of-sample data testing). The system should hold up under all these tests.

However, just because they are out-of-sample data, this still does not mean that the system will perform well in the future. But at least with out-of-sample testing, the probability of having over-optimized is reduced.

Net profit	Percentage	RSI period
424.59	42.46	7
355.30	35.53	6
259.69	25.97	8
221.18	22.12	9
206.50	20.65	10
67.63	6.76	11
0	0	1, 12–24
−10.09	−1.01	5
−156.18	−15.62	2
−159.11	−15.91	3
−213.43	−21.34	4

Table 7.4 Optimization results

hot tip! I find it useful to keep one set of data which I use to develop my trading system and ideas, and two sets of out-of-sample data. I use one of the out-of-sample datasets for fine-tuning my system, and one for the very, very last test. That way I never run out of "clean" untested data.

Summary

As you have seen there is a lot to consider when deciding on trading systems. Of course, you could just take tips overheard on the subway/tube/metro but where's the fun in that? In this chapter we have focussed on the importance of personality to selecting a trading system, a much neglected issue. It is something you could ignore, but you would then never achieve your optimal level of profits.

8

Key principles of strategy making and testing: Some problems

Online trader problems

■ Thinking about creating my own system. Where to begin? What are the steps?

■ What problems could I encounter and how should I side-step them?

■ Do I really need to be able to program a computer to create my own system? Where's the fun in that?

■ What do other online traders have to say on creating systems?

Later in the book we will look at some tried and tested strategies. However, while some people just like to eat their cake, others like to cook it, too. In other words, you may not want just "off-the-shelf" systems and strategies, you may want to develop your own. In this chapter we go through key principles and problems you may encounter in developing a robust strategy from scratch. In subsequent chapters we go on to examine how to resolve those problems. See, it's simple: first problem, then solution. I strongly recommend a good cup of coffee, however, before diving into this chapter.

Fig 8.1 Ameritrade daily bar chart

Step 1 Heads up: Price

Before we can formulate a trading system, we first need to have a look at some historic price charts for the product. So, for example, if we are interested in trading short term in stocks, then we would start with some stock price charts, for instance an Ameritrade chart for the past, say, year (see Fig 8.1). Of course you could take more than one year of daily data.

Obviously, we need charts of the product and time frame we will be trading. If we are trading stocks for the short term, we would work with stock charts showing daily price bars. Chapter 35 shows takes you through some of the best web-sites and software for displaying price charts.

Step 2 Entry and exit: Mark the chart

The next thing to do is mark on the chart where you would have wanted any system to get you into the market and where you would have wanted the system to have got you out of the market. See Fig 8.2 as an example. The entry and exit points you choose may be different. But, essentially, before you mark the chart these are some points to consider:

■ You want buy signals to be generated just as a big move starts.

■ A "big" move is a matter of trading choice, but obviously it is one which if you had entered would be sufficiently large to overcome commissions and "slippage" and leave a healthy profit.

■ The corresponding sell signal has to be as close as possible to the peak of the move to extract as much profit as possible.

Remember, this chapter and the whole process is for someone wanting to develop their own systems from scratch. If all this is turning your mind into mush, you could always just follow the ready-made systems that appear later in the book. The rest of us won't think you've wimped out.

Fig 8.2 has signals which were placed "by eye." In fact, in the next chapter we shall look at some web-sites and software which can do the same for you automatically. Indeed, you will be introduced to software that can calculate the optimal profits you could have earned in a theoretically perfect system with 20–20 hindsight. The aim of such an impossible signal generator is to give you a template against which to compare your own system's signals, to see how close they are to perfection.

To illustrate the fact that your choice of buy and sell signals is a matter of personal choice, an equally valid equivalent to Fig 8.2 may look like Fig 8.3.

Fig 8.2 Ameritrade with buy and sell signals

	Trade 1	Trade 2	Trade 3
Entry price (approx.)	$7	$10	$55
Exit price (approx.)	$12	$60	$165
Profit/loss (after $16 round turn commission) on purchase based on $5000 equity for each trade	$3554	$24 984	$9884

Table 8.1 P&L for signals in Fig 8.2

How do I choose where exactly to place the buy and sell signals?

The major difference between Figs 8.2 and 8.3 are that buy and sell signals on Fig 8.3 are better suited to a trader who is looking to develop a system which does not keep him in the market for as long as those signals in 8.2 would. Hence the signals are a lot closer together.

Total profit for a system if it could have generated the signals shown in Fig 8.2 is $38 422 after commissions. On an equity of $5000. That's a return of 768 percent in under one year and just going long (see Table 8.1).

Fig 8.3 Ameritrade with different buy and sell signals

Total profit for a system if it could have generated the signals shown on Fig 8.3 is $24 549 after commissions. On an equity of $5000. That's a return of 491 percent in under one year and just going long (see Table 8.2).

A simple buy and hold strategy would have produced around $125 000 profit!

But before you get all excited, remember this is based on the hypothetical signals, with hindsight. And why would a book about short-term trading make such revelations about buy and hold strategies? Well, you need to trade to make money, however it is made.

Why do we look at such signals? Well, we are going to try to find a system to fit the signals, and this small illustration shows that where the buy and sell signals are can make a very big difference to the bottom line. The better you understand the nuts and bolts of system manufacture from the bottom up, then, hopefully, the better the system you can design and the more money you can make.

Before you throw the book away in favor of a "buy and hold" strategy, let me remind you of one reason why short-term trading is popular. The downside when buy and sell

	Trade 1	Trade 2	Trade 3	Trade4	Trade 5
Entry price (approx.)	$9	$10	$17	$26	$66
Exit price (approx.)	$12	$18	$33	$58	$174
Profit/loss (after $16 round turn commission) on purchase based on $5000 equity for each trade	$1649	$3984	$4688	$6144	$8084

Table 8.2 P&L for signals in Fig 8.3

signals are closer together is generally that the profit levels between entry and exit are lower. So why would you want a system with signals closer together? This goes to the heart of why we would trade in the short term at all, and is a question all traders ask themselves. There are several reasons we may want buy and sell signals closer together.

As long as we can overcome commissions (which in online trading are minimal anyway) you have the opportunity to capture the upward parts of all moves and be out of the downward elements, and therefore make a relatively little amount (relative to buy and hold sometimes) on each trade (because the time between entry and exit is small) but make a lot cumulatively (because you are doing a high volume of trades). To illustrate this point check out Fig 8.4.

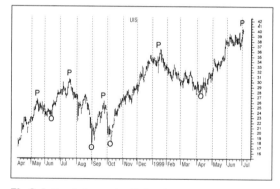

Fig 8.4 Unysis buy and sell signals

Total profit for a system if it could have generated the signals shown on Fig 8.4 is $9896 after commissions. On an equity of $5000. That's a return of 198 percent in under one year and just going long (see Table 8.3).

On a buy and hold the corresponding profit is $3308. And that's why we trade short term – to make a buck on the ups, and side-step on the downs.

	Trade 1	Trade 2	Trade 3	Trade4	Trade 5
Entry price (approx.)	$18	$24	$20	$20	$29
Exit price (approx.)	$26	$29	$25	$35	$39
Profit/loss (after $16 round turn commission) on purchase based on $5000 equity for each trade	$2200	$1024	$1234	$3734	$1704

Table 8.3 P&L for signals in Fig 8.4

To further make the point about what we are trying to achieve when trading shorter term consider Fig 8.5. Imagine you bought at the start of the period and sold at the end. In all three cases you would have made the same amount of profit over the same time. But, only in the first two instances would a non-buy and hold strategy have had the potential to make more money, because it may have entered at the lowest point and exited at the highest.

With 20–20 hindsight we could say when we should have just adopted a buy and hold strategy and when we should have adopted a more active short-term trading strategy. Since we can't foresee the type of market, we have to play the odds as suggested by Table 8.4.

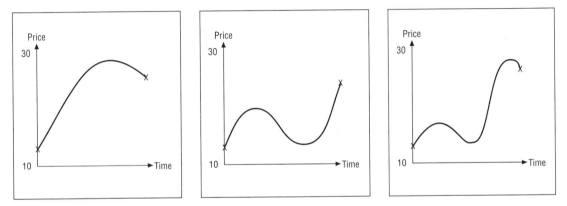

Fig 8.5 Non-buy and hold strategy at work

Stock trend	Strategy likely to produce best results
Up	Buy and hold
Sideways	Active
Down	Active

Table 8.4 Playing the odds for best results

Step 3 Overlaying indicators

For those unfamiliar with the most popular technical analysis indicators, I recommend they read Chapter 35 first.

So, we have our chart marked with areas where we would like our indicators to indicate

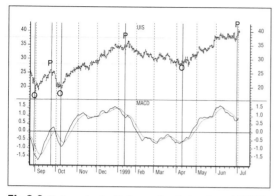

Fig 8.6 Unisys chart with buy and sell signals and MACD

buy and sell signals. Our next step is to take the chart and add indicators to look for good fits. We'll worry about "tweaking" and optimization later, but for now let's look at an example (see Fig 8.6).

The vertical lines in Fig 8.6 coincide with where we would want the indicator to suggest buy and sell signals. Here, I have chosen the MACD purely for illustrative purposes. Anyone familiar with the MACD and how it operates (or anyone who has read Chapter 35 on technical analysis) will see that the vertical lines are quite close to indicator buy and sell signals.

Let's assume for the purposes of illustrating the point of how indicators may be used that we will apply the following trading system rules for the MACD:

1   Buy where the MACD is below 0 and moves above its own moving average (the dotted line).

2   Sell where the MACD moves down across its moving average unless not already in an open position.

3   A protective sell stop is placed at a loss of, say 15 percent.

By changing indicator parameters we could probably get it to be even closer – a process called optimization. But we'll come to that in the next chapter.

But all is not bliss

Now we come to the problem with using just one straightforward indicator. The indicator also appears to give buy and sell signals in places we did not indicate on our price chart. Fig 8.7 signifies "extra" buys and their corresponding sells based on our three rules.

While our system is basic and crude, the point is the same: on closer inspection the signals generated by merely taking a technical indicator will not produce particularly good results, especially when compared to the potential profit available in theory.

So what are we to do to improve matters? Well, that's where the beginner moves to the next level. We now appreciate that trading life is not simple, that god is in the detail and we need to be somewhat sophisticated.

But all this is not to say technical analysis is useless, that complicated strategies are better than simple ones, or that the MACD is useless. In fact, I prefer simple strategies to complicated ones, and the MACD is one of my favorite indicators. The point of this

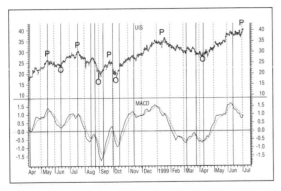

Fig 8.7 Unysis chart with signals generated by a simple MACD system

step-by-step exercise is to show that in trading system construction the answers are to be found elsewhere – beyond the very basic. Where that elsewhere is will be revealed next.

Use the power of the (computing) force

If that cup of coffee is getting cold, you may want a refill – especially if you have brainache about now.

One of the best ways to see what trading systems may or may not work and play with their parameters is to have specialist software do it for you. In Chapter 9 we profile some of the most popular and best software for systems development and testing, and what you should look for in the software and web-sites.

Multiply your resources

To overcome some of the deficiencies of oversimple strategies the advanced trader uses multiple time frames and multi-indicators. The reasoning behind this and how it operates is described in Chapter 12.

Summary

In this chapter we have highlighted some problems with simple technical analysis. First, too many buy and sell signals can be generated, thereby reducing profitability. Second, without a computer, trying to find the best, "optimal," parameters can be a tedious and near impossible task. So what is an online e-trader to do?

In the next chapter we shall examine some web-sites that provide solutions to our trading strategy development problems, and which should, therefore, increase profitability.

9

Software for creating and testing systems: And then Gates said unto man: "Let there be powerful software"

Online trader problems

- Do I need trading software to create my trading system?
- What is the best software for creating trading systems and for charting that most of the other online traders use?

Having in the last chapter seen some of the problems in creating and then optimizing trading systems for maximum profit, what we really need is software to do all the hard work for us, especially if you lazier than a rug on tranquillizers. And lo! Such software exists.

In this chapter we examine what you should be looking for in such software, how to use it, with examples to familiarize yourself with the power of the programs and the potential for creating and testing your own systems. We will also look at the top names in the industry, and how to get hold of some of the goodies. Towards the end of the chapter we look at software especially for options analysis. Finally, all such software needs daily and historical price data, and we want reputable sources for them. So, who are the best sources?

What to look for

We are looking for value-for-money software from the best companies in the industry that provide the most easy-to-use and comprehensive trading systems creating and testing tools. It's that simple. While we are at it, we may as well ask for software that also charts markets and indicators. Oh, some ready-made systems would be nice too.

hot tip! **If they have built it, it must be needed**

By seeing the kinds of features top software provides, e.g. optimization, you can get a good idea of what you should be looking to do when developing your own systems.

Systems creation and testing features

There are certain things we want from our software that makes creating and testing systems that bit easier. Remember, first we create the system, then we test it, next we optimize it.

We want software to:

- Help us write trading systems e.g. how to put into software language "Go long when moving average one crosses moving average two and the momentum indicator is in positive territory and the weekly MACD is also above its moving average."

- Test our systems, i.e. calculate how much money we would have made, or lost, if we had traded the system.

- Allow us to analyze the test results by having the software plotting where we should have bought and sold, and P&Ls of each trade.

- Automatically optimize our system by comparing profitability for each possible combination of parameters. (Too much gobbledegook? It becomes clearer later, honest.)

- Allow us to compare trading systems.

hot tip! Remember, technical analysis is an art. You can't incorporate market feel, experience. Although some people do prefer mechanical systems which remove all human decision making.

Indicator builders

Does the software allow you to create your own indicators? This can be useful if books or magazines describe new indicators, and provide the coding for you to enter into your software to try out for yourself, or if you just want to test a few ideas out.

Building your own indicators is not for everyone; it can be complex, tedious, and require some proficiency at math. Most good software has the key building blocks you would need to express the elements of most indicators. To try to make indicator building a little bit easier, software often has key terms in dialog boxes which you can simple add by clicking. Good software comes with textbook explanations of how everything works.

This is what the moving average convergence divergence indicator (MACD), which plots the difference between two exponential moving averages, looks like in a popular software package:

```
Mov(close, 12, E) - Mov(close, 26, E)
```

example ▌ Indicator language

The language used to plot a custom indicator is usually "pigeon English." For instance, typing "close – mov (close, 15, simple)" will plot a line that subtracts the 15-day moving average from the close of each day.

System development

Check to make sure you can create your own system, that is specify trading rules by which you can enter and exit the market. Some enhancements to look for:

- Stops: Can you enter "stops" on specified losses (in dollars or percent), periods of activity (i.e. so you are not left long or short in a security for long period of time), on specified profit levels (again, based on dollar amounts or percent) or trailing stops (a stop that is activated when a certain amount of profit is lost)?

- Commissions: Can you specify commission levels in advance so your profit and loss reports for the system are more accurate?

- Position specification: Can you tell the system to consider only long, only short or both positions?

- Margin specification: Can you specify if you can trade on margin so as to give a more accurate profit and loss report?

- Equity line: It would be useful for analyzing your system if a cumulative track of your equity were plotted along time (see Fig 9.1).

expert advice ✔ Phil Flynn, Vice President, Alaron Trading

"The other thing about great traders is their discipline, sticking to their plan. What I have done to be more disciplined is to become more mechanical. I take the pressure off myself. I let the markets tell me when I am right or wrong. It becomes a lot more easier if you can make it non-personal. This is the position, this is the price, this is the target, this is the stop."

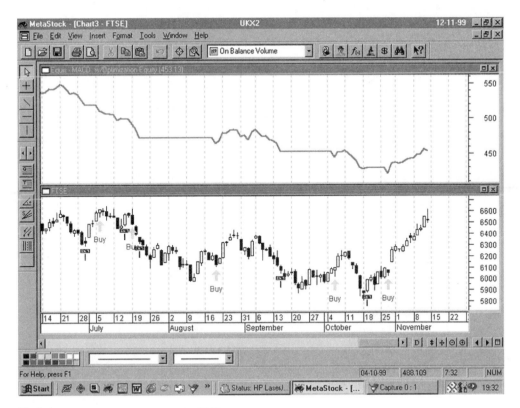

Fig 9.1 Equity line for a test using the MACD

Optimization

Optimization is where the computer tests numerous values to find the most profitable one. This is good. We want this in our software, please. Consider a simple system. You go long when the price is above the five-day moving average and exit when it is below it. If you then optimize this system, the computer may say that you earn the most profit by using a 10-day moving average on this particular security instead. And that is optimization. The bottom line can be quite startling. By changing the parameters you could go from a loss-making system to a profitable one.

A good software package will report back the following for each of the parameters it tested:

- total net profit
- percent gain/loss
- buy/hold profit (i.e. how much you could have made if you just bought and held)

- average profit per trade (average win and average loss)

- total number of trades (number of winners and losers)

- largest win and loss

- average holding time to gain a win

- most consecutive wins and losses

- average consecutive wins and losses

- total time out of market

- average time out of market

- maximum drawdown

- commission paid.

Fig 9.2 Part of a trading system report from TradeStation by OmegaResearch

As you can see there is a wealth of fascinating information (see Fig 9.2). You soon realize that net profit is not necessarily the only thing to consider. For instance, what if you placed 100 trades and lost on 99 and won on one. Even if you showed a net profit would you want that system or one where you showed a lower profit but won around half the time? More about this later.

Securities screening

Now, this is not what happens to you when you apply to join the CIA. This is far more important than national security. You want your software package to:

- Go through all your securities and list all those with buy and sell signals according to your system. That way you can put your feet up while your overworked computer sweats it out.

- Go through securities and rank them according to performance.

---

smug trader

Get off your butt

To be a truly smug trader and trade well, you have to do more than just let your computer find your buy and sell signals. You need to look at price charts yourself, and treat them like a symphony with new notes added each period. Feel them, caress them . . . well, you get the idea. Understand by observing how the price and indicator changes daily. That way you will have a better, deeper understanding of the market and I am afraid that is something a computer cannot inculcate. Mind you, did you ever see the film *Demon Seed*?

- Go through securities and rank them according to whether they have triggered buy signals on your system and on additional filters, e.g. has a buy signal been triggered according to your own system and has the price moved above its 50-day and 200-day moving averages?

- Allow you to customize the screening process so you can have the computer look for particular changes in the securities.

- Alert you when a signal has occurred.

Other features

Essentially, any software we want should have as many of the following features as possible. These are some of the features top online traders would look for in their state-of-the-art trading software. Afterwards, we will analyze the top names and check out their sites.

Markets

We are obviously going to want software that can handle data about the market we are particularly concerned with, be it stocks, options, futures, indices. Top-notch software can handle all this and more.

Data frequency

Don't forget to double-check that the software version handles intra-day or end-of-day data respectively, depending on the types of trading you are intending. Most intra-day traders also need end-of-day data for their analysis, but the converse is not true. Fortunately, most software that offers intra-day data also offers end-of-day data.

Data included

Are the data you will need daily included in the price of the package or do you need to get them from a third-party supplier, and, if so, is your software compatible with the top data providers. The software we examine are all compatible with the best third-party data providers.

Data downloader

Do you need extra software to download data from the third-party data provider, or is that included in the price of the software?

Data cleaner?

Does the software come with a feature which scans all downloaded data for errors and automatically corrects errors such as price highs and lows and dates out of sequence? It can be incredibly annoying if your charts are incomprehensible due to corrupt data. The best software automatically scans, detects, and corrects.

Data formats

Can the software read a variety of data formats so allowing you a wider source of data provider? You obviously do not want to be stuck with some esoteric "never heard of it" data format.

Charts

The more types of charts the software can display with the data, the better. Obviously, all can display bar charts, but you want Japanese Candlesticks, Market Profile (which is very popular with professional traders, but very few software packages are capable of producing it), Kengo, Equivolume, Point & Figure, to name but a few.

Indicators

Again, the more indicators that come with the package, the better, since it gives you options to play around with. Most come with the obvious ones such as momentum, stochastics, etc.

Ease of use

How easy is the package to use? To test this you need a demo version. For instance, most people are used to working on Windows, and therefore software designed to have the look and feel of a Windows package, e.g. drag and drop, right click functionality, icons, etc., is going to be a lot easier to learn quickly and more intuitively.

Over-fitting

When testing systems there is the obvious danger that by "tweaking" and optimizing the system you may have fallen foul of "over-fitting." That is, the system works for the data at hand, but not as well on "out-of-sample" data.

For that reason it is important to test the system on lots of different time period and sample data. I prefer to keep one set of data for the final test after all other optimization has been completed. That final test should be in line with preceding results, otherwise all may not be well at the ranch and a return to the drawing board may be called for.

chat box 9.1

Should I paper trade?

From a trader on Silicon Investor on 5.6.1999

Many people begin their quest for day trading success by being conservative and paper trading. After a few weeks or months, they develop a "successful" method of trading and get the confidence to begin trading with a real account using real money.

Unfortunately, a funny thing tends to happen on the way to the bank. They find that they consistently lose money. Why? Well, the "real" world is not nearly as easy as the paper world. The reason is 100 percent related to liquidity. The only difference between paper trading and real trading is getting your orders filled.

This is easily done with paper trading. Simply assume you can buy at the inside ask (seems conservative, right?) and sell at the inside bid. Further refine your paper trading assumptions by assuming you will get filled at whatever the inside bid/ask is after a delay of five or 10 seconds from (paper) order placement (seems even more conservative, right?). Regardless, you will likely find that it is much easier to paper trade than to trade for real.

Why bother paper trading? It sounds like paper trading is a waste of time. Not so fast. I can assure you that any system that loses money while paper trading will lose money even faster during real trading. In this respect, paper trading is very valuable. Why waste real money by trading any system that cannot be consistently profitable during paper trading? Also, you can develop a huge amount of knowledge and experience while paper trading. And in addition, paper trading is cheap!

Don't waste your hard-earned capital on a system until you develop the confidence that it can be successful while paper trading. NASA uses flight simulators for a reason. They don't send astronauts into orbit simply with the confidence that they think the astronaut may possibly know what to do at the right time, perhaps.

If you find a successful system, there will be plenty of time to make your millions in the future, don't worry about not making money today. I am a firm believer that paper trading *will not* adequately simulate real trading. But I believe paper trading is an absolute requirement for any new trader who wants to be successful, but cannot afford to lose a fortune trying. Paper trading will not assure success, but it will limit the losses while you search for it.

Once you find a "successful" system, carefully attempt a few trades in the real market. Does it trade as well as it paper trades? Why or why not? Can you improve you order routing skills to make it trade as well? It is hopeless to get this system to work at all in the real world? If successful . . . GREAT! If not, you found out cheaply . . . Move on to another system or refine your current system based on what you have learned.

Checklist for reducing the risk of over-fitting:

- ·The rise in cumulative profits should be gradual and gentle, not with volatile spikes.
- Test the system across different time frames.
- Test the system on different market conditions: uptrends, downtrends, and non-trending markets.
- Test the system on different securities.

Top software sites to try before you buy

Having teased you with all the wonders of modern software, now is the time to stop being coy and name some names. Table 9.1 names some names, web-sites, and prices (at time of print). All these products are best of breed, no second-rate time wasters here.

Product*	Company	Address	Cost	Charting
Metastock	Equis	www.equis.com	$349	✓
OmniTrader 3.5	Nirvana	www.nirv.com	$395 (futures) $695 (stocks)	✓
TradeStation	Omega Research	www.omegaresearch.com	$2399	✓
Trading Expert Pro	AIQ Systems	www.aiq.com	$1295	✓
Window on Wall St Day Trader	Window On Wall St	www.windowonwallstreet.com	$1499	✓

* Check out the web-sites for latest versions.

Table 9.1 Naming names

Options analysis software

Whether they use fundamental analysis or technical analysis or a combination of both, and whether they trade stocks, futures, indices, or currency options, many options traders also use special options analysis software which helps them in making their trading decisions. Such software relates specifically to the technicalities of options. The details of the sites explain what the software does. This will, of course, make most sense to you if you have an understanding of options, for which see the Appendix 2 and the educational sites in Chapter 37.

expert advice ✓ **Phil Flynn, Vice President, Alaron Trading**

"The best thing to do when you have a trading plan that is working is to think very, very carefully before you make a single variation. I guess being somewhat mechanical is the best way to avoid that situation. If you change anything that is working you have to make sure it is not your ego doing it. You have to make a very solid decision that this is to improve the system as opposed to taking bigger risks for the sake of it. Have it written down before you change it so you can always return to the original plan."

Although it is often possible to trade successfully without such software, the calculations should be undertaken by options traders whether they use the software or not. Consequently, such software is most useful if:

- You plan to undertake more complex strategies, e.g. butterflies, rather than simple calls and puts purchases.
- You are not confident (despite reading Appendix 2 and following the options educational sites listed in the book) with the mathematical calculations.
- You require to do the calculations speedily.
- You would prefer a graphical representation of likely option scenarios.
- You are concerned you may be missing out on greater profits by using different strategies.

In this section the most popular sites are listed and also those options analysis software vendors considered best.

What to look for

When considering options analysis software there are certain things it needs to be able to do to be more than a mere unnecessary add-on. Table 9.2 provides some comparisons.

Option-pricing model
The software will calculate a fair value for the option based on industry-standard option pricing models. This can be a useful benchmark guide to compare prices with the market price.

Auto-position search
Good software should be able to search, based on the user's trading objectives, which options strategies are the most suitable. The search should be based not only on common strategies, such as call and put purchases, but also less common one such as butterflies and strangles.

Name and web address	Option-pricing model	Auto-position search	Option breakdown	Position chart	Probability calculator	Products *	Major quote vendors	Other features	Demo/trial	Price
OptionStation (Omega Research) www.omegaresearch.com	✓	✓	✓	✓	✓	csifb	✓	Alert	✓	$1794
Option Vue V (Option Vue) www.optionvue.com	✓	✓	✓	✓	✓	csifb	✓	Portfolio tracker	✓	$1695
Optionscope (Equis) www.equis.com	✓	✗	✓	✓	✗	csifb	✓			$49.95
Option Pro (Essex Trading Co) www.essextrading.com	✓	✓	✓	✓	✓	sf	✓	Portfolio tracker	✓	from $795
Options Lab (Mantic Software) www.manticsoft.com	✓	✗	✓	✓	✗	csifb	n/a		✓	$89.95
OptionTrader98 (AustinSoft) www.austin-soft.com	✓	✓	✓	✓	✗	csifb	✗ included	Portfolio tracker	✓	$395

* c = currency options; s = stock options; i = index options; f = futures options; b = bond options.

Table 9.2 Table of comparison

Usually, the user can enter his assumptions about target price, volatility, expiry. The software will then apply each strategy to the assets available, given the user's assumptions. A list should then be produced ranking each strategy by corresponding likely profit (and sometimes maximum profit, risk). The more ranges the user can input, the better. For example, instead of having to input a target price, can the user input a range, or can the user input a date and, based on the underlying asset's historical volatility, will software use the most likely price at that date?

Option breakdown

Any software in this category should be able to totally analyze any given option providing information such as volatility, Greek risk measurements (delta, gamma, vega, theta, rho, lambda), time and intrinsic value, open interest.

Position chart

This can be a helpful visual aid. It graphically shows how the position's profit/loss profile will look over time. Software should display "what if" scenarios based on the user's own assumptions so a best, worst and most likely case scenario can be built. These charts help understand risk better.

Probability calculator

This calculates the probability of the underlying or option price being at a certain price level by a certain time (input by the user).

Major quote vendors supported

We obviously want a software package that supports data downloads from the major quote vendors. That reduces additional costs. It also means that we are not tied to the software provider's own data.

Other features

These can be a useful but non-essential bonus. Two common ones are pager alerts, i.e. you are paged when certain price targets are met. The second common feature is the portfolio tracker – to track your option positions (see Fig 9.3).

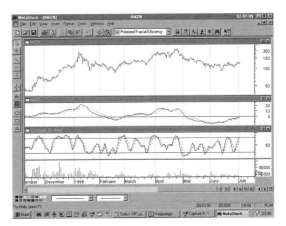

Fig 9.3 Polarized fractal efficiency

> **hot tip!** **Check it out**
>
> Although many of the top options analysis software providers provide the same services, after all there are only so many ways to calculate an option's theoretical fair value, it is the way they display the information and how user friendly the software screens are that make the major difference. So, make sure you take the time, and have the patience, to try their demos first.

Summary

Many, many moons ago when TV was new technology, the moon was not yet American, and people thought Nixon would be good in the White House, traders used to undertake technical analysis with pen and paper. They would carefully collate data and plot them. Now, there is something to be said about this, and sometimes I will take a price chart and follow each bar with my finger and see how the indicator reacts – to get a feel for the motions of prices. Nowadays, with powerful computers to perform our technical analysis for us, we can do a lot more, very quickly.

In this chapter we have seen some of the advantages of using software as part of a trading system. It certainly has become an essential tool for the online trader and given the relative cheapness of some software, I find it extremely useful for getting a quick feel for how a security is performing, and for testing out ideas.

10

The anatomy of a price rise and strategy rules

Online trader problems

- What is it about price moves and indicators that makes making profits so difficult?
- If I know this what can I do to avoid problems?

In this chapter

Making trading rules by which to enter, let alone exit, the market, can sometimes feel like trying to solve the Rubik Cube: you get one bit right (for instance, the number of losing trades is low) only to find that another bit is not quite right (the profits from your remaining trades drop). In this chapter we examine the nature of a price move and what you should know before designing your own rules or using someone else's.

Price moves

If you are looking to go long the market, then, ideally, you want an indicator that will get you in as close to the bottom of the rise as possible. The problem with many indicators is that they are either too early (so that the market keeps dropping after you enter, only for you to find that it knocks out your stop-loss, or to find you should have entered later to make more money) or too late (in which case you often find you make very little profit because the bulk of the move has gone) or, worse, the signal is so late the trend has reversed (see Table 10.1). Don't worry, there will be pictures to go with the words (see Figs 10.1–10.8).

Consider the nature of the start of an upward price move (see Fig 10.5).

	Indicator or entry rule triggered too early		Indicator or entry rule triggered too late	
Price action	Price continues dropping after entry, then rises	Price continues dropping after entry, then drops some more	Price has only a little further to rise	Price turns around and now starts to fall back
Consequence	Little profit. You miss out on some profit	You make a loss	Little profit	You make a loss

Table 10.1 Price moves and indicators

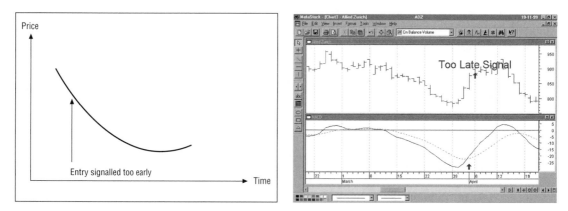

Fig 10.1 Indicator too early   **Fig 10.2** Indicator too late

The price stops dipping and rises a little. At point x some indicator, let us say the momentum indicator, will signal a buy. It could be any indicator, but for this illustration we are assuming that a signal is generated at that point. When you develop your own rules you will find that some of your tests result in a signal at that early point. At point

Fig 10.3 Start of an upward price move

y, another indicator, let us say the stochastic, will generate a signal.

Now as things stand one of three things could happen. From point y the price could dip and move higher, or it could dip and dip lower, or not dip and just keep rising. As matters stand, all things being equal we do not know what will happen when we are at point y. Of course, looking at other indicators and factors we may conclude that one event is more *probable* than another, but we never *know*. That is what makes trading difficult. It is all probabilities.

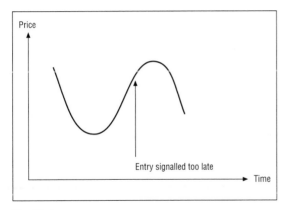

Fig 10.4 Price dips

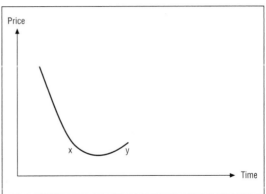

Fig 10.5 Price moves higher

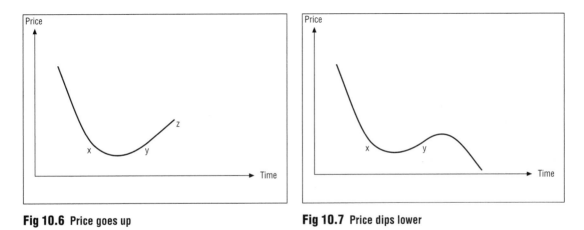

Fig 10.6 Price goes up

Fig 10.7 Price dips lower

If the price dipped and then dipped even lower and you entered at x on the indications of the momentum indicator then by the time you got out you would not suffered as big a loss compared to getting in at point y. The other benefit of getting in at point x is that if the price actually dips and rise, then you would make a bigger profit than if you got in at y, and also would probably not ever go into negative territory.

So you prefer indicators that give a buy signal at x over those that give it slightly later at y? But that seems too obvious. Well, the problem with indicators that give buy signals at x is that they are triggered by a small price rise that can occur so often in everyday declines, i.e. it generates many false signals. The small price rise that triggers the buy signal at x, does not trigger the signal at y. So y avoids lots of small losses. We now have a trade-off to face.

The early indicator gives us more profit compared to the later one if the price continues upward, and less of a loss if the price dips after triggering the later indicator. But all this comes at the expense of having more losing trades that are avoided by the later indicator.

What should you do?

The prime concern in any system is what makes more money, the system triggered at x or at y and that is the determinant. I have often found that the indicator giving the buy signal at y is the one that is more profitable because it avoids all the false losing signals of the signal at x. So that is settled, then, is it?

The problem is that as soon as you get the signal at y you can do one of two things the next morning:

1 You could buy on the open. This is not recommended because what if you had waited and saw the price fall, you could have saved yourself from a bad trade or entered later at a better price.

2 You could wait to see if the price rises and then buy. This is what I prefer to do. But if only life were that easy. What do you do if the price does indeed fall from the open, but at the close your indicator still says buy?

Well, you go with what the price is doing, not what the indicator is saying. If the indicator says buy and the next morning the price falls, you should not buy.

When do you get in?

I would wait for the price to break the preceding day's high, or break the level it reached when the buy signal was first given. (I know all this seems convoluted, but you will encounter these questions and wonder what on earth to do, so persevere.) This way, if the price keeps falling, you are OK because you never got in. But, on the downside, all this waiting means you could enter at such a late stage that the whole move has expired (see Fig 10.4).

It is this that may well make you think the market is out to get you and you feel it has led you up the garden path like some teasing amorous lover, only to have the door slammed in your face before you could get . . . some. Another analogy is the market as a bucking bronco trying to throw you off. Fear not, she teases everyone, do not become paranoid, that is the way of the markets.

Now look at Fig 10.8 again.

Do you get in at x, y or z? I prefer the indicator that gives the signal at y, and if the price dips immediately after the signal is generated, I try to get in as soon as possible on an uptick (i.e. slight price rise) but not as late as z. This way I miss the losses incurred by getting in too early at x and too late at z.

Fig 10.8 When did you get in?

Summary

In system and trading rule design you will definitely come across the problem in Fig 10.8, so it is good to know it exists; others have had to deal with it. It involves trade-offs, but ultimately the guiding decision is "what makes the most money in the long term?" Remember, you may not always encounter this problem, the price may just go up and up and up and not dip until well after you have got buy signals from your system. But on the whole, price rise and dip and indicators come in three flavors; early, intermediate, late. I have tried to convey what I believe generally to be the optimal strategy.

Online trading strategies for stocks, futures, and options

11

Essential technical analysis strategies for online trading

Online trader problems

- How do I know which securities to buy?
- Even if I know what to buy, when is the best time to buy it, so I reduce the chances of the stock going down right after I have bought it?
- What are the signs a security is "tanking," i.e. ripe for a fall?
- What is this thing "technical analysis" people keep talking about?
- I can't be bothered reading a load of accounts, analysts' reports and dull stuff like that before deciding what to buy. What should I do?
- How do the big institutions use technical analysis?

Vast books have been written on TA (check out the reading list (Appendix 5) for some of the best), so this is a refresher chapter for people who may need reminding of some of the key concepts of technical analysis. But it is also for all those newbies who need to get up to speed about TA. I am not going to go through every single analytic method known to man and beast. I am going to focus on the techniques I use, that are the most popular, and that the major institutions use. There will be no discussion of the latest esoteric method developed by some whacky maths professor out of Lima who swears that TA, mixed with a bit of sun-spot gazing, produces great trading results. No. You only get the good stuff here.

I love TA, and trust me, this stuff is so straightforward once you get the hang of it. I have explained it to Oxford professors and 14-year-old students. Remember throughout that TA is simply a way of trying to find out when to buy low and sell high. The software and sites discussed in Chapters 9 and 39 will allow you to easily plot charts, indicators, and trendlines.

The rationale for technical analysis

As we noted before the reason for using TA is to know when to buy low and sell high. It tends to work best over a time frame of a few days to a few weeks, so is ideal for short-term trading. Many of the indicators and methods of analysis we will examine are trying to determine when traders may have overreacted and therefore have sold too much stock too quickly or vice versa and therefore afford us the opportunity to enter or exit the market at the best time to maximize profits.

But TA does not always work. Nothing in the markets always works – as far as I know – although I understand George Soros may have a better idea than most what often works. Whenever we use TA, or any other form of analysis, we are, in fact, looking for points where there is an increased *probability* of a price move.

Some tools used to determine high-probability price move areas

Charting

Let us start at the beginning, and as simply as possible. The first thing all technical analysts will do is put up a price chart. There are many, many types. Check out Figs 11.1, 11.2 and 11.3.

Bar charts are the most popular ways of depicting prices. The length is determined by the extremities of the high and the low. The horizontal line on the left of each vertical line represents the opening price, and the horizontal line on the right represents the close.

In Japanese Candlesticks there is a "body" and a line (like a wick). The body is a rectangle drawn between the open and close of the day. It is shaded black if the close is lower than the open, and white if the close is above the open. The wick is added to join the high and low of the day. Of course, if there is no price movement after the open then there will be no body or wick, just a horizontal line.

I won't bore you with point and figure charts, or for that matter Renko or Kagi – bar charts and Candlesticks are by far the most popular and all we need to know before we undertake a PhD in TA.

Trendlines

A trendline simply joins a series of higher lows or lower highs. Uh? Look at Fig 11.4. We see the line joining higher lows. Drawing trendlines is best treated as an art and you should not look for exact points, but get a feel for where prices are hitting the approximate narrow area around the line and then moving back up. What trendlines try to represent are areas where there is a relatively increased probability of a price move off the trendline.

You would not trade off the trendline, but rather use it as one piece of evidence when determining likely price moves. More of how to do this later.

Support and resistance

You will often have read or heard the phrase "prices met stiff resistance today and could not break through the [xx,xxx] barrier." By drawing support and resistance levels we are again trying to determine areas where prices are *probably*, but not *certainly*, going to

Fig 11.1 Bar chart

Fig 11.2 Japanese Candlesticks

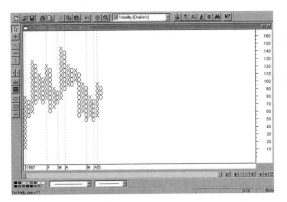

Fig 11.3 Point and figure chart

Fig 11.4 Trendlines

behave in a particular way. See for instance Figs 11.5 and 11.6. They depict support and resistance levels respectively. So for instance, when the price approaches the resistance area it has greater difficulty getting past that area, and you may decide you want to exit your position (if you are holding one) at that point.

Like trendlines, they must not be thought of as set in stone. They are liable to move, and can be penetrated intra-day or maybe even in a couple of days. They should perhaps be thought of as zones of probable price action. In a moment we will look at how to use this to actually trade.

With trendlines and supports and resistances, the probability of a price move in a particular direction increases the longer the trendline has been in "force," i.e. not been penetrated but merely had the price touch it and then bounce of it. So if a trendline has six points over a six-month period where the price did not pass through it but instead touched and moved in the opposite direction, this would be a strong signal that the price will do this on the seventh approach. Have a look at Fig 11.7 which should remove the clouds of foggy ambiguity from your mind.

Fig 11.5 Support

With supports and resistances what we are seeing is a battle between buyers and sellers. For instance, at a resistance level sellers may have decided they will start selling a security at that level because it is overpriced, and buyers are too few to do much about it. So the price has to retreat as selling increases. If the buyers increase in number and size at the crucial point (i.e. go for a push through the line of resistance with reinforcements) then the price may break through with the force of a broken dam, marauding buyers, pushing the price up higher,

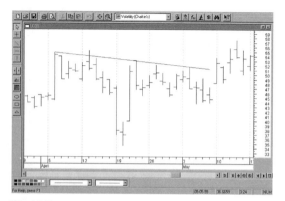

Fig 11.6 La résistance

Fig 11.7 Probability of a price move

and short sellers who had not anticipated the breakthrough now have to buy back their positions to limit their losses, thereby becoming buyers and pushing the prices even higher again.

This is one reason why the price often jumps at breakouts with a sharp rise, a gap up in price, and increased volume. Watch for these things and you will soon get a feel for price action around supports and resistances.

Support and resistance trading strategies

One strategy traders use with, say, resistances is to wait to see if the resistance is broken, and if it is, then on the basis that all those people who did not expect it to be broken would be wrong and now have to go with the side of the break, price should break through resistances, when they do break through, with a significant rise, i.e. first look for a penetration or breakthrough of the resistance. If there is one, then it should be followed by a big move (i.e. breakout).

So what counts for penetration? Given market volatility you could get prices piercing a trendline or support or resistance but then close back above it. For this reason, some technical analysts only draw trendlines and support and resistance levels based on closing prices, because intra-day prices are too erratic to mean a real penetration has occurred. Others say the price must close for two or three days in a penetrating position. (I hope you are not reading this chapter in bed, there is a danger your concentration may be distracted.)

An alternative method of trading is to wait and see if the trendline is *not* broken, and then trade in the direction of the rebound.

Role reversal

When a support or resistance level is broken it tends then to reverse its role and become a resistance level or support level respectively (see Fig 11.8). This is a common occurrence and the same rules about resistances and supports apply as before.

Trendline, supports and resistances can be drawn on any time frame, whether the charts you are using are three-minute or weekly. You would first determine the time frame you intend to trade and choose the bar charts appropriate to that. For instance, if you intend to hold a position for only a few days then you would use the daily charts.

Fig 11.8 Role reversal

hot tip! **Always more**

Always use more than just trendlines in making trading decisions, unless you have a liking for losing money. Remember too, trading using TA is an art and should not be thought of as providing scientific entry and exit points. You cannot, without psychic abilities, get in exactly at the very best price. All technical analysts try to be as good as possible, and that means being merely good enough. With the markets there is no 100 percent perfection. Again, you are not dealing with certainties but probabilities and that is why you need stop-losses.

Pullbacks

After a breakthrough of a support or resistance the price will often "pull back" to the trendline it just broke through. You have to be careful of this because you may think the move has ended, in which case you may exit an otherwise profitable trade prematurely. Unfortunately, you will not know if it is a pullback (which could also be used as another opportunity to enter the trade if you missed it first time) or a false breakout, until it is too late. So the key is to set stop-losses, and watch the prices like a hawk. If the price breaks through, then pulls back to near the support line again, is it now starting to go back through the support line and continuing on as if it had never broken through (i.e. a false breakout), or is it starting to return in the direction of the breakout? Feel free to take a break, look at Fig 11.9, think it over, have a snooze, and return to this.

Reversal pattern strategies

Reversal patterns are chart patterns which historically have tended to precede a reversal in prices. Again, they are added to our overall evidence of what the price may do, which then gives us a better idea whether we should exit a position or enter one. So let's do a run down. If you like what you see then you should definitely learn more before trading by picking up some of the technical analysis books in the recommended reading.

Fig 11.9 Pullback

Fig 11.10 Head and shoulders

Head and shoulders strategies

An anatomical pattern this. Have a look at Fig 11.10 for a nice example. It is not always as clear cut.

This is a common pattern on bar charts and fairly reliable. The horizontal line represents the "neckline" and you must always wait for it to be broken for it to be a head and shoulders position. The pattern can occur on a slope. The price is supposed to reach as far below the neckline as the top of your head is from your neckline.

The position can also occur as a bullish pattern if it appears as an opposite or mirror reflection. In that case, the price would break up through the neckline. In many ways you can think of the neckline as a support and trade the pattern like a trendline break, mentioned earlier.

Tops and bottoms strategies

A bottom is the opposite of, wait for it, a . . . top. The top occurs where the price rises to a resistance level, falls back, and then rises again, and yet again falls back. The volume on the rise to the second peak should be lower than the volume on the rise to the first peak. This is because buyers are getting weaker at pushing the price up. Valley to peak should be at least 15 percent to represent a proper top. As buyers lose numbers and heart, the sellers push the price down and a reversal occurs (Fig 11.11).

Triangle strategies

Fig 11.12 shows a triangle. For a price reversal on the upside the horizontal line appears above the ascending diagonal line. We are then looking for a breakout of the horizontal line. To trade the pattern you can treat it very much like a breakout pattern from a resistance level.

The above is an ascending triangle, the descending triangle is an exact mirror reflection and that would represent a price breakout to the downside. In the ascending triangle

Fig 11.11 You're the tops   **Fig 11.12** Triangle

pattern, buyers are willing to pay increasingly higher prices but at the resistance level their willingness subsides and sellers come in. Near the pinnacle of the triangle, the buyers overcome the sellers and a breakout occurs.

Volume should be decreasing to the apex and then increase on breakout as the marauding purchasing invaders impeach the sellers' line of defence. The triangle pattern occurs quite frequently, and the price target is as far above the horizontal as the mouth of the triangle is wide! Why that should be the price target is a bit of a mystery.

Saucer strategies

The pattern for this is shown in Fig 11.13. It represents a gradual change in opinion about a stock. Although saucers are rare, if you can spot them as the price is rising they can be an additionally confirmatory indicator of a trend change. There are no price targets for this pattern so exit needs to be determined more by rising stop-losses or exit points determined by other technical methods we discuss in the following.

Fig 11.13 A flying pattern: the saucer

Continuation patterns

These patterns confirm that the current direction of price movement will continue. They can represent a pause in price and so can be used as a good point to step on before the escalator starts moving up again.

Rectangles: not a square strategy

The rectangle is simply where the price action moves sideways between a support and resistance level after a rise. It can be thought of as a resting place where buying and selling troops stop for a moment to reconsider price levels, some start profit, while other late comers get on board.

A strategy for this is to trade it in the same way you would any other breakout of a resistance (forgotten? We discussed it earlier in this chapter.) Once the breakout occurs then prices should continue onward and upward. Unlike just a plain breakout of a resistance level, the fact that there has been a rectangle formation first and a price rise before it, adds to the likelihood that a breakout from the resistance will occur and be significant.

Flag strategy: Flying the flag for more of the same

A flag can appear in an uptrend or downtrend. See Fig 11.14 for an example. The flag looks like a rectangle rotated diagonally upward and is preceded by a downtrend. The flag is where, instead of a sideways move after a downturn, buyers for a while outgun sellers and cause prices to rise, as they believe prices have oversold, but the sellers soon return as prices rise. The flag is important only after the bottom of the flag is pierced – so wait for that. Then you know the market will fall further and you saw a flag. If it is not pierced you simply have a reversal.

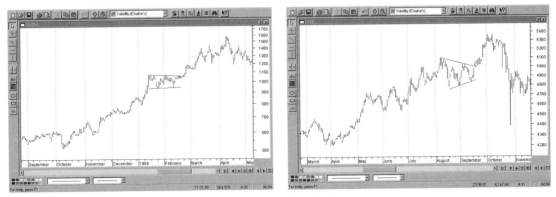

Fig 11.14 The price continues to flag   **Fig 11.15** Pennant

Pennant strategy

The pennant is like other continuation patterns in that it forms as a breathing space in the battle between buyers and sellers. In Fig 11.15 you can see a clear example.

The pennant in Fig 11.15 shows a rising trend followed by a price move where two boundary lines converge – representing the battle between buyers and sellers. Volume should decrease to the apex and increase on the breakout of the upper boundary.

You can treat the breakout of the upper boundary in the same way for trading as we discussed before about trading breakouts generally. The pennant makes a breakout more likely to result in a continuation, than does a simple breakout without a pennant.

Momentum-based strategies

Momentum is a generic term I am using here to discuss four similar indicators: stochastic, momentum, MACD, and RSI. The reasoning behind all momentum indicators is that a security price moving in a particular direction tends to slow before reversing direction. Therefore, if we can pinpoint where it has started slowing, we can be ready for the reversal and plan our strategies accordingly. Think of prices like a ball thrown in the air, before the ball falls it tends to slow down.

Plotting these indicators is simplicity itself on either the software detailed in Chapter 9 or the charting web-sites in Chapter 33. So worry not about that. For now let us just concentrate on the principles and how we can use these indicators in trading.

Time frames

All the indicators mentioned so far are based on mathematical operations undertaken on price. You do not need to worry about what the specifics are, but for those interested, the reading list is the best place to find out. These formulae have one or two, sometimes three variables that affect how the indicators are displayed and the time frame for which they will give the best signals. Again, most software and sites already incorporate as default settings the most popular values for the variables and so, again, you do not need to worry about that either. You can then just experiment with different variable values to see what produces best results. So onward to the issue of how to interpret these indicators so that you can base some strategies around them.

With each of the following you would rarely base a buy or sell decision on just the one indicator. We are always looking for as much evidence as possible about a price move in a particular direction and towards that end we shall see how a professional TA would do it.

Overbought/oversold strategies

All the momentum indicators can be used to indicate how overbought or oversold a security is. For illustration let us stick to oversold, which is the opposite of overbought. We say a security is oversold when selling has forced the price down so much that it should bounce back. So how do the momentum indicators measure this?

Looking at Fig 11.16 which plots the momentum indicator, we would say that the security is oversold when the momentum indicator is near its extreme lows relative to its other lows. Now you can get more precise and say that the security is oversold if the momentum is below a specific figure.

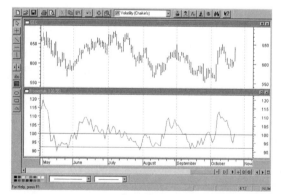

Fig 11.16 Momentum indicator

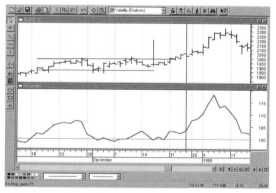

Fig 11.17 Oversold momentum

Trading strategy

One way to trade oversold signals is to buy the security when the momentum indicator moves up from being oversold. Now this is way too simple a strategy to be consistently profitable. So why am I telling you, and why is it too simple?

Even though it is too simple a strategy in itself, it is a useful piece of evidence to add to the whole melting pot of which way we think prices may go. It is too simple because momentum indicators often go oversold, go up a little out of oversold territory, and then become oversold again. Also, we must remember that price has to be our ultimate indicator, and we must wait for the price to move up also, because the momentum indicator could continue up, but prices continue down.

One way to use this evidence in conjunction with other evidence of an impending price move may be if the momentum is oversold and just starts moving up, the price is in a rectangle formation and just starts a breakout. You would have more confidence in the move because you have two independent strategies confirming that the move is less likely to be a false move (see Fig 11.17).

Positive divergence

Improving on oversold signals is positive divergence. Check out Fig 11.18. A positive divergence occurs when the momentum indicator (whether the RSI, MACD, momentum, or stochastic) makes a higher low, but the price does not.

Trading strategy

One popular strategy is to buy as the momentum and the price rise after the price makes its higher low. This is not foolproof, but is more reliable and more favored by technical analysts than simply oversold signals.

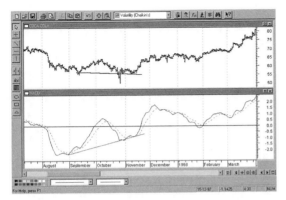

Fig 11.18 Positive divergence

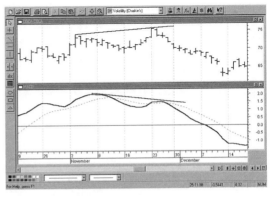

Fig 11.19 Negative divergence

Negative divergence

Fig 11.19 illustrates a negative divergence. The momentum indicator makes lower highs while the price does not, or even higher highs. As the momentum indicator then starts to fall from its high (which should be in overbought territory), the price should also start to fall. Again this is a stronger signal of an impending price fall than just a straightforward plain old oversold signal.

Trading strategy

Go short or exit a long position as the price and momentum start to dip lower. To avoid a bad signal, you could incorporate a rule like "the momentum has to fall from an oversold position and the price has to break the previous day's low before you exit or go short."

Reverse divergence

The reverse divergence is a variation on the negative divergence theme. It occurs when the price makes lower highs, but the momentum makes higher highs, deeper into oversold territory. Fig 11.20 depicts an example. The price should fall with the momentum indicator now.

Trading strategy

You can decide to exit or go short as the momentum and price both move downward from the momentum's oversold position.

Momentum trendlines

Trendlines on momentum indicators, as in Fig 11.21, can sometimes give clues to possible price movement where no trendline can be drawn on the price chart.

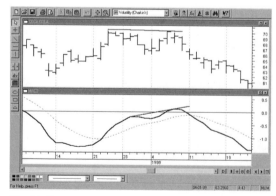

Fig 11.20 Reverse divergence   **Fig 11.21** Mo' better trendlines

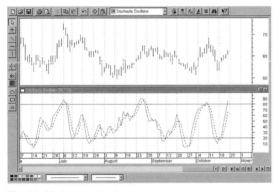

Fig 11.22 Stochastic chart

Trading strategy

The trendline on the momentum can be used in the same way as in normal price indicators. So, for instance, a resitance level on the momentum indicator may give a good indication that a price reversal is imminent. The same cautions with corroborating indicators and price confirmation apply as before; i.e. make sure you have another indicator or chart pattern confirming the bearishness and wait until prices fall.

Stochastics

While the stochastic is a momentum-based indicator and the interpretation and strategies already examined can be applied to it, there are also some specific to it because of its design. Fig 11.22 shows a stochastic and price chart.

%K crosses %D

With the stochastic you can see there is a solid line (%K) and a dotted line (%D) line. Don't worry about the mathematical formulae that generate them. Stochastic followers will consider a buy signal when the %K crosses up through the %D in an oversold territory as in Fig 11.22. A sell signal is when the %K crosses down through the %D and both are in overbought territory. When combined with the other pattern above, such positive divergences can be quite a powerful indicator.

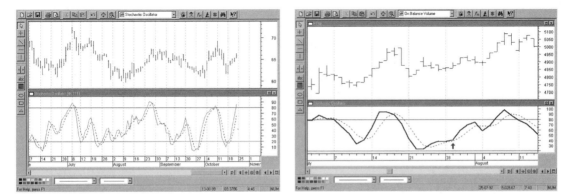

Fig 11.23 False divergence

Fig 11.24 False divergence with a bullish pattern

False divergence

This pattern occurs when the %K approaches the %D, looks like it is going to cross it and be a buy signal, but instead just teases us by kissing it and rebounding off it. This can be a strong signal of a price continuing to fall. Fig 11.23 shows an example of this. It can also occur as a bullish pattern as in Fig 11.24.

Stochastic compared to the RSI and momentum indicators

I tend to find the stochastic less prone to false signals which see me enter only to have the price not do as expected. The stochastic is not a volatile indicator and gives smoother, "easier to read" lines. I like it.

The weaknesses in stochastics, momentum, and RSI

If we understand the weaknesses of certain indicators, we can then, hopefully, avoid traps of poor trades, and compensate for those weaknesses by adding new indicators which do not suffer the same weaknesses. The stochastic, momentum, and RSI can all waver in the oversold or overbought regions for prolonged periods when a trend is continuing onward in the same direction. So, you could get a false signal to sell prematurely during an uptrend, as the oversold indicator suggests a sell signal. Fig 11.25 illustrates this problem.

This in turn raises the issue of how we can solve this problem. One way is not to act on a signal until the price confirms it. So, for instance, you would not act on a sell signal by the momentum indicator unless the price closes lower than the previous day's low and then opens the next day and moves yet lower. Another way to avoid the premature signal is to observe both the momentum indicator and the MACD. So let us turn now to the MACD. Not a bad link, eh?

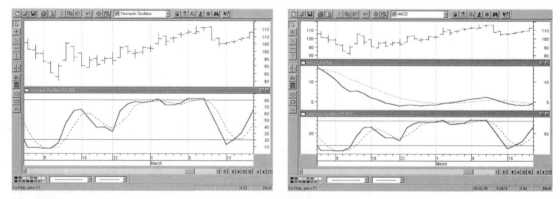

Fig 11.25 False sell signals in stochastic   **Fig 11.26** Moving average convergence divergence

MACD (pronounced Mac-D – like the famous chain of burger joints)

Not named after a Scotsman, but standing for the moving average convergence divergence, the MACD by its mathematical construction tends not to suffer from the problems of the other momentum indicators. Fig 11.26 illustrates this.

The dotted line is the moving average of the MACD and is called the signal line. A crossing of the solid line from above in the overbought region can be interpreted as a sell signal, as can a move up through the dotted line when in the oversold signal.

Trading strategy

The MACD tends to give fewer buy or sell signals than the other momentum indicators. I tend to use it to avoid the problems with the momentum indicators giving premature signals. So, for instance, in Fig 11.27 we see the momentum indicator suggests a buy signal, but the MACD is dropping so sharply that it overrides the momentum signal.

Why not use MACD all the time? Well, I think it works best when combined with other momentum indicators, because the MACD is a little slow and tends to give buy signals a bit too late. So a better strategy is to buy based on the momentum indicators as long as the MACD is not falling sharply, and possibly has even just started moving sideways. See Fig 11.28 for an illustration.

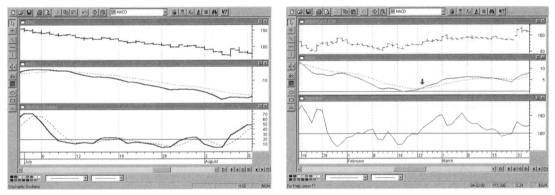

Fig 11.27 Momentum override   **Fig 11.28** MACD in combination

Summary

To summarize this long chapter, we have looked for indicators of relatively high probability that the stock price is going to move one way and not another, and the rest is detail. It is something you should re-read, as one read is unlikely to be enough. Now you deserve a break.

12

Multiple time frames and indicators: Multiplicity for high-probability returns

Online trader problems

- Having got a system, how can the risk of a loss be even further reduced?

- What advice do other online traders give about using multiple time frames and multiple indicators?

- Which are some good online sites where I can plot multiple time frames and indicators?

---

chat box 12.1

Good traders do it many times

Posted by a trader on Silicon Investor on 10.6.1999

For those who position trade, it would be useful to use both the daily and weekly charts in your analysis. Many times you will see a good buying opportunity in a stock that is declining on the daily chart but is in a solid uptrend on the weekly chart. The key is being familiar with the support and resistance price areas. As the price starts touching its support price areas, people start buying again and shorts start covering. The key is the direction of the weekly chart. If it's up, the ultimate resolution of the daily chart will be up. If it's down, the ultimate resolution of the daily chart will be down.

Multiple time frames

The principle of multiple time states that if there is a convergence of technical indicators across different time frames then that suggests a greater probability of a price move. Sounds a bit convoluted. Let me explain . . .

Imagine a short-term system based on a stochastic indicator using a daily bar chart. For the purposes of this illustration we can give it %K values of 5 for time periods and 3 for slowing, and %D value of 3. (If you are unfamiliar with the stochastic oscillator, see the chapter on indicators.)

In this system a buy signal is indicated when the stochastic crosses 20 to the upside. A sell signal is generated when the stochastic crosses 80 to the downside. The system is kept overly simple so we can concentrate on the principle under discussion (Fig 12.1).

Imagine now that we are at the point numbered 2. Should we buy E-Bay at that point, based on the stochastic indicator? All other things being equal it appears that since the stochastic indicator is turning up from an oversold position, breaking the %D line, and the stock is on an uptrend then this would be a good point at which to go long, and so we may go long at the open of the next bar, approximately $47 (see Fig 12.2).

But fast forwarding we see that that was not a particularly good purchase (see Fig 12.3). So the issue arises: Is there any quick, simple way of augmenting a particular system?

Well, if at the point of entry we had looked were on the same stochastic indicator but on a weekly bar chart we would have seen what is displayed in Fig 12.4, namely a stochastic indicator that is oversold, just broken through the 80 level and its own moving average. A very different perspective indeed! That may have tipped us off against entry based purely on the daily chart. The same principle can be applied if you intra-day trade. As well as three-minute chart, for instance, you may also want simultaneously display 10-minute charts. When I day trade futures I have multiple windows open to ensure similar

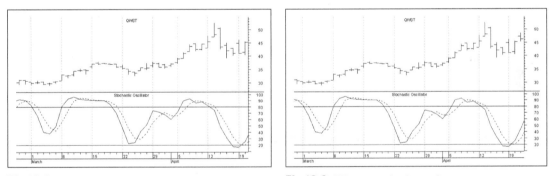

Fig 12.1 QWest

Fig 12.2 QWest, one day forward

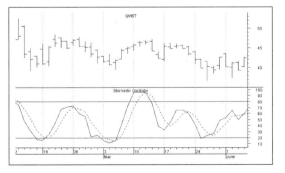

Fig 12.3 QWest – fast forward!

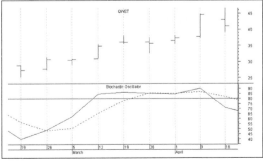

Fig 12.4 If unsure, stay clear

signals on all windows, so I am more assured of a move in the direction I desire. Remember, if unsure, stay clear.

What is the interrelationship between the two (or more) time frames?

My view is that the longer time frame operates as a background force against which the shorter time frame acts. While the shorter time frame reacts to day-to-day forces, the longer time frame is relatively unaffected by these. The shorter time frame is being pressured in a particular direction by the longer time frame, although occasionally an event can be so significant, e.g. a law suit, that it operates on the weekly time frame from the daily (see Fig 12.5).

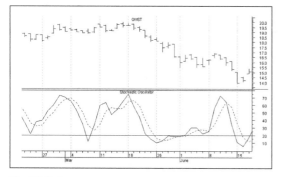

Fig 12.5 Downward pressure on the daily stochastic

In the figures we have just looked at, the weekly stochastic, which was overbought and turning down, was applying downward pressure on the daily stochastic and so the price could not move as it may otherwise have done.

Another example

Consider the QWest chart (see Fig 12.6). Based on the same simple indicator and the information in the figure should we buy? The stochastic is oversold, broken above the 20 percent mark and heading higher. However, the figure shows quite a fall in price recently and we cannot be too sure that it may not continue falling.

Now examine Fig 12.7, which is the same information but on a weekly chart. The stochastic reveals an oversold reading, but does has yet to turn above 20 percent, and break the %D line. If we wait a further week (Fig 12.8) we get a stronger signal at which point we may want to go long.

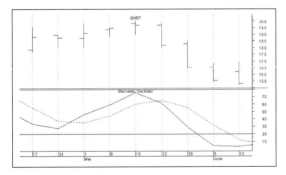

Fig 12.6 QWest – to buy or not to buy?

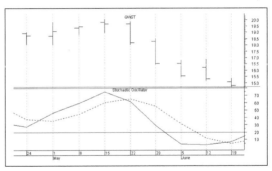

Fig 12.7 QWest – weekly info

---

chat box 12.3

Time travel for day traders

Posted by a trader on Silicon Investor on 8.6.1999

One of the most fundamental techniques I have found beneficial for day trading stocks is to learn to watch an issue simultaneously in multiple time frames. Many seasoned, successful stock traders have learned to do this. The day chart is the most important to fully understand and monitor. Before I enter a trade-off of an intra-day chart (or Level II action; usually it's a hybrid) I will look at the day chart (in reference to the past 3–5 days) and ask myself if I still want to enter. When trading stocks intra-day (even for scalps), I watch the 30-minute, five-minute, and one-minute charts (occasionally a tick-chart, but less in the past couple of years as I've integrated Level II). The best set-up is to have a screen with day chart, 30/5/1-minute charts, all on the same screen. I do display volume on every time frame and consider understanding volume in relation to price to be extremely important to stock-trading success (another topic).

On each chart, I run a 10, 20, 40, and 50–period moving average. As Linda Raschke says: "Always watch price relative to something else." The best "something else" is the MA. It represents a normalized reference point. So, when a stock is a certain percentage away from a given moving average, it tells you a lot. You learn more that's repeatable that way. For example, when a stock gets out in front of its 10-period moving average (although it may stay extended for a while), it is inevitably much more vulnerable to pullbacks. Universally – it applies on the day chart, and intra-day (intra-day, for smaller pullbacks). When you're watching stocks on multiple time frames, the higher time frames "filter out the noise," and provide you with greater perspective, leading you to trade in the right direction, and to always be aware of the trend.

Does it work, would the purchase have produced a good profit? Check out Fig 12.9 (daily) and 12.10 (weekly). You will note that the whole rally is confirmed far better on the weekly chart than on the daily chart, which can be used to override the daily stochastic signals when it reached overbought levels but the price kept going up.

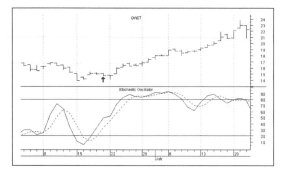

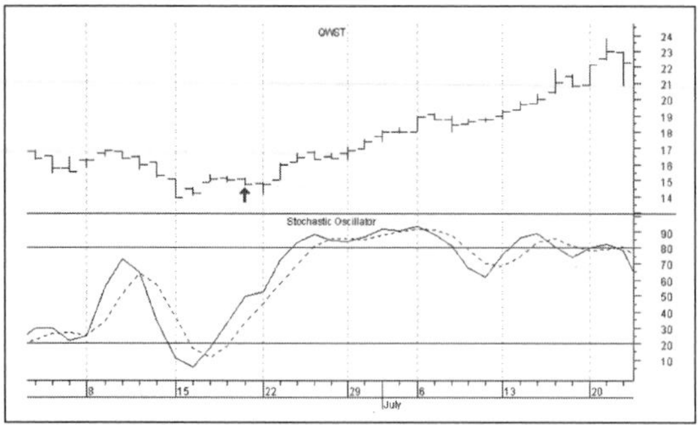

Fig 12.8 QWest – another week, a stronger signal

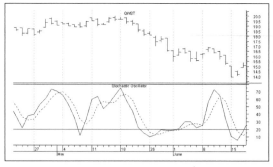

Fig 12.9 Daily QWest

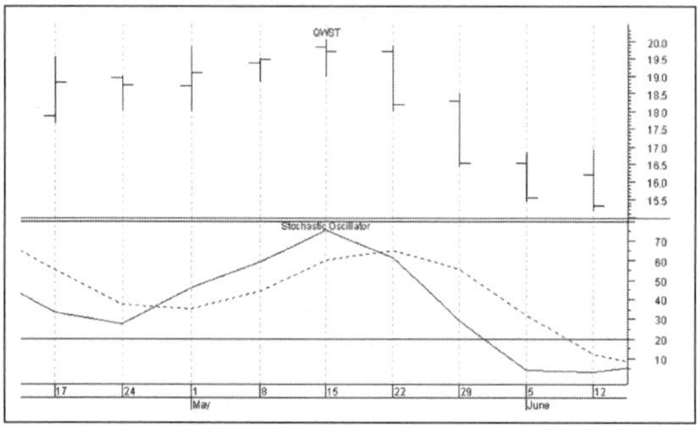

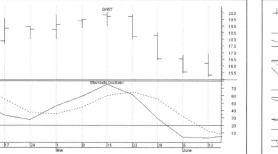

Fig 12.10 Weekly QWest

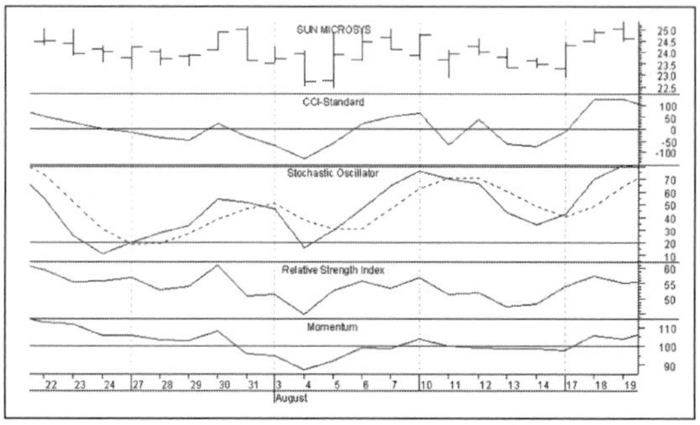

Fig 12.11 Sun Microsystems with momentum and MACD indicators

Multiple indicators

Traders base their decisions on the information available before them. That is not to say that volumes and volumes of information is essential – after all, at some point you have to stop pontificating and pull the trigger. But there is a balance between too little information and too much.

Most systems do not rely on just one indicator. They would use a series of analytical methods and charting techniques to determine the best moment to strike. Consider Fig 12.11. This is a daily chart of Sun Microsystems with a momentum and MACD indicator displayed.

Examining the figure if we were looking to go long we may reason that there are some good reasons for entry:

■ The momentum indicator is oversold and moving up.

- The momentum indicator is showing positive divergences (it is making higher lows) which is bullish.
- The short-term trend appears bullish.

Let us now look at the same chart but with three additional momentum-based indicators (see Fig 12.12). Now we see a different picture and may well reason:

- The CCI indicator is in oversold territory and turning down.
- The stochastic indicator is in oversold territory too and turning down.
- The RSI is moving down and is slightly oversold.

So, what to do? Let us fast forward a few days to Fig 12.13.

It seems clear that, with the additional information the multiple indicators gave, we had a better picture. Of course, I used an example which illustrated the point, and there are ample cases where even using a million indicators could not save a poor entry. But the idea is that multiple indicators reduce the number of bad decisions.

A problem with having more information is that when some of it is contradictory it can lead to indecision. Then you find that if you had stuck to one indicator you may well have entered the trade and made a bundle. However, the real issue is whether, by using multiple indicators, you save more from having not entered bad trades compared to the amount you have missed making by not having just one indicator. In my experience, the rewards in terms of avoided bad trades with multiple indicators outweighs the missed profits that would have accrued from following just one indicator. I know it sound like gobbledegook, but it makes sense if you read it one or two hundred times.

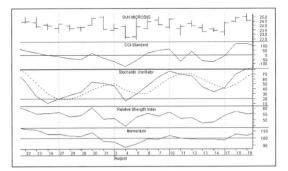

Fig 12.12 Sun Microsystems with more indicators

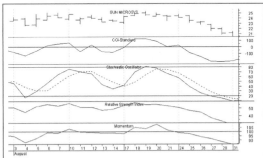

Fig 12.13 Fast forward time again!

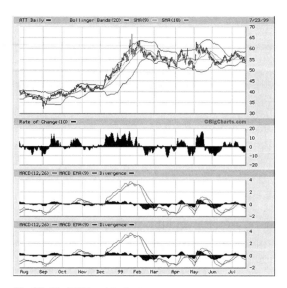

Fig 12.14 AT&T on bigcharts.com

Fig 12.15 British Airways on the British E*Trade

Some good web-sites

www.bigcharts.com is an excellent resource for multiple time frames and multiple indicators simulatenously. (See Fig 12.14.) Ask Research at www.askresearch.com also allows multiple indicators but is slightly more difficult to handle. For our UK friends www.etrade.co.uk offers good charting for UK stocks (see Fig 12.15). As you can see the UK charting site is getting to be as good as its American counterparts. Cup of tea?

Summary

When trading, I use multiple time frames and multiple indicators on the screen. I will have several windows open simultaneously and arranged on the screen to permit this. The way to do it online is to have multiple browser windows open. If you are using software, all the top analytical ones listed in the software chapter allow simultaneous multiple indicators, if not simultaneous multiple time frames.

13

IPO or NO: Strategies for trading IPOs

Strategy risk level: moderate

In this chapter

Initial public offerings, when a company offers some or all of its shares to the public at the offer price in order to raise capital, have been much in the news. We all wish we had bought some Amazon, AOL, E*Trade, Schwab at the offer price. The offer is made by select institutions to select individuals and so most people cannot buy at the offer price and have to wait for the shares to start trading. However, these IPOs often explode far higher than the offer price on the first day of trading and buying then can very much feel like missing the boat, as Table 13.1 shows.

Name	Offer	Day 1
Yankee Candle Co.	$18	$24 1/8
Commerce One Inc.	$21	$61
Ask Jeeves	$15	$64 15/16
Clarent Corp.	$15	$25 1/2

Table 13.1 Some IPOs offers vs. Day 1

So what strategies can be used to profit from IPOs?

Strategies which are not that effective

Try to buy at the offer price

The best way to take advantage of an IPO would be to buy at the offer price before the shares are publicly traded and so before they rise. Underwriters price IPOs expecting at least a 15 percent rise on the first day so as to ensure the offering is considered a success and there is demand. This presents two problems.

First, it is very difficult as a retail investor to get any shares before they start trading. You would need to have an account with a broker who has been selected to sell the shares. To find out who they are you can look on the "underwriting" part of the IPO company's SEC registration. They are usually the big institutional banks such as Lehman Brothers or the discount brokers who have a distribution agreement, such as E*Trade, Wit Capital, Schwab. But see chat box 13.1.

---

chat box 13.1

No IPO

From Scott McCormick on Investorville on 12.2.1999

Online brokers claim to be leveling the playing field for IPO investors, giving them a chance to get in at the offering price. But this isn't really happening. Just as with retail brokers, the best customers are getting the shares. E*Trade gives its professional-edge customers ($25/mo) first shot at the shares, Schwab gives their active traders (24 trades/yr) first shot, and DLJ requires $100k in assets.

Second, even if you are allocated some shares, "flipping," which is the practice of selling very shortly after they are initially traded, is highly discouraged by brokers, to the extent that you may be excluded from future IPOs by them. But holding onto them may not be a very good strategy, either (see chat box 13.2).

---

chat box 13.2

IPO flip or NO

From Bill Tarr on Investorville on 25.5.1999

Just heard an interesting stat. The average for the 52 internet IPOs so far this year:

First trade vs. offering price: up 114%

Current price vs. First trade: down 26%.

So, if buying at the offer price to sell on day one is a no-no, either because it is murder trying to get the stocks, or because flipping could see you barred from future issues, what can you do?

Try to buy on day one

This is not a good idea as chat box 13.1 reveals. On day one many IPOs often fall in price. Check out Fig 13.1, which shows the Goldman Sachs IPO, and Screen 13.1 which shows Europe's largest internet play "freeserve."

The main reasons why buying on day one is such a bad idea is that, first, the price hits the day's high in the morning session as all the hype surrounding the issue finds a means of expressing itself through initial buying of the stock. With the buyers then dried up, the price can go in only one direction. Amazon.com traded below its offering price a week after its high on the first day of trading. Onsale also fell below its offer price in a few weeks, only to rise 500 percent later in the year.

---

chat box 13.3   **Buffet's advice**

From Art Vandelay on Investorville on 11.5.1999

Warren Buffet said something very interesting about IPOs last week that I thought I'd share (note that this isn't verbatim).

The problem with initial public offerings is that they're carried out when the seller (the company) feels it's most advantageous to do so – in other words, when it can ask a relatively high price for its shares. Why in the world would you want to buy something at a time and price of the seller's choosing, thus virtually assuring yourself of not purchasing the asset at an attractive price?

It's almost a mathematical impossibility to imagine that, out of the thousands of things for sale on a given day, the most attractively priced is the one being sold by a knowledgeable seller. As an example, consider Goldman Sachs' canceling of its IPO amidst the global economic turmoil in the fall of 1998. Goldman gave you a perfect buy signal . . . the brokerages have doubled since then. I doubt those who bought Goldman when it went public will do as well.

Fig 13.1 Goldman Sachs IPO

Screen 13.1

Try to sell on day one

Of course, if so many IPOs fall on day one, why not short the issue on the basis you could buy it back cheaper later? I do not recommend this, it is a very high-risk strategy. Period.

Strategy that is effective

Table 13.2 summarizes the strategy that works for pullback IPOs.

Minimum experience level	Risk level	Product types	Typical time scale	Key web-sites
Beginner–intermediate	Intermediate	Stocks	Few days to weeks	www.ipomaven.com www.ipocentral.com www.ipo.com www.ipo-network.com

Table 13.2 Pullback IPOs – strategy summary

Strategy aim

We want to wait for the IPO to come off its highs of the first few days and then enter as it starts to rise again.

Products suitable for

Stocks

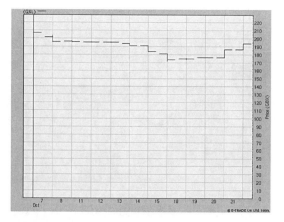

Fig 13.2 Look out for pullback

Entry and exit points

The set-up

First of all use the web-sites listed here to find the dates of new IPOs. Then monitor them on the technical analysis web-sites listed in that chapter.

Find a stock that opens 20 percent higher than its offer price. Look for the price to start pulling back after day one. The pullback may take anything from two to six days. It is made of lower lows and no higher highs compared to the preceding day (see Fig 13.2).

Entry

After the pullback on the third or fourth day, place a buy stop order to take you into the market 1/16 above the previous day's high price. To reduce risk, you could place it 1/8 of a point above.

Exit

Your stop-loss is at the previous day's low. Use trailing stops to reach a profit, e.g. the trailing stop could be the preceding day's low, or the low two day's ago.

Examples

See Fig 13.3 of a full-blown example of the strategy.

Optimization

The problem with going long IPOs is that so little is often known about these companies compared to stocks that have been trading for a number of years. However, one way to reduce risk is to see who the underwriter is, from looking at the web-sites listed, and buying, based on their reputation. The biggest names whose IPOs perform the best are Goldman Sachs, and Merrill Lynch, Morgan Stanley Dean Witter.

Where the strategy failed

Fig 13.4 shows an instance of things not quite going to plan.

Fig 13.3 Pullback strategy in detail

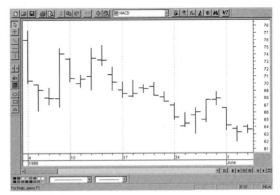

Fig 13.4 Things didn't quite go to plan

Some good web-sites

IPO Maven ***

www.ipomaven.com

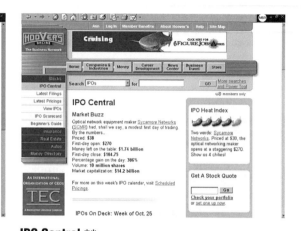

IPO Central **

www.ipocentral.com

IPO.com ***

www.ipo.com

The IPO Network **

www.iposyndicate.com

Summary

IPOs can be an exciting time for both entrepreneurs behind a company and traders having a stake in the company. Sometimes, they are exciting for traders for all the wrong reasons. Traders hear lots of hype about a company, but have little trading history. The risk of investing in such a company is exciting because of the risk, and that is the wrong type of excitement for a trader to seek. You need to be very cautious of the hype and hoop-la surrounding a new issue and remember there are only so many potential Yahoos!

14

Intra-day pivot-point strategies

Strategy risk level: high

In this chapter

Pivot points are popular among many professional futures floor traders, especially those trading index futures products such as the S&P 500. They can be considered as support and resistance levels. Most writers on pivot points and users of them will say that if pivot points work it is due to their widespread use acting as a self-fulfilling prophesy, rather than some graphical depiction of some subtle mass trader psychological behavior at key price points. But, if it works, then it works.

Strategy that is effective

I consider this a high-risk strategy precisely because it relies on usage by lots of other traders to work, rather than having some more "substantial" basis such as momentum indicators which measure trend slowdown as an advance indicator of reversal. Although the calculations could be applied to non-intra-day and markets other than futures, I think it is best to apply it to those markets alone, because that is where everyone else we are relying on to make the strategy work uses it (see Table 14.1).

Minimum experience level	Risk level	Product types	Typical time scale	Key web-sites
Intermediate	High	Futures, options on indices	Intra-day	www.tradehard.com www.bigcharts.com

Table 14.1 Intra-day pivot-point strategy summary

Strategy aim

To profit by taking a view on short-term directional price changes based on pivot-point figures.

Products suitable for

Futures

Options on futures

Futures and options on futures

Since with pivot points you are looking to trade-off levels, it helps if those levels are wide apart. Consequently, the best futures markets on which to pivot are those with a wide daily trading range, such as the S&P 500 index, soyabeans, wheat, and Treasury bonds, Dow Jones futures, FTSE futures and other major market indices futures.

Entry and exit points

We need to calculate pivot points first of all (see Fig 14.1). To get tomorrow's figures, we need today's high (h), low (l), and close (c) values.

Daily pivot   (p) $= (h+l+c)/3$

Resistance 1   (r1) $= (2*p)-l$

Support 1   (s1) $= (2*p)-h$

Resistance 2   (r2) $= (p-s1)+r1$

Support 2   (s2) $= p-(r1-s1)$

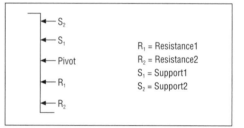

Fig 14.1 Calculate your pivot points

Entry

Buy when the market moves up through the daily pivot and short when it moves down through the daily pivot. If you prefer trading breakouts you may want to go long, not at the pivot, but a break of r2, or go short on a downward break of s2 (or short on the break of s1 with a profit target of s2).

Exit

The support and resistance levels can be used as exit points – either as stop-losses or profit targets. If you go long as the market moves up through the pivot, you could set a stop-loss at s1 and take a profit at r1. Alternatively you could take half-profits at r1, move your stop-loss up from s1 to the pivot, and aim to close the other half of your position at r2.

As you can tell, there are lots of variations you can use when using pivots.

Examples

Consider Fig 14.2 which shows the daily bar for Tradehard.com. Now consider Fig 14.3 which shows the intra-day chart with pivot points and the various resistance and support levels marked on it based on the values derived from Fig 14.2.

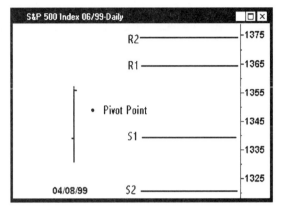

Fig 14.2 Tradehard.com   **Fig 14.3** Intra-day chart with pivot points

Optimization

To lower risk, I make a note of pivot-point levels, and use them as something to look out for and be aware of in my intra-day futures trading, but not something on which solely to base my trading decisions. For example, if I was short the S&P 500 and so momentum indicators starting to show a positive divergence (bullish) and the price was starting to consolidate, then, if that was also a pivot point, it may well be the factor that tilts the balance in favor of an exit. Another way of reducing risk is to look at the broader daily trend and only place trades in the direction of that.

Some good web-sites

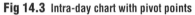

Tradehard (www.tradehard.com) provide a daily list of pivots, and supports and resistances, saving you the trouble of having to calculate them across markets. www.bigcharts.com is good for displaying intra-day charts. For other web-sites displaying intra-day charts see the chapter on technical analysis web-sites.

Summary

Pivot numbers and their corresponding support and resistance figures can be useful additional information for the off-floor online trader to have in front of her as she monitors the market. I would urge using them as part of a broader system. Since the trades are intra-day, disciplined stop-losses are essential. I like to have a pad with the various supports, pivot points, and preceding day's close, as well as longer term key support and resistances noted in chronological order, making it easier to view.

15

Retracement strategies: Hold yer horses ▶▶

Strategic risk level: moderate to high

In this chapter

After sharp price rallies there are often equally sharp price retracements. This strategy aims to profit from the retracement and is popular among contrarians (see Table 15.1).

Strategy that is effective

Minimum experience level	Risk level	Product types	Typical time scale	Key web-sites
Beginner–intermediate	Intermediate–high	Stocks, options, futures	2–10 days (can be used intra-day but more difficult)	Any charting sites (see Chapter 35)

Table 15.1 Retracement strategy summary

Strategy aim

This aim of this strategy is to benefit from stock price reversals (or pullbacks) after a sharp price move up or down. Take a look at Fig 15.1 which depicts Amazon (AMZN). You will note a sharp, unsustainable rally then a pullback. It is this pullback that we want to profit from. The price could equally have fallen, and we would seek to profit from a "bounce." For simplicity, we will concentrate on pullbacks.

So why not just try to get in on the rally?

There are several responses to this:

■ We may well be in on the rally using a different system, but now we want to add extra profit by profiting from a move in the opposite direction, too.

■ We have missed the rally, or not have a particularly good system for rally entries.

Tell me more about retracements

Like all trading strategies, this one has followers and it has detractors; those that believe and those that do not. One theory is that, after a rally, prices tend to retrace by certain amounts. They argue that prices tend to retrace 25, 50 or 75 percent. Actually, anything more than a 50 percent retracement of a 50 percent retracement should perhaps be called a reversal, but that is not important. The downside to this theory is that you are not guaranteed such a reversal. Moreover, you would not know in advance if the reversal were going to reach, say, 50 percent after reaching 25 percent (see Figs 15.2, 15.3, 15.4).

Other retracement enthusiasts swear by levels which coincide with Fibonacci numbers: 38.2 percent, 50 percent, 61.8 percent. The problem is that by the time you plot both

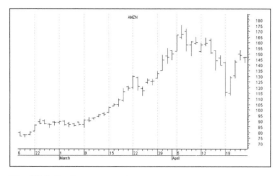

Fig 15.1 Pullback on AMZN

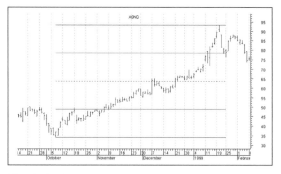

Fig 15.2 A typical 25% retracement

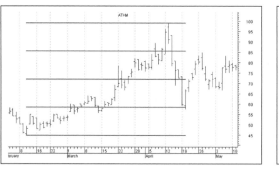

Fig 15.3 A typical 75% retracement

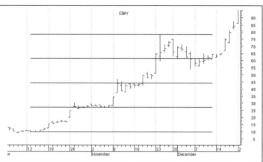

Fig 15.4 Price failing to reach 50% retracement

quadrants and Fibonacci ratio you are left with a lot of quite close retracement levels, and it can feel like the price can retrace to anywhere.

Deeper retracements occur when weaker holders become sellers as prices start falling. The retracement slows and stops as new buyers enter the market, tempted by the lower price.

Products suitable for

Futures

Stocks

Options

Futures

The major indices often rally and pull back and futures on them can be a good play for this strategy. You can use either intra-day or intra-week pullbacks. However, for intra-week pullbacks, since you would be holding the position overnight, it increases the risk you are exposed to. Your margin requirements are greater too (Fig 15.5).

Stocks

For pullbacks after a rally, this requires shorting the stock and that, of course, is more technical and difficult than simply going long. Stock shorting should only be attempted by the intermediate-level trader.

To get a good return with stocks requires a larger amount of money invested. Looking at Fig 15.1, if you had called the trade perfectly, and sold short say 60 shares of Amazon at around $173, and bought them back at $115, you would have a return of $3480 in 14 days.

Fig 15.5 Dow Jones Industrial Average June 1999 future

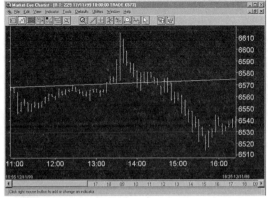

Screen 15.1

Options

Strategy

Since the strategy is short term in duration, our greatest returns are likely to come from a straight long options position (e.g. long put for a pullback after a rally).

Option time

We want the price move to have maximum effect on the option and so a near month option with about one month to expiry is best. Anything shorter and time erosion is likely to be too great, anything longer to expiry and the option may not move as much as we would like.

Option strike

An option out of the money is more risky than one in the money in the event of the pullback failing to materialize, and so I would suggest the option which is just in the money.

Risk reduction strategies

You could reduce risk by:

- using a longer to expiry option
- a deeper in the money
- hedging the long position, say a long put, with a short lower strike price put, the idea being that if the stock rallied instead of retracing, the loss you suffer on the long put can be offset, to some extent, by being able to buy back the short put at a lower price and hence making some money on that.

Entry and exit points

The set-up

Before we can trade the retracement, we need something to retrace, i.e. a sharp rally. Since we will be looking for at least a 25 percent retracement of the rally, we need to make sure that any rally is big enough that the point we *enter* to the point of a 25 percent retracement of the rally is worth the risk we will be taking. So, we need to know three things:

- Where the rally starts.
- Where it ends.
- Where we enter.

Look at Fig 15.6. Those three points are marked. We will examine later how we know when to enter the trade. The question of where the rally starts could be defined in detailed mathematical terms, but I think it should be kept a question of art. Generally a rally starts when the price stops making lower lows and starts making higher highs. You'll know it when you see it, because you are looking for big rallies, and if you can't spot big rallies by looking at price charts, then trading is not a good pastime for you to indulge in. You would be looking for an isolated low; a bar which is preceded and followed by bars with higher lows.

The rally ends at the highest high before the entry signal. Obviously, you have to wait for the entry signal before you know the rally has ended on this definition. It will help if you look at Fig 15.6. With this strategy things are far easier to understand when seen than when described. We want an entry signal to get us in as close as possible to the start of the retracement.

Now look at Fig 15.7, which divides the rally into four equal parts. Each level represents 25 percent of the rally. As you can see from the end of the rally to a 25 percent is where the entry signal occurs. So that is not a feasible strategy on this occasion. We have two choices: either wait for another opportunity, or look for the price to drop to the 50 percent retracement level. The entry to the 50 percent level gives us enough profit, we calculate, and so continue.

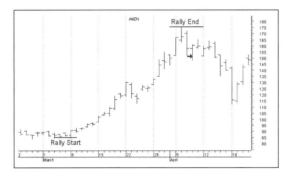

Fig 15.6 The set-up

Fig 15.7 The entry signal

Entry

Conditions before entry:

- Set-up established (and so price failed to make a higher high). Call the highest high "Bar 1."

- Bar 2 fails to break the high of Bar 1.

- Bar 3 breaks the low of Bar 2 but not its high. Enter when Bar 3 breaks the low of Bar 2.

You could have lots of variations on this for entry. For instance, you could enter on the open of Bar 3, not waiting to see if it breaks Bar 2's low. You could enter if there is no new high for three consecutive bars. The problem I have found with other permutations is that you either enter too early, and so find that the rally had not really ended, or you enter too late and find slim pickings. Entry is an art and requires balance so you are neither too early nor too late.

Exit

Exit points can vary but one of the following should serve you well:

■ Exit when the high of the day is greater than the two-day high (you could just exit if the high today is greater than the high yesterday, but I find that leads to too many false early exits). By the same token, waiting for the two-day high to be broken can lead to a late exit and loss of some of the accrued profits.

■ Of course the usual rules about stop-losses apply (see Chapter 33).

Warnings of impending doom

Before the exit signal occurs there may be early warnings of a possible reverse. One such early warning is when the price hits the retracement level. Sometimes the retracement level can be a support level. Beware of the price hitting supports, too.

Optimization

Use momentum indicators

To finesse entry signals I often look at momentum indicators to see if they are showing signs of an impending pullback. For example, is the momentum indicator oversold and moving down? Are any of the indicators failing to make new highs with the price (i.e. showing a divergence)? Was the failure to make a new high triggered by a news announcement? (Very often a news announcment will trigger and end a rally. The announcement starting the rally could be something like a new product announcement, and the one ending it could be something like negative broker comment a few days later on the product.)

Fig 15.8 shows how the stochastic indicator, in oversold territory, turning down, and making a negative divergence, confirms the retracement entry signal.

Use longer rallies

The immediate rally that you are examining is usually part of a longer move. If the retracement levels of the longer rally coincide with those of the shorter one that can be an important extra signal that the market may well pull back to that level. Fig 15.9 shows that the longer rally retraces 25 percent where the shorter rally retraces 50 percent.

Where the strategy failed

As I keep repeating, no strategy is perfect and you must appreciate the fallibility of any strategy so that you are not mistakenly holding the belief that you cannot lose. If you enter a position with the experience of how the strategy can lead you astray, you will be better able to enter cautiously and exit in time.

Here are some conclusions from my experience, which will save you a lot of time. The main shortcomings of this strategy are three-fold:

1 Moves where the distance from entry to a 25 percent retracement level is sufficiently profitable to merit taking the risk are quite rare. That is another way of saying the rally is not big enough.

2 Very often by the time an entry is indicated the price is already at the 25 percent retracement level.

3 Quite often, by the time an exit is indicated, a lot of the gains may have been given up.

Fig 15.8 illustrates the first of these points.

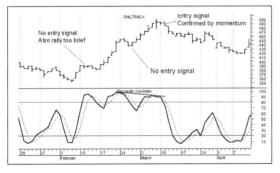

Fig 15.8 Using indicators to confirm entry signal

Fig 15.9 Retracement of a longer rally

Some good web-sites

Web-sites on which you can monitor price charts are ubiquitous on the web. Some of the best ones for clear bar charts and also permitting technical analysis are listed in Chapter 35. One such charting site is www.bigcharts.com (see Screen 15.2).

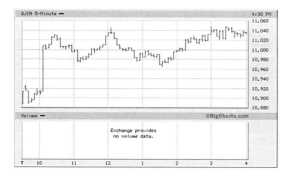

Screen 15.2

Summary

The retracement trade can be a good short-term trade. However, it is risky because you are looking to be contrarian at the peak of a rally. It requires courage and daring, but good old-fashioned rules of money and risk management discussed in other parts of this book must never be forgotten. The strategy really works best when there has been a steep rally, there is a relatively large distance between the entry and 25 percent retracement level, and the momentum indicators show weakness. But, as with all strategies, and I will say it yet again, it is never 100 percent certain.

16

Pullback onto trend strategies

Strategic risk level: moderate

In this chapter

This strategy is closely related to the retracement strategy, in that it is seeking to take advantage of the swings in prices that occur after a sharp move (see Table 16.1).

Minimum experience level	Risk level	Product types	Typical time scale	Key web-sites
Beginner	Low–intermediate	Stocks, options, futures	2–10 days, can be used on intra-day price charts	Charting sites, www.tradehard.com

Table 16.1 Trend pullback strategy summary

Strategy that is effective

Strategy aim

Unlike the retracement strategy, the aim of this strategy is to get you back onto a trend as the pullback ends and the trend resumes, because as you are entering at the pullback end, you would be getting a relatively good price. One of the dangers is that you enter prematurely, and the pullback continues (or worse still, the pullback is a reversal and the trend does not resume).

Products suitable for

Stocks

Futures

Options

Stocks

Since we are looking for a short rise after the pullback the amount of stock we would need to buy would be relatively high. This increases the risk of loss should the strategy fail, and so options may be a better strategy. We would also have to be very careful with our money and risk management when buying such a large quantity of stock for a short price rise. So it is particularly important you read those chapters carefully if using this strategy.

Futures

This is a particularly popular strategy with intra-day futures traders.

Options

See the options chapters for options basics.

Strategy

Since this is essentially a strategy to take advantage of an upward price move, the optimal strategy I would recommend is going long a call.

In or out of the money?

The further out of the money the calls are, the greater the risk of losing all your money from a move in the wrong direction or a small move in the correct direction. Your percentage returns compared to the probable percentage losses will be unsatisfactory. Slightly in the money options will probably have the best reward:risk ratio. Too far in the money and if the stock moves in the correct direction the percentage return will not be that great, because the option would be so highly priced due to its intrinsic value.

Time to expiry

If you are expecting the price to have exhausted its move in 1–3 weeks, I would suggest an option with at least 10 weeks to expiry, otherwise time decay will erode the price too sharply. An option greater than 16 months out of the money and you will be paying so much for it in time value that your percentage return will not be very good.

How to reduce risk

The usual strategies here:

■ Sell a further out of the money call (which can be bought back more cheaply if the market falls thereby offsetting losses on the long position).
■ Buy a deeper in the money option so your percentage lost is not so great (although your percentage gain on a winning move will be reduced, too).
■ Buy an option with longer to expiry, so time decay does not work too strongly against you; the pay-off is a lower return on investment.

Entry and exit points

The set-up

Look for a stock that has an established trend and wait for it to make a relative high. Wait for it then to make three consecutive days of lower lows and lower highs (see Fig 16.1). Jeff Cooper, who favors this strategy, confirms the strength of the stocks trend by looking for a relative strength index (RSI) reading of 95.

Entry

Cooper recommends long entry on day four, 1/16 of a point above the day-three high. A stop can be placed near the day-three low. A stop is very important to reduce the risk inherent in this strategy. These rules stop you entering trades which would not have succeeded (see Fig 16.2).

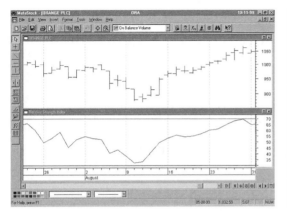

Fig 16.1 RSI reading confirming strength of stocks

Fig 16.2 Place a stop to reduce risk

Exit

The strategy does not have a specific exit. You could develop your own. I look for a lower close relative to the preceding day then place a stop 1/8 or 1/16 of a point below that day's low.

Example

Another example of the strategy in play is provided at Fig 16.3.

Optimization

Since you are looking for a good entry point on a pullback to buy for an uptrend there the main issue relates to how you could improve picking the best opportunities.

Because you are looking for a strong uptrend stock, an examination of the longer term chart and fundamentals as well as the weekly chart and its technicals should reveal how healthy a company and trend is in place. See Chapter 12 for more details on how longer time frames can work on shorter time frames.

Where the strategy failed

Take a good look at Fig 16.4; it shows you what can go wrong.

Fig 16.3 Another example of using the strategy

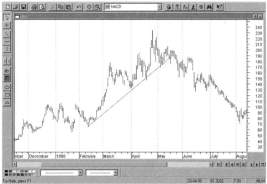

Fig 16.4 When the strategy fails

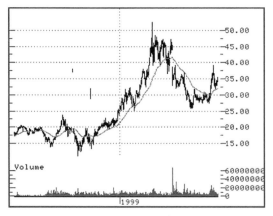

Screen 16.1

Some good web-sites

A site which lists stocks which are ready for a pullback strategy is the Tradehard site, at www.tradehard.com.

Summary

Getting onto a good trending stock is the route of much online trading stock. This can be a good strategy to get you in at a good price. As always it is not a 100 percent strategy and success also depends on placing stops and reducing risk.

17

Japanese Candlestick entry and exit strategies: From the Land of the Rising Sun

Strategic risk level: low

In this chapter

I once said I was a fan of Japanese Candlesticks to a banker. He promptly asked me if the Japanese use a special kind of wax and if the candles were fragrant! He obviously thought I had some unusual hobby involving candlewax.

As your system provides an entry or exit signal, an often excellent way to confirm the signal or get an advance warning of an impending signal is to use Japanese Candlestick formations. In this chapter we examine some key formations and how you might use them as part of a system to finesse them. Appendix 2 lists the most common formations and Appendix 5 lists some of the best books on the subject for more in-depth analysis.

Strategy that is effective

For those who have never come across a Japanese Candlestick, they are a way of displaying open, high, low, close information different than conventional western bar charts. What is more they have great names like "hanging man," and that has to be good (see Table 17.1).

See Figs 17.1 and 17.2. Both display the same price information, but one is in western bar chart format, the other in Japanese Candlestick format.

Minimum experience level	Risk level	Product types	Typical time scale	Key web-sites
Beginner	Intermediate. Low if used as part of a system	All	All	www.iptc.com www.iqc.com www.equis.com

Table 17.1 Japanese Candlestick strategy summary

Fig 17.1 Price information in western bar chart format

Fig 17.2 Price information – Japanese Candlestick style!

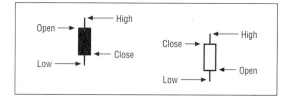

Fig 17.3 How the Japanese Candlestick works

A Japanese Candlestick is composed of a body and "wick." The body size is determined by the open and close. The body is shaded black if the price closed below the open, and shaded white if the price closed above the open. The wick measures the high and the low for the period (see Fig 17.3).

Strategy aim

To make use of centuries of experience of traders who have noted that certain price formations tend to precede price moves up, down or sideways. We want to augment our systems by overlaying this simple technique.

Japanese Candlestick formations can be used in several ways:

- to confirm or contradict a system signal to enter a market
- to confirm or contradict a decision already made about being in the market
- to confirm or contradict a decision already made about being out of the market
- to provide an early warning to exit a trade.

Products suitable for

Futures

Options

Stocks

Because Japanese Candlesticks are a way of displaying prices they can be used irrespective of the product.

Entry and exit points

I recommend using it as a reference. Here I have depicted some of the most common ones and examples of the little fellas in action (Figs 17.4–17.9).

Fig 17.4 Engulfing bear

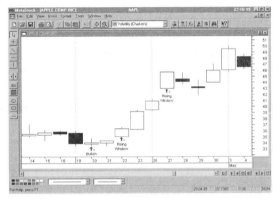

Fig 17.5 Rising window

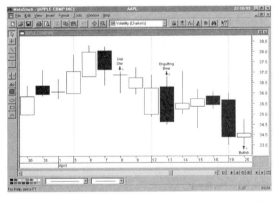

Fig 17.6 Doji star

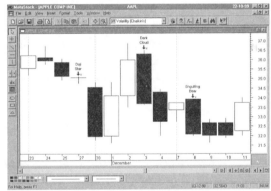

Fig 17.7 Dark cloud

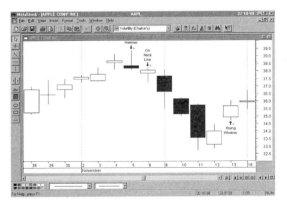

Fig 17.8 On neck line

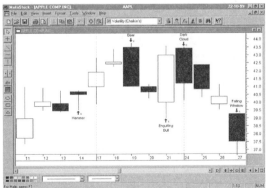

Fig 17.9 Hammer

Optimization

Few traders would rely on Japanese Candlesticks alone. Most use it as part of an overall system. They would look for a convergence or confluence of signals, both from their system and from Candlesticks, because this would increase the probability of a move, and we are looking for high probability and low risk all the time.

Convergence of indicators

Examine Fig 17.10. The stock is Amazon and on April 27 it hits a new high, but the stochastic in the bottom window has failed to make a new high with the price. This is a bearish indication. What is more the price closed below its open, another bearish sign.

On April 28 we see the MACD (middle window) has failed to make a new high with the price, the price has dropped further, and the stochastic has broken its own moving average, turning down from an oversold position. Now we are getting ready to go short the market, or exit any long positions. On April 29 we note there is a negative divergence in the MACD and Amazon has produced a "falling window" pattern. Now, as well as the convergence of momentum indicators, we also have the Japanese Candlestick confirming our bearish suspicions.

Remember, no one candlestick is being used as definitive, it is simply being used as greater evidence on which to base our decisions. Trading is about probabilities, not certainties, and Candlesticks help give us slightly more information about how probable a particular market move may be.

Convergence of Candlesticks

You can also look for additional confirmation of your view by examining it to see if there are a lot of candlesticks in a vicinity all suggesting the same thing. For example, see Fig 17.11.

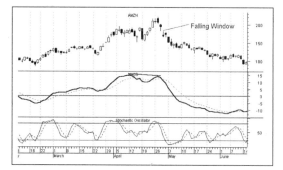

Fig 17.10 Bearish indicators on Amazon

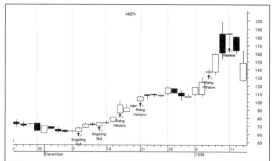

Fig 17.11 Convergence of Candlesticks

Where the strategy failed

Candlesticks give an indication of what has *tended* to happen in the past given a particular Candlestick formation. They do not say what the size of the move will be, whether it may be large or negligible, or whether it will occur at all. That is why a convergence of indicators is so important and a strict stop and money management system. To prove the point have a look at Figs 17.12–17.13. I like to look at where indicators have failed to bring me down to earth to remind me that there is no "Holy Grail" and that no matter how tempting and "can't fail" a position can look in the future, it can fail and I must stick to a discipline plan.

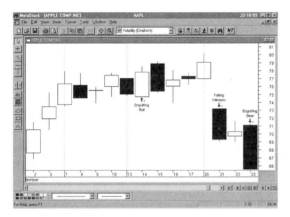

Fig 17.12 Strategy failure due to engulfing bull, falling window and engulfing bear

Fig 17.13 Strategy failure due to hammer

Some good web-sites

Some good charting sites allow the display of Japanese Candlesticks as well as traditional bar charts. Take a look at the ones in the charting web-sites section. www.equis.com also goes through some of the basics of Japanese Candlesticks charting.

For a specialist site on Japanese Candlesticks that offers educational material, trading strategies, books and charts see www.iptc.com – it is a bit slow but worth persevering with. IQ Chart which does real-time intra-day charts also displays these in Candlesticks, and for a fee has a Candlestick recognition system.

Screen 17.1

Screen 17.2

Summary

Oriental candlewax aside, Japanese Candlesticks can be an excellent additional source of valuable market information and I recommend their use. I, personally, do not centre my trading decisions around them, but instead look at them as one of the last things before making a decision. I love their elegant simplicity. In that regard, I am much like a Japanese Candlestick myself.

Most of the web-sites listed under the technical analysis web-site chapters and the systems software chapter will display price charts in Candlesticks at the click of mouse button, some software such as Metastock even scans price charts and labels the charts with patterns – which is the software I have used. (It is to plotting price charts by hand what taking steroids is to 100m runners – just makes the job a lot easier.)

18

Earnings strategies: Show me the money ⟩⟩

Strategic risk level: low

In this chapter

What moves share prices? If we knew that we would be sitting on a beach in the Bahamas. But one thing is for sure, the unexpected moves prices. The unexpected may be new information about a stock, such as earnings, and it can have a short sharp effect on stocks. Such moves can be tradeable for the short-term trader. We can be even more astute than that; the way the price moves after earnings can tell us a lot about future direction. When we speak of earnings we are talking about "earnings consensus" which is the average of all the analysts' earnings estimate. It tends to be the consensus figure that is more relevant, as opposed to the specific earnings figure of any one analyst.

Strategy that is effective

The strategy does not require you to set up your own research desk, second-guess the analysts at Salomon Brothers, and place a position before earnings are announced on the basis that analysts may have got it wrong. The share price can do several telling things after an earnings announcement. If earnings were in line with expectations, we would expect the stock price to be relatively unchanged. If it moves up, it could mean the markets were relieved their expectations were met, and the outlook could be brighter for the company. If the price moves down after, in line with expectation earnings, then it could be that the market was hoping for the stock to beat its estimates, and is quite disappointed (see Table 18.1).

More interestingly, we will look at what it means if a stock moves up on poorer than expected earnings or down on better than expected earnings information. Soon after an earnings announcement, analysts' up and downgradings follow through and reinforce or dampen any price move – adding to the possibility of a short-term trading profit opportunity.

Minimum experience level	Risk level	Product types	Typical time scale	Key web-sites
Beginner–intermediate	Intermediate	Stocks, options	Intra-day to a few days	www.firstcall.com www.zacks.com www.whispernumber.com

Table 18.1 Earnings strategy summary

Strategy aim

The strategy here tries to profit from post-earnings price moves.

Products suitable for

Stocks

Option

Options

Since we are anticipating movement in the underlying stock, earnings news could be a useful short-term leveraged strategy. We would be holding the stock for a short time – until the market digests the earnings information which could be a few hours, to more likely a few days (when the analysts come in with regradings), so do not anticipate too much time decay in the price of the option. An option with six weeks to expiry should be fine. But do consider the issue of how to choose the best option, as described in the section on options in the book.

Entry and exit points

The set-up

Find and monitor from the web-sites in this chapter stocks with forthcoming earnings announcements. Make a note from the same site of expected earnings. On the morning after the earnings announcement is made (assuming earnings announcement made the preceding day after market close), make a note if it is greater than or less than analysts' expectations. We will ignore (for this strategy) stocks which are line with analyst expectations.

Entry

If the earnings were better than expectations, go short (or buy a put) when and if the price goes below the previous day's low. This way, only if the stock falls on better than expected earnings, would you go short, i.e. only if the market is giving a very bearish evaluation on the earnings.

If the earnings were worse than expected, go long when and if the price passes the previous day's high. Again if the price rises on worse than expected earnings, the market is telling you that it is happy with the stock.

Exit

There are no special exit rules, so you could exit on a break of the preceding day's low if you are long, or you could exit on a trailing stop.

Example

Fig 18.1 shows an example of the strategy in motion.

Optimization

For those positions where we are looking to go long, we would be even more comfortable if there was an uptrend and other indicators (such as momentum indicators) suggested the stock was oversold and ready for a rise. The opposite holds true for going short, of course.

Where the strategy failed

This is a risky strategy to the extent that the size of the move is unknown, and a volatile market could hit your entry only to leave you nursing a loss if the market then moves in the opposite direction. To reduce this risk we enter on the low or the high of the preceding day, but it can all still end in tears, as Fig 18.2 shows.

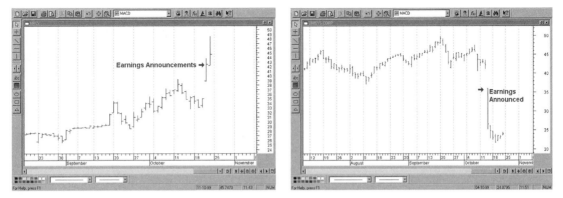

Fig 18.1 The strategy in motion   **Fig 18.2** It can all end in tears

Some good web-sites

The following sites provide all the earnings information you could want for trading this strategy. These sites provide earnings calendars so you can plan ahead. Most earnings announcements come after market close at 4.30pm but occasionally occur during market hours.

Whisper Numbers ✳✳✳

www.whispernumbers.com

This is an excellent service. The sites home page blurb explains it best:

The hottest indicator driving stocks today is the "Whisper Number." A projected earnings number above or below the consensus estimate. These numbers, until now only available to Wall Street's top analysts and savvy traders, are now available for you.

What's the buzz on the street? Find out what's being said behind closed doors, in the back alley, and on the floor, but . . . shhhhhhhh . . . don't tell anyone, the Whisper Numbers are here.

So idea is simple, the consensus and the whisper are two different things, and, of the two, the whisper is more likely to impact price. In this strategy, you can use the whisper number instead of the earnings figure.

Zacks ✳✳✳

www.zacks.com

A key earnings specialist site that categorizes upside and downside surprises, and by what percentage, so is very useful for this strategy.

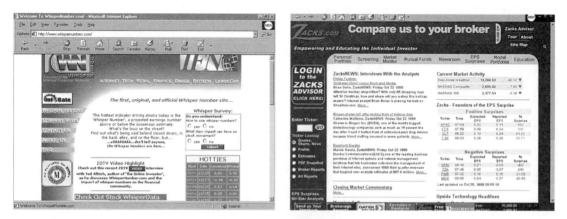

Screen 18.1   **Screen 18.2**

Screen 18.3

First Call ✳✳✳

`www1.firstcall.com/us/usnav.htm`

A very well-known earnings information provider. Top-quality information. More directed towards institutions than the Zacks site, I feel.

Summary

This strategy relies on the fact that new market information can lead to price moves in the short term. Any purchases nevertheless require close monitoring, because the new information will only act on the stock price for as long as it has not become fully incorporated into it.

19

Day trading futures: Momentum strategy

Strategic risk level: moderate

In this chapter

This is a simple strategy to take advantage of intra-day price moves in liquid futures contracts such as the S&P 500, or Dow Jones indices futures contracts.

Strategy that is effective

Table 19.1 summarizes the strategy discussed in this chapter.

Minimum experience level	Risk level	Product types	Typical time scale	Key web-sites
Intermediate	Moderate	Futures	Intra-day	www.iqc.com

Table 19.1 Momentum strategy summary

Strategy aim

To find the optimal entry point before a short price move up or down.

Products suitable for

Futures

Futures

This is an intra-day strategy, and since it requires momentum to be profitable we need to restrict it to liquid contracts.

Entry and exit points

The set-up

You can use five- 10-, 15- or 20-minute bars. Let us assume 10-minute bars are being used. Wait for the price to be above the 15-period moving average.

The entry

Enter on one tick above the previous bar as soon as the three-period RSI falls below the 30. If that has not occurred in the next two bars, do not enter.

The exit

The stop-loss can be the low of the preceding bar. For a profit exit, you could use a trailing stop or the preceding bar's low or the low of two bars ago.

Example

See Fig 19.1 for an example of the strategy in motion.

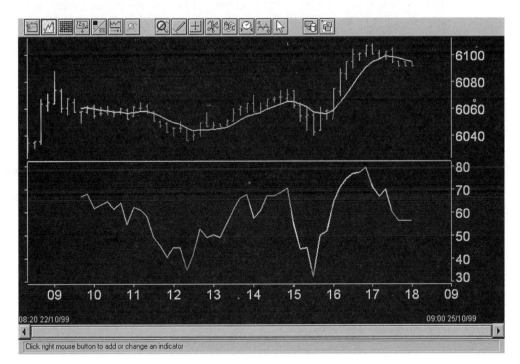

Fig 19.1 The strategy in action

Optimization

The probability of a move up can be increased if you look for other chart patterns such as double bottoms, or indicator patterns such as positive divergences. (See Chapter 11 for a reference to these.)

Where the strategy failed

Fig 19.2 shows how not to go about it.

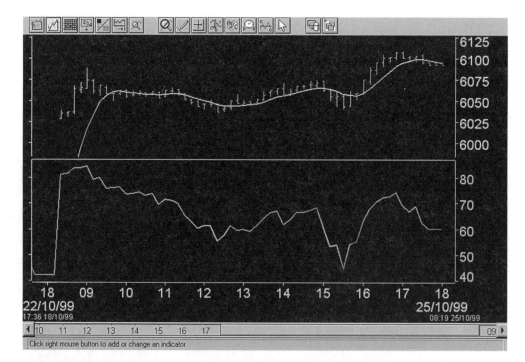

Fig 19.2 Strategy failure

Some good web-sites

You need real-time price charts of futures contracts which allow the display of the RSI, so good sites might include www.quote.com and www.iqc.com.

Summary

Stops are an essential aspect of this strategy. It's essentially "letting the profits run and cutting the losses short." What I like about this strategy is that it uses two indicators: the moving average, and the RSI, together.

20

Cup and handle: Traders get imaginative

Strategic risk level: moderate

In this chapter

The cup and handle strategy is based on a chart pattern made famous by the technical analyst, William O'Neill. Unlike ancient mariners who gave the constellations romantic names such as Cassiopeia, lonely technical analysts gave chart patterns more mundane names. In this chapter we explore how you might find and exploit this pattern and useful web-sites for seeking it out among the constellations of securities.

Strategy that is effective

Table 20.1 summarizes the cup and handle strategy.

Minimum experience level	Risk level	Product types	Typical time scale	Key web-sites
Beginner	Low to moderate	Stocks, futures and options	Intra-day to several weeks	www.tradehard.com

Table 20.1 Cup and handle strategy summary

Strategy aim

To time entry after the formation of a handle part of this formation so as to capture the subsequent upward move. The pattern often occurs as the "breathing space" during a rally, and after the handle is formed, the rally or uptrend may resume.

Products suitable for

Stocks

Futures

Options

Futures

This pattern can exhibit itself on intra-day charts, and so lends itself well to intra-day futures trading.

Options

See the options chapters for options basics.

Strategy

Since this is essentially a strategy to take advantage of an upward price move, the optimal strategy I would recommend is going long a call.

In or out of the money?

The further out of the money the calls are, the greater the risk of losing all your money from a move in the wrong direction, or a small move in the correct direction. Your percentage returns compared to the probable percentage losses will be unsatisfactory. Slightly in the money options will probably have the best reward:risk ratio. Too far in the money, and, if the stock moves in the correct direction, the percentage return will not be that great because the option would be so highly priced due to its intrinsic value.

Time to expiry

If you are expecting the price to have exhausted its move in one–three weeks I would suggest an option with at least 10 weeks to expiry, otherwise time decay will erode the price to sharply. An option greater than 16 months out of the money and you will be paying so much for it in time value that your percentage return will not be very good.

How to reduce risk

The usual strategies here:

- Sell a further out of the money call (which can be bought back more cheaply if the market falls, thereby offsetting losses on the long position).
- Buy a deeper in the money option so your percentage loss is not so great (although your percentage gain on a winning move will be reduced, too).
- Buy an option with longer to expiry, so time decay does not work too strongly against you; the pay-off is a lower return on investment.

Entry and exit points

The set-up

1 The stock must be in an uptrend. You can check for this visually or define an uptrend as a stock above its 50-day moving average.

2 A cup formation needs to have been created.

3 A handle should follow the cup (see Fig 20.1).

Entry

Go long when the market continues on its uptrend by "breaking the handle."

Exit

There is no defined exit point, but you could wait for a lower low to be made, or two consecutive lower lows, or use some other indicator, e.g. the MACD, to signal an exit.

Example

Fig 20.2 shows a cup and handle.

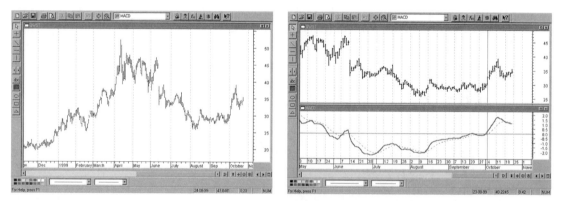

Fig 20.1 Cup formation

Fig 20.2 Cup and handle

Optimization

The key to profiting from the pattern resides in two factors:

1 Why the cup formed.

2 The solidity of the breaking of the handle.

The cup is actually the price falling. At that stage we would not know if it was a reversal, or a cup and handle formation. If there appears to be fundamental news to suggest that although a cup has formed the company has undergone a reversal of fortune, as opposed to mere profit taking due to its recent rally, then you may want to reconsider the play.

You will want to ensure the breaking of the handle is not false and so will want to rely on other indicators as confirmation, for instance, are there any positive divergences on the momentum indicators? Was their increased volume breakout associated with the price break that broke the handle?

Where the strategy failed

Fig 20.3 shows an example of failure. Heed its salutory tale well.

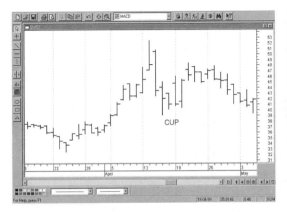

Fig 20.3 Revenge of the China

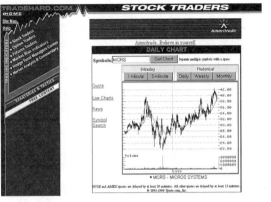

Screen 20.1

Some good web-sites

The well-respected technical analyst, Dave Landry, is a follower of this strategy and www.tradehard.com is a site that scans stocks for the appearance of this pattern.

Summary

Like all chart patterns this one is prone to failure, but what is good about it is that when it works it permits you to get on board a trend. A pretty pattern to be sure.

All this talk has made me thirsty. Cup of tea?

21

Breaking-out strategies: True or false?

Strategic risk level: moderate

In this chapter

Fig 21.1 Trading on price breakouts

Trading on price breakouts, that is when the price moves out of an area of consolidation or makes a new high or low (as in Fig 21.1), is a very popular strategy among online traders. However, because of false breakouts it is not as simple as it once was, and the strategy has had to become more sophisticated and complex than it used to be. In this chapter, we start at the basics and move onto the advanced aspects of the strategy, and finally the types of online sites you would want to visit if this strategy tickles your fancy.

Strategy that is effective

Table 21.1 summarizes the breaking-out strategies.

Minimum experience level	Risk level	Product types	Typical time scale	Key web-sites
Beginner–intermediate	Low–moderate	Stocks, futures, options	Few days to weeks (can also work on intra-day charts)	www.iqc.com

Table 21.1 Breaking-out strategy summary

Strategy aim

We are looking to profit from a price moving out of a consolidation area or a previous relative high. We may also be able to profit from false breakouts. It appears that the "turtles" taught by Richard Dennis may well have made their fortunes using a breakout strategy. For those who do not know, Dennis is a very famous and highly successful trader, who trained some non-traders in his methods. These were his "turtles"; human to be sure, and not amphibian, despite what some people may say about traders.

Products suitable for

Stocks

Futures

Options

Stocks

The good thing about using this strategy for stocks is that the price rise may be generated by a strongly trending stock that has temporarily consolidated. That then may be a short-term reaction with a company that is fundamentally healthy. Now, although in the short term we focus on technicals, it is always good when we are going long on a company that is fundamentally sound too, because that reduces the risk of a negative move.

Futures

Intra-day futures charts regularly show breakouts and trading breakouts are as popular a pastime for the floor traders as trading false breakouts.

Options

See options basics.

The options plays on this strategy are the same for trades where you are expecting an up move – long calls – or a down move – long puts. I would not recommend the high-risk strategy of naked writing options to take advantage of either anticipated price moves. Because of the increased probability of false breakouts a vertical bull spread (e.g. long call plus short a further out of the money call) may be a good idea. More complicated strategies tend not to make money because of commission costs.

Entry and exit points

The set-up

There is no special set-up for this strategy; you can go straight to the entry criteria.

Entry

There are several different entry criteria.

Normal strategy

Enter on a new 10-, 20-, 40- or 50-day high. (For shorting the market you, of course, do the opposite and look for the respective lows.)

Raschke-Connors Strategy

Larry Connors and Linda Bradford Raschke – two of the industry's most respected traders, tutors and writers – describe in their excellent book, *Street Smarts* (M. Gordon Publishing, 1996), a slightly more elaborate entry for what they call "the Turtle Soup Strategy," to take advantage of false breakouts. Remember here their aim so go long despite a new low, because they consider the breakout to be false:

Day One: *The market has to make a 20-day low four or more days after a previous 20-day low. The close for this latest low day has to be the same or lower than the preceding low day.*

Day Two: *Place a buy-stop order (i.e. to enter the market) at the last 20-day low. If the order is unfilled during the day you cancel it.*

What I like about this entry rule is that you are allowing market action to take you into a trade and not any indicator such as ADX, etc. The most important indicator is, after all, price. This entry rule reduces the risk of being wrong about the breakout being false, because if it is genuine then the buy-stop order should not be activated. One could research breakouts and see where a buy-stop order should be placed, given the likely price action for a true and for a false breakout.

Fig 21.2 A Raschke-Connors entry

The other good thing about the Raschke-Connnors rules are that in practice it can work well with the market cycles and be triggered by the buy stop when the cycle turns direction (see Fig 21.2).

Exit

Normal strategy

There is no specific exit, and so you could use other indicators to determine an exit point, e.g. momentum indicators, a trailing stop, or the price failing to make a new high. Worry not, momentum indicators are discussed in the chapter on technical indicators and trailing stops in the chapter on stops.

I look for two consecutive lower lows, but if the momentum indicators show negative bearish divergence, or there is a piece of negative fundamental news I may get out after one lower low in the price. I also may set a trailing exit at a certain percentage point below the highest high reached since I entered the trade. So if I entered the trade at 100, and four days later the market reached 130 at its high and then the next day went to 120 I may have exited because 120 is more than 5 percent (my exit level off the high) below 130 (the high reached since my entry).

Raschke-Connors Strategy

Place a sell stop-loss order one tick under the lowest of the lows of day one and day two. Plus look to get out based on trailing stops.

Example

Fig 21.3 shows a breakout trade.

Optimization

Many markets

Since you are looking for breakouts, if you monitor too few markets then you will have too few breakouts to trade. So you must monitor several securities if using this strategy.

False breakouts

The popularity of the system has led to false breakouts being a common occurrence (see Fig 21.4). For example, a security may be near its 50-day high. Traders seeing this on the floor may start offering the stocks at higher prices (i.e. the price the retail customer buys at and the price at which the floor trader or market maker sells to them at) in the hope of selling stock to breakout traders at the higher breakout prices. Next, the floor traders will drop the bid in the hope of buying back the stock cheaply. As the bid drops, the breakout traders panic and sell out.

Fig 21.3 A breakout trade

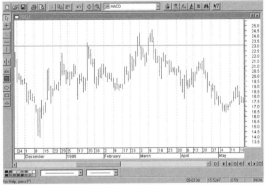

Fig 21.4 The false breakout

Gauging the market to determine if true or false breakout

Trading in the opposite direction to the initial breakout is often called "fading" the breakout (fading because you are moving away from it!). Are there any signals online traders can use to determine if there is going to be a true or a false breakthrough? With none of these factors is anything guaranteed, but the probabilities may be slightly favoring one move over another.

Indicators

If, at the point of breakout, the indicators suggest bearishness that may well be a good reason to fade the breakout.

Market background

If the major indices are bearish and the sector looks overbought you have some cause for caution on a breakout.

News

If the breakout follows a news item of positive news that could be the spur for a breakout.

Chart patterns

See the chapter on technical analysis for chart patterns.

If the breakout occurs near the base of formations such as a head and shoulders, or double top or bottom formation that may give you an idea of the nature of the breakout.

Volume

A price move confirmed by unusually high volume suggests that the price move is less likely to reverse in the near term. If the breakout occurs on high volume that should increase the possibility of a true breakout.

Where the strategy failed

The problem with illustrating strategy failure here is that a failed breakout is a false breakout. The true failure is when near a breakout level a price moves sideways, neither true nor false (see Fig 21.5).

Fig 21.5 Next day confirmation

Next day

Instead of entering as soon as the new high is made, you could enter if the market closes at a new high and moves up on the open the next day. That way you get additional confirmation. This is the method I use.

Some good web-sites

Charting sites are, of course, needed to monitor prices, and they are listed in the chapter on technical analysis web-sites.

Summary

It is unfortunate that the breakout pattern is not as easy as it used to be. To trade it effectively now you need to monitor chart patterns, and possible sector and market background. The rise of false breakouts makes the need for tight stop-losses and risk and money management even more important when using this strategy.

22

Online strategies from the net: Lists and sites that supply trading opportunities

Strategic risk level: moderate

Online trading problems

- How can I search for securities that may be good short-term trading plays?
- Which sites list securities which may be good plays based on trading strategies?
- Which are the best web-sites for doing this?

In this chapter

When searching for short-term trading plays, online traders have discovered that securities exhibiting certain characteristics may have a tendency to be good candidates. But what are the characteristics they need to display and how, out of the thousands of securities, do we find them? That is what is in this chapter. There are two types of sites in this group. Those that list securities based on some criteria entered by the user (filters) which the site then uses to screen securities. The second type of site provides lists based on its own strategies. Many sites do a mix of both.

Whatever the results produced, this is the starting point for further research; it is a means of saving you having to search hundreds of stocks manually. With this shortlist produced by the web-sites always make sure you check the price charts, and understand what you are expecting the price to do and follow the risk and money management advice in the relevant chapters of this book. Look for confirmation of any anticipated price move in other technical indicators, the price and other time frames. Remember, the lists of stocks generated by the screen do not tell you price projections.

> **hot tip!** You do not need to be overwhelmed with researching every stock that gets listed by a screen. Limit yourself to 25, 50 or 100 depending on the time you have and want to spend.

We will examine and review some of the top sites and look at some of the criteria (filters) you could input to search (screen) out securities for those short-term plays (see Fig 22.1).

We also explain these strategies so you are not restricted to any one site and get a feel for why something is used. The sites are chosen based on the following criteria:

- ease of use
- free if possible; if they charge, must be very good value for money
- sites with pre-built searches preferred
- the number of search variables the better
- the number of securities scanned
- focus on short-term strategies.

Fig 22.1 Typical search filter

---

expert advice ✓ *David Landry on the top-notch Tradehard.com site*

"Some of the best traders I know only look at a few lists. You might want to concentrate on the ones that fit your style of trading. For instance, I like pullbacks and cups and handles."

Screening based strategies

Short-term strong and high analyst rankings and surprised earnings

Table 22.2 contains a summary.

Minimum experience level	Risk level	Product types	Typical time scale	Key web-sites
Beginner	Low–intermediate	Stocks, options	Several weeks to several months	www.wallstreetcity.com

Table 22.1 Strategy summary

Strategy aim

This searches stocks with recent strength based on higher earnings that surprised the market in the last month. Moreover, these stocks have high analyst rankings as well, so should continue upward, at least in the short term. The idea is that these stocks have very recently surprised the major institutions on earnings and as they re-evaluate their strong recommendations, and possibly buy more of the stock, it should rise in price to incorporate the new earnings information.

Products suitable for

Stocks

Options (the possibility of continuing strength or weakness opens the way for a call or put strategy)

Screening criteria

■ Analyst consensus as high as possible to strong buy

■ Earnings surprises as many as possible in last four quarters

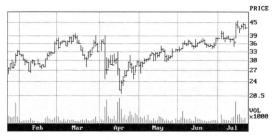

Fig 22.2 Mercury Interactive Corp (MERQ)

Some good web-sites

Which web-sites you can use will depend very much on the search criteria that web-sites offer. This is one of the searches available on the Wall Street City site, which is an excellent site that also provides back-tested results for the strategy based on market capitalization of stock. Fig 22.2 shows one of the stocks to be found using this search criterion on the Wall Street City site. Note the stock has virtually doubled since April 1999 to July 1999.

Recent technical strength and strong growth

Table 22.2 contains a summary.

Minimum experience level	Risk level	Product types	Typical time scale	Key web-sites
Beginner	Low–intermediate	Stocks, options	Few days to few weeks	www.wallstreetcity.com

Table 22.2 Strategy summary

Strategy aim

To take advantage of any impending price move up on a stock that has shown recent (30 day) increased volume, high growth.

Products suitable for

Stocks

Options

Screening criteria

- Strong growth based on projected earnings, historical earnings, cash flow, and sales
- Technical strength of a stock, using MACD, relative performance (1 week), and moving average breakout (10 day)

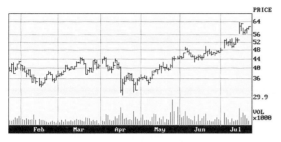

Some good web-sites

Again, I used Wall Street City for this, although your criteria for the filters could be different. Fig 22.3 was produced by the search. Another stock that doubled in price in a few months.

Fig 22.3 Veritas software (VRTS)

Room to grow (by Sharon Crayne on Stocktables)

Table 22.3 contains a summary.

Minimum experience level	Risk level	Product types	Typical time scale	Key web-sites
Intermediate	Intermediate	Stocks, options	Few days	www.stocktables.com

Table 22.3 Strategy summary

Strategy aim

Here we are looking for stocks that have made new highs but have a high degree of accumulation and have not doubled in price in the past year, on the basis they have some room to grow.

Products suitable for

Stocks

Options

Screening criteria

- Relative strength greater than 30 (see the chapter on technical indicators if you need a refresher on this indicator)
- EPS greater than 30 (so the stock has strong fundamentals)
- A/D greater than five (this is a measure of the degree of accumulation)
- New high

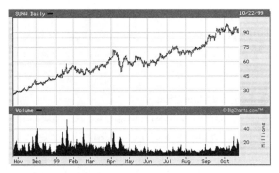

Fig 22.4 Stocktables

Some good web-sites

www.stocktables.com. Although this site is a little difficult to handle it does focus on short-term screening criteria (see Screen 22.2).

Strong stocks/recently weak

Table 22.4 contains a summary.

Minimum experience level	Risk level	Product types	Typical time scale	Key web-sites
Beginnner	Low	Stocks, options	Few days	www.wallstreetcity.com

Table 22.4 Strategy summary

Strategy aim

We are looking for stocks that have had a long-term strength, but have recently shown weakness which may then be an opportunity to enter for a spring back to the longer term trend. Of itself the list of stocks is just those that may turn up. We would want price confirmation and confirmation from other indicators as well, of course.

Screen 22.1

Screen 22.2

Products suitable for

Stocks

Options

Screening criteria

■ Relative 18-week performance as low as possible

■ P/E ratio as high as possible

■ Relative performance three year is as high as possible

Some good web-sites

Wall Street City provides a pre-built search for this category, but warns that you need to use the list results as a starting point for further research.

Engulfing patterns

Table 22.5 contains a summary.

Minimum experience level	Risk level	Product types	Typical time scale	Key web-sites
Beginner–intermediate	Intermediate	Stocks, options	Few days	www.moneynet.com

Table 22.5 Strategy summary

Strategy aim

This is strategies based on Japanese Candlesticks. Engulfing patterns are either bullish or bearish. It is essential that any stocks showing this formation are then further researched, for instance, using the principles of technical analysis described in this book. It is strongly unadvisable to trade simply on the signal alone.

Products suitable for

Stocks

Options

Screening criterion

■ Bullish/bearish engulfing pattern

Screen 22.3

Some good web-sites

Reuters MoneyNet http://www.moneynet.com/content/MONEYNET/HotStockList/HotStockList.asp. The MoneyNet is an excellent site. The Hot Stock List is accessed through the "research" section.

Fundamentally and technically weak

Table 22.6 contains a summary.

Minimum experience level	Risk level	Product types	Typical time scale	Key web-sites
Beginner	Low–intermediate	Stocks	Few days – weeks	www.wallstreetcity.com

Table 22.6 Strategy summary

Strategy aim

Here, we look for stocks that have historically been high, but may have slipped in recent times and may be ready for a revival that we could take advantage of. Least squared (LSQ) deviation reveals the position of the stock price to an LSQ line over various time periods, stated as a percentage, and is a barometer of under- and overvaluation for a stock. If a stock is trading off its LSQ line, that stock is undervalued based on history. Of course, history does not necessarily repeat itself, and the LSQ line can shift down if the price remains low for long enough.

Products suitable for

Stocks

Screening criteria

■ Least squared deviation one year is as high as possible

■ Relative performance 18, 26 week is as low as possible

■ MACD as low as possible

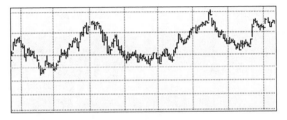

Fig 22.5 Wall Street City

Some good web-sites

Once again, Wall Street City provides the filters to enable filtering based on this strategy (see Screen 22.1).

Momentum screens

Table 22.7 contains a summary.

Minimum experience level	Risk level	Product types	Typical time scale	Key web-sites
Beginner	Low–intermediate	Stocks, options, futures	Few days	www.alphachart.com www.wallstreetcity.com

Table 22.7 Strategy summary

Strategy aim

We are looking to screen for strategies showing oversold on several momentum indicators of time frames simultaneously. Don't forget the chapter on momentum indicators and using multiple time frames and multiple indicators.

Products suitable for

Futures

Stocks

Options

Screening criteria

- Nine-, 14-, 25-day RSI < 0
- MACD crosses above its nine-day signal
- Stochastic oscillator %D crosses above %K
- Momentum is negative

Some good web-sites

Alphachart is one of the few sites that provides the appropriate technical indicators for searching securities matching this criterion. Alphachart is also easy to use and free. Wall Street City also can be screened for high and low momentum stocks.

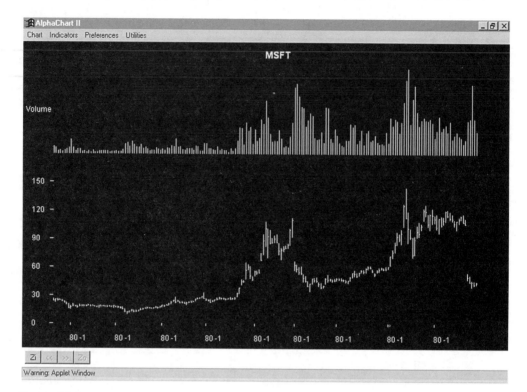

Screen 22.4

Breakout strategies

Table 22.8 contains a summary.

Minimum experience level	Risk level	Product types	Typical time scale	Key web-sites
Beginner	Low	Stocks, options	Few days	www.moneynet.com

Table 22.8 Strategy summary

Strategy aim

When prices break out of a consolidation that can often trigger a sharp move. You can think of a consolidation phase as a tug of war between buyers and sellers. The breakout signals a victory to one side or the other depending on whether it is an upside or downside breakout. Rather like a battleline that is breached, the subsequent victorious hordes can move quite quickly and fairly, particularly as those who previously took an opposing view may turn tail and join the victors.

Breakout trading can be risky because of the danger of false breakouts (see Fig 22.6), making the use of stops all the more important. When it comes to breakout a stop could be placed just inside the consolidation area on the basis that a genuine as opposed to false breakout would not see prices return to the consolidation area in the short term.

We discuss breakout strategies in a separate chapter but for now I want to introduce you to this useful search which can list the candidates.

Products suitable for

Stocks

Options

Futures

Screening criterion

■ Breakout from consolidation

Some good web-sites

Web-site screening for this phenomenon is particularly useful, because searching through thousands of stock for this pattern "by eye" can take a very long time. Again, the MoneyNet site uses this screen (see Fig 22.7).

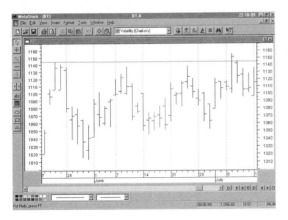

Fig 22.6 A false breakout displayed on MoneyNet

Fig 22.7 Breakout on MoneyNet!

Summary

Lists produced by screens can be a very useful starting point for further investigation, but the warnings at the start of the chapter cannot be overstated. Now I am going to be accused of being repetitive. You must ensure that you apply all the other principles of trading when working with such lists.

23

Bollinger Bands strategies: Wait for it to get tight

Strategic risk level: moderate

In this chapter

There is a theory, which, simply put, states that things revert to their mean (i.e. average), so if something sways too far from its average then there should be an increased probability that it will revert to its mean. Bollinger Bands attempt to capture whether

Fig 23.1 Your best Bollinger, please

a stock is far more or far less volatile than its norm, and therefore whether that should change. They can also be interpreted on the basis that if a stock is hardly moving, then it can only do one thing – move. On the basis of this information, we should be able to trade the security. I know it seems a bit far-fetched and long-winded, but it does make a lot of sense, and it is one of the indicators I always add to my armory (see Fig 23.1).

What is particularly useful is that is not a momentum indicator, but a volatility one, and so adds an extra dimension to our trading perspective, offering independent confirmation or corroboration of other indicators based on different theories. Read on to see how to interpret this indicator.

Strategy that is effective

Table 23.1 summarizes Bollinger Band strategies.

Minimum experience level	Risk level	Product types	Typical time scale	Key web-sites
Intermediate	High if used in isolation. Lower if used as part of a system with other indicators	All. Needs liquid securities	All short	www.wallstreetcity.com www.bigcharts.com www.etrade.co.uk

Table 23.1 Bollinger Bands strategy summary

Strategy aim

To buy as volatility starts increasing, as long as we know which direction the stock is going to move in.

Products suitable for

Futures

Options

Stocks

Options

Since we are looking for the price to become more volatile, but may not know the direction, we could buy a call and a put, and try to profit from a price move in either direction, closing out the option which is in the wrong direction. Also, as volatility increases, the option price should increase simply due to that alone. However, buying two lots of options means twice the commission costs and spreads involved and time decay, so we have to be absolutely sure about our option math and whether the risk reward is worth it. See Appendix 2 to brush up on options decision-making process.

Entry and exit points

Bollinger Bands envelope the stock price and are plotted at standard deviation levels above and below a moving average. The standard deviation is a statistical (no, don't switch off just because I said "statistical") measure of how far, on average, something deviates away from its own average. And now, in English.

First, take the price. Next, plot its moving average (you recall, the average of the price over the last x days). Next, work out how far the current price is from the moving average. Take this figure and calculate on average how far the price is from its own moving average. Plot that.

Don't worry too much about this. The idea is that if something has moved away a lot further than it normally does, then it should stray back to where it normally (on average) is.

We are not too concerned whether the theory holds up to close scrutiny. Our concern is whether the reality holds up to close scrutiny.

Entry

The Bollinger Bands contract when the security is going through a period of low volatility, i.e. the standard deviation around the mean price is low, in other words, the price is on average not moving too far away from its own average price. Sharp price moves tend to follow such low volatility as the volatility has only one way to go – up. We have to wait for the price to confirm price direction (see Fig 23.2).

Fig 23.2 Entry

Exit

For projecting price targets I often find that the price moves from one Bollinger Band to the opposite one, sometimes, however, it will pause or reverse at the middle band. I often do not look for Bollinger contraction but instead will just look for medium-side bands and a momentum buy signal, on the basis that the momentum suggests buy, and with the price on the bottom Bollinger, and wide enough bands so that when the price goes to the top band, I should have a nice profit (see Fig 23.3).

chat
box 23.2
A trader on Silicon Investor on 8.6.1999

You noted that when price moves above a certain MA (i.e. 10-period) that it tends to pullback. Rather than using MAs, as you do, I use Bollinger Bands to look for overbought (oversold) conditions. When I see a stock jump outside the upper band I look to sell, if long (or go short) and if it falls below the lower band I look to go long (or cover a short). Do you not think Bollingers would further validate your MA analysis? I tend to use stochastics and/or RSI to confirm what I might see with Bollingers.

chat
box 23.3
A trader on Silicon Investor on 12.6.1999

Location and direction determine trading phase

1 *Upper vs. lower action*
Location of price bars determines the strength of the current phase. Price within the upper band signifies power while price within the lower band signals weakness.

2 *Price direction*
Direction of price within the band identifies convergence and divergence with the current trend. Rising price within the lower band and falling price within the upper band signal divergence while rising within the upper and falling within the lower signal convergence.

3 *Trend testing*
The lower band, middle band (center average) and upper band represent support/resistance for the trend. Reversal of any band increases odds that price will expand in the reversed direction and return to the last band crossed or touched.

Penetration through the center band increases directional momentum

1 *Crossing from below center to above*
Uptrend increase in strength. Observe directional movement of the upper band as price approaches.

2 *Crossing from above center to below*
Downtrend increase in weakness. Observe directional movement of the lower band as price approaches.

Bands open in response to awakening trend

1 *Climbing the ladder*
If the angle of the upper band rises in response to approaching price, expect a series of upward price bars, each riding higher along the top band. This is an uptrend in progress. Conversely, price striking into a horizontal upper band predicts reversal and resistance.

2 *The slippery slope*
If the angle of the lower band falls in response to approaching price, expect a series of downward price bars, each pushing lower along the bottom band. This is a downtrend in progress. Conversely, price striking into a horizontal lower band predicts reversal and support.

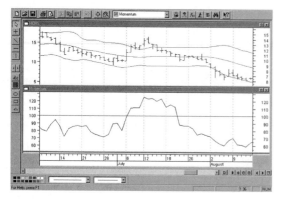

Fig 23.3 Exit

Optimization

You can get a clue to price direction move by looking at momentum indicators. If the Bollinger is contracted and the momentum is starting to turn up in oversold territory, that could mean a bullish move upwards.

Where the strategy failed

Like all strategies, this one is prone to failure. The thing to watch out for is reversal at the middle band. You have to watch the price and other indicators to see if they give a clue to future price direction; are they all bullish, or, on a balance of probabilities, as close as you can tell bullish?

Some good web-sites

Charting sites offering Bollinger Bands and the display of other indicators are the best here. For USA, check out Big Charts (www.bigcharts.com) and Wall Street City (www.wallstreetcity.com) and for UK, try www.etrade.co.uk.

Summary

Displaying Bollinger Bands can be done by either the three internet sites, or other ones in the chapter on technical analysis charting, or software mentioned before. The variables for the Bollinger are usually entered by the chart providers as default values, and I tend not to play with these.

It is a display on the price, and so I figure while I am looking at the price there is no harm in having the B–bands on as well.

24

Strategies for price gaps: Mind the gap! ⟫

Strategic risk level: moderate

In this chapter

There cannot be a trader who has not seen a price gap. (See Fig 24.1, just in case.) How can we take advantage of these in our trading?

Strategy that is effective

Table 24.1 summarizes strategies for price gaps.

Minimum experience level	Risk level	Product types	Typical time scale	Key web-sites
Intermediate	Intermediate	All	A few days	See Chapter 35

Table 24.1 Price gap strategy summary

Fig 24.1 The gap

Strategy aim

Gaps are a result of a sudden unexpected news item forcing significant volume change. Something important is happening. We want to buy or sell to take advantage of this move. In technical analysis terms, gaps tend to be closed, except when they are not! Useful, eh? What this means is that we can enter a strategy based on the fact that if we can determine beforehand a gap is going to be closed, then we place a trade; if we can determine it is not, then we can place a trade in the opposite direction.

Products suitable for

Futures

Options

Stocks

Entry and exit points

Entry

The market opening is far more important than the close. As Grant Noble states in *The Traders Edge*: "Virtually every floor trader that is not sick or on vacation seems to be there on the opening. That's not the case during other trading hours. Even the close often finds many floor traders on the sideline or already home."

The set-up for trading an opening gap is a very bearish announcement after market close the day before. This could be an analyst's report or an earning report if you trade stocks, for futures traders in indices it could be inflation reports.

Now wait for the market to gap open lower than the previous day's close. It is the fear of the gap from the previous close that leads many futures traders (myself included) to close out positions during the day and not hold them overnight. That does not apply to stocks, of course. They gap open less frequently, and I may sell before a major announcement if I am a "weak long," i.e. someone only just holding on.

Now for the entry signal: Look to buy one tick above the previous day's close. See Fig 24.2 for an illustration. What we are looking for here is that after the bearish announcement most of the public will have placed their sell orders with their brokers ready for the market open. The market, therefore, gaps lower. But then there should only really be buyers left, so it should

Fig 24.2 Look for the entry signal

move up. Floor traders not being stupid, contrary to popular rumor, wait for this and then buy, which is what we want to do.

If, however, the security continues falling then we are protected anyway because our buy order is not triggered. The danger we have is if the price rises to trigger our buy order, then falls. To protect against this we have a stop-loss in place in accordance with our money management rules.

---

chat box 24.2

A trader on Silicon Investor on 30.6.1999

I once tried to sell a big DELL position thinking it was 3:01pm. I had lost an hour somewhere and it was really 4:01pm. I never had a position that big overnight before. Sure enough, the next morning DELL was set to open three points below my entry. I sold into it, just happy to be relieved of the pain. The stocks went straight up from there all day, well past my original entry point.

I won't forget the pain in my stomach watching the spread drop that morning before open. I forgot all my rational knowledge of the numbers and market sentiment and acted on instinct. Wrong.

Understanding that mentality is one reason buying into morning gaps sometimes makes for complete no-brainer winners. Some gap downs are very low risk when you have confidence and understand your market: the prior moves and swings on the stock (the TA numbers), overall sentiment and reading between the lines of the news for the decline.

Inexperienced traders are better off avoiding these types of entries but many of us who have been around for a while have seen the same crap over and over again. Many morning games are redundant. Market makers and insiders are not particularly original in their strategies. In other words, they'll tell the same lies as often as they can get away with them.

Exit

Place a protective stop-loss in accordance with your money management rules, alternatively at the low for the day. There is no exit rule directly associated with the strategy, so you can use your own, such as exiting on a stochastic indicator sell signal (see Fig 24.3).

Optimization

Because this is a very short-term trade it tends to work best in leveraged markets like futures markets. However, for stocks you could use it to enter a stock you had been eyeing up anyway. Alternatively, if you were already long a stock and hit with this negative news, you can use this strategy to make sure you do not exit at the open (i.e. potentially worst price) but, instead, wait for a price improvement.

Where the strategy failed

My usual warning, watch out for whipsaws (see Fig 24.4).

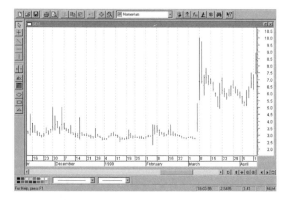

Fig 24.3 Gap strategy in operation

Fig 24.4 Watch out for whipsaws

Some good web-sites

Ideally you want sites which clearly tell you analyst's recommendation, changes and earnings announcements as well as news items. Try these.

MarketGuide ***

www.marketguide.com

Very easy to get the information you need to trade this strategy. News flow up to date.

Screen 24.1

CBS MarketWatch ✳✳✳

`www.marketwatch.com`

Another excellent US site. Sometimes the text can be a little small, but other than that, lots of company news and info.

E✳Trade UK ✳✳✳

`www.etrade.co.uk`

A good selection of news and economic as well as company news straight from AFX. Plus charting allows you to plot the charts, too.

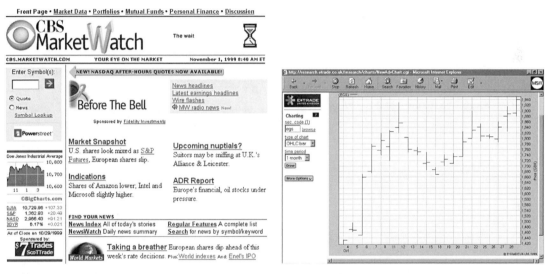

Screen 24.2   **Screen 24.3**

Summary

For stock traders, this strategy is probably going to help in reducing the likelihood of exiting at the day's worst price after some bearish news. For futures traders, it can be a useful entry mechanism for the start of the day.

25

Volatility strategies: If it moves, jump on it ▶▶

Strategic risk level: high

In this chapter

Buy low and sell high is the trite cry of traders. For the price to get from one level to the other we rely on volatility. Here we are trying to predict volatility increases, and, therefore, price changes.

Strategy that is effective

Table 25.1 summarizes volatility strategies.

Minimum experience level	Risk level	Product types	Typical time scale	Key web-sites
Intermediate	Intermediate	All	A few days	www.tradehard.com

Table 25.1 Volatility strategy summary

Strategy aim

Get into a security just before a volatility rise which should see the price change. We do not know the direction of the move, only that one is imminent, and so must take care to ensure we see the direction first, otherwise we may end up on the wrong side of a move.

Products suitable for

Futures

Options

Stocks

Options

Since we are unsure of price move, we could go for a put and call; either as part of a guts, strangle or straddle strategy. (See Appendix 2 if unsure what these exotic terms mean.) But we must be careful, since any price move is likely to offset the additional commission costs.

Entry and exit points

Entry

Look for short-term volatility reading as being quite low. Look for a longer term volatility to be quite high. On the basis that the short-term volatility has to increase to revert back to its longer term trend, buy as the price makes a break out of current trend (see Fig 25.1).

Exit

Exit based on money management rules, a trailing stop or another indicator, e.g. MACD indicating a sell.

Optimization

Wait for a decided price move in one direction or the other to avoid false moves. You can also combine with other indicators.

Where the strategy failed

Slight degree of risk here in that volatility alone requires a bit of bravado, I feel, and can remain in a low volatility state for prolonged periods (see Fig 25.2).

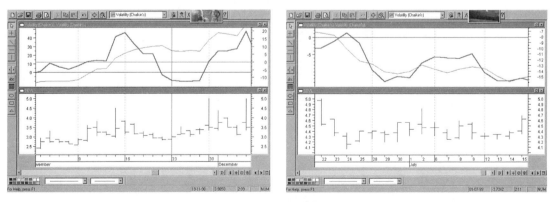

Fig 25.1 Entry   **Fig 25.2** Exit

Some good web-sites

To plot volatility indicators usually requires specialist technical analyis software as mentioned in Chapter 9. But a great site for listing securities that may be ripe for a volatility explosion is Tradehard.com.

Summary

Volatility trading requires a degree of experience and skill and is not for the novice. You would only be holding positions for a few days at a time, and you need to monitor the position carefully each day. So do make sure you paper trade beforehand.

Electronic day trading strategies

26

Electronic day trading: Warnings, cautions, and pitfalls

Online trader problem

- What issues should I be aware of about electronic day trading?

There has been a frenzy about electronic day trading. Well, I am going to tell it as it is. I am not trying to sell any product or service, so you are going to get the objective truth. Also, I want to make this clear above all else: You cannot start electronic day trading after reading one book, or even two books. It is a very difficult activity, as you are about to discover. But, before we go into what it is and strategies relating to it, let us go through some strategies.

Just facts, please

Day trading results in high commissions

As you will see in the next chapter, day traders try to profit from small price moves. To make that a worthwhile profit they need a combination of two things: First, they need a lot of capital to plough into the trade so that multiplied by the small price it results in an acceptable profit; second, they need to trade a lot, so those small profits become something respectable. Trading often incurs commissions, and lots of it.

Not through online brokers

Online brokers are not set up for day trading, you have to use the types of firms mentioned later in this chapter. Using online brokers and an ordinary internet connection will not give you the speed of execution you need. The New York State Attorney General once had to launch an investigation into online brokers because some day traders lost money by trying to day trade through ordinary online brokers.

Any specialist day trading firm should be checked by you to ensure it can handle day trading, and is reputable.

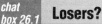

Losers?

From a trader on Investorville on 26.2.1999

Consider this: what percent of people who play blackjack lose money? If they only play one hand, 52 percent. If they play for an hour, maybe 70 percent. If they play for a day, maybe 85 percent. The only ways to win at blackjack in the long run are to count cards or to cheat. The question is, is there a card-counting or cheating analog in day trading? If there is, it's not widely known, because if it were then it would no longer work.

And winners

From a trader on Investorville on 4.4.1999

What's all the fuss over day traders about?

Seems to me the people who claim we lose more than we make are the people who never come close to making what we do. Altho' I confess it wasn't all made on day trades alone, sometimes we held on for as long as a week, nevertheless we were able to pay off the $128 000 we owed on the house. In Jan, we cleared $270 000 on CMGI alone, in one day. OK, that doesn't happen every day. But we sure make enuff, and we're way ahead in the game. And OK maybe it is gambling? So what?

Very few do it, despite the noise

According to the Electronic Traders Association there are only 4–5000 electronic day traders, i.e. professional day traders trading 30–40 times a day. That compares to nearly 8 million online traders trading between twice a day and twice a month.

For what it's worth

From a trader on Silicon Investor on 23.6.1999

1 Keep reading everything you can get your hands on, and then re-read it including various threads on SI.

2 Subscribe to *Stocks and Commodities* magazine. Lots of good info and education in it.

3 Go to the Pristine Daytrader site, www.pristine.com, and read the free education, print it out and re-read if you want to. Give some consideration to signing up for the Pristine Lite newsletter daily picks. Twenty bucks a month, and worth every penny. Good picks and they try and teach you as they go.

4 PAPER TRADE for at least three, maybe six months and do it seriously so that it will be a learning experience.

5   Position trade (swing trade, short-term trade) for at least six months before you start trying to day trade. If you don't understand position trading, there is a good chance that you will get killed trying to day trade. When I'm talking about day trading, I'm talking about getting in and out in a few minutes and being happy with 1/4 or 1/2 point, not buying in the morning and selling in the afternoon and trying to pick up a couple of points. Everyone seems to have different explanations of what day trading is.

6   Learn everything you can about TA (technical analysis), if you are going to do short-term trading, you have *got* to understand charts and indicators or you're dead meat.

Most lose money

The North American Securities Association concluded a seven-month study in 1999 and condemned day trading firms for conducting "get rich quick" marketing. If they tell you it is easy, and you can make a fortune and you can work your own hours, and you believe them, then you need to transfer your funds to a more saner member of your family. Beware day trading firm advertisements!

The study found that the largest loss on a single trade was $81 522, and the high number of trades involved meant on average you needed to produce a 56 percent return just to break even. The same study found that 70 percent of day traders lose money.

expert advice ✓ **Arthur Levitt, Chairman SEC, on 4.6.1999**

On the other end of the spectrum are so-called "day traders," whose time horizon for moving in and out of stock positions is measured by minutes, if not seconds. Some argue that day trading is really nothing more than speculation. And speculation is not new to our markets. Personally, I don't think day traders are speculating because traditional speculating requires some market knowledge. They are instead gambling, which doesn't. Historically, short-term trading has been an activity filled by a relatively small number of professional traders.

I am concerned that more and more people may be undertaking day trading strategies without full appreciation of the risks involved. No one should have any illusions of what he is getting involved in. I know of one state that recently found that 67 out of 68 day traders at a firm lost money.

Mental fatigue

Day trading requires concentration and focus, sometimes for hours on end, rather like an air traffic controller. So, unless you have been an air traffic controller, be aware of this difficulty. It is an activity similar to forex trading at an institution. Forex traders and air traffic controllers have a early burn-out age.

Those who may have started reading this chapter thinking that the majority of day traders make lots of money for doing very little will now have a clearer picture of the truth. We now move on to examine in detail the mechanics of electronic day trading, including exactly what it is.

---

chat box 26.4

The trials and tribulations of a new trader

A trader on Silicon Investor on 23.6.1999

My current situation is spent learning two endeavors;

1 How to day trade.

2 How to position trade.

I started this process last August by reading many of the popular day trading books. I have aggressively studied Elder's book, even working through the study guide questions.

Given my full-time job (software engineer) and that I live in Phoenix, I have used MB Trading (Jan–Feb) and now Polar Trading (May–June) to try to day trade the first 1 1/2 hours of the opening before I go into work.

Other than my disastrous overnight trade of NITE (from 48 to 33), I have been focussing on scalping. My day trade plan is to scalp trade to cover costs. I have been taking advantage of the $5.00 commissions. I have not been profitable, but I have learned quite a bit.

My primary goal is to learn day trading without losing huge amounts of cash. I am well capitalized, so I know I can do significant damage. I seem to have a different challenge than many traders. I have the captital, but I don't have 12 hours day to learn "how to trade."

My position trading plan is currently applying the BTTT (SI–Befriend The Trend) techniques (thanks, Thomas!). I am trying to force myself into entering a new position every other day.

I use the word force as I believe this is the crux of my current problems. Being an engineer, I could always be certain of the outcomes of any situation I might encounter. However, with trading, I cannot be certain of the outcome of any action I take. And this has been a real problem for me.

I have read the recent bios of many of the contributors to this thread and have noticed a pattern that most of the successful traders have been working hard at this for several years. My challenge is to accelerate this learning curve to minimize the time and that initial drawdown.

My biggest question is "How do I get the experience and wisdom that Trader Alan, Palo Alto Trader, and Eric P. have acquired (after many years of effort) in a much shorter time frame?

I am not expecting to find an answer to this question, but I am looking for techniques to condition my thinking, and apply what I learn. I can read this information, mostly understand the content, but I don't have ability to quickly condition myself to evaluate trading situations using this information (in real time).

So, I want to position trade, but I don't have the confidence to make more that two trades a week. So, I try scalping (CSCO only) with a day trade broker in order to make more trading decisions and build up my confidence. I find myself staring at numbers all morning having no idea how to succeed. I enter trades and enforce my discipline by taking 1/8 point loss. By the time I get out, its 1/4 loss or more on 100 shares. Two or three trades and I'm down $100 . . . every day.

After a few days of taking hits, I spend my days just watching the numbers. Then I realize that I am spending 2+ hours a day just watching charts and MM activity and not studying all the other valuable sources of information available. I also realize that I haven't successfully transformed myself into a morning person who thinks crystal clear at 6:30 am.

I am currently trying to condition myself to get out of a trade properly (position trading). I have been agonizing over the issue of giving a trade enough room, and not taking a loss (the break-even stop). Last week, I traded TCAT at 54 7/16. It went in my favor up to 56 and then traded as low as 51 1/2. I managed to get out at 53. My initial stop was 51. I agonized over a winning trade turning into a loss, but the trade was still above my initial stop-loss. I got out with a loss and sold a winning position to get out even. Taking the loss isn't so much my biggest concern, but rather the agonizing over what to do. I am seeking ways to condition myself to doing the right thing quickly and confidently.

27

Day trading: The Level II screen and acronyms

Online trader problems

- What is all this online trading talk about?
- Exactly how are they (supposedly) making money then?

The aim of this chapter is to give an overview to the curious about what electronic day traders actually *do*. Those whose interests are aroused and want to take things further should visit the web-sites I refer to later and the reading in Appendix 5.

What is going on here, then?

First, electronic day traders are, well, day traders. They close, or at least are supposed to close, their positions the same day and do not hold them overnight. So, it requires you to give up your day job and get in front of the computer for a start. Got that? No two ways about it. If you are still interested, read on. Since this section is an introduction to the whole phenomenon of day trading, I am not going to pad out the chapters with historical background.

Understanding prices is very important to understanding what electronic day traders do. Stocks are quoted in the format of bid ask, or bid offer. The bid is the price a member of the public would receive on selling the stock, and the offer is the price they would have to pay. The bid is less than the offer, and this is the spread. The person selling to you at the offer, and buying from you at the bid, is pocketing the spread.

I am going to define electronic day traders as separate and distinct from online traders. Online traders use the internet to place trades through an online broker such E*Trade that then executes the trade. They buy at the offer price, and sell at the bid. Most intend to hold the stock for at least a few days. The electronic day trader makes money from selling to the public at offer and buying at the bid, although they may also ride and profit (or lose) from any price movement in the stock.

ECNs, SOES, and other acronyms

Electronic day trading is about having direct electronic access to order books so you can buy or sell directly with the other party without using a broker, thereby allowing you speed. There are four ways to get electronic direct access: SuperDot (for NYSE), Small Order Entry System (SOES) and SelectNet (for NASDAQ) and ECNs. ECNs (electronic communication networks) make bid and offer prices on the stock. On listed exchanges (NYSE, ASE), the specialists make bids and offers, too, and on NASDAQ, the market makers do so. SuperDot and SelectNet are electronic order routing systems, i.e., they route orders to get them executed.

Listed exchanges are in a centralized location such as New York; NASDAQ is an electronic screen-based exchange not located in a single location and is called a negotiated market.

jargon			
	SuperDot	NYSE	Market makers and ECNs
	SelectNet and SOES	NASDAQ	Specialists and ECNs

The market makers may be institutions like Merrill Lynch and Goldman Sachs. An important thing to remember is that their best and brightest will be posting the bids and offers, i.e. Ivy league or Oxbridge boys and girls who have gone through one million interviews and an army assault course to get the job. Remember this, it is important a little later on. These institutions are good at what they do, we know this because what they are supposed to do is make money, and they do.

ECNs (like Island, Tradebook, Instinet, Archipelago, SelectNet and others) are trading networks through which a few brokers provide access to the public. They let you act as a market maker and pocket the spread. So far, so painless, eh? Okay, let us move on to the next piece of the puzzle – price.

Whichever way you trade, you must find out the latest rules and methods of operation from the exchange (through its web-site), or the broker providing the software for the system used. For example, the five-minute restriction on all further orders in the same security by the same customer, means you can't buy more IBM on SOES within five minutes of buying it the first time around.

SOES

You can only enter orders up to a maximum of 200, 500 or 1000 in size depending on the stock. This is the TIER size. The hard part of day trading is knowing if the market maker is a net buyer or seller or just displaying his TIER size.

chat box 27.1	**NASDAQ vs. NYSE**

From a trader on Silicon Investor on 5.6.1999

Daytrading NYSE versus NASDAQ stocks

Nasdaq advantages:

1 Fast executions on ISLD

2 Ability to see Level II data for depth of market

3 Ability to trade after hours using ECNs

Nasdaq disadvantages:

1 SOES useless in stocks that are moving

2 SNET useless in stocks that are moving

3 ISLD trading can result in partial fills (seven shares, etc.)

4 Market makers only showing firm quotes for 100 shares

5 17-second delay given to MMs before they must update quote

6 Even if alone at the inside bid/ask and multiple executions take place at your price, you won't necessarily get filled, as payment for order flow brokers simply fill their orders by matching your price

NYSE advantages:

1 The NYSE exchange specialist is forbidden from executing an order for himself in preference to filling an existing limit order on his book (i.e. from a customer)

2 Your limit order has equal standing with all other limit orders on the NYSE book. No bypassing your order on NYSE, orders filled based on order entry time

3 You will never get filled with seven shares out of a 1000-share order!

4 The stocks move slower, and may be more easy to predict direction

5 The posted quotes are "real," and therefore give you a realistic hope that they can be executed against (i.e. no 17-second phantom MM)

NYSE disadvantages:

1 Order executions can be much slower due to the trade being filled manually by the specialist using the SuperDOT system, typically 10–60 seconds (sometimes longer)

2 The specialist does not have to show the full size of the bid/ask on the book

3 Payment for order flow firms can bypass your limit order on the NYSE book by executing their customer trades for themselves on regional exchanges

4 Lower volatility means less movement and thus less profit potential for "perfect" traders

5 No ECNs mean larger spreads

ECNs

Each ECN allows different functionality. For example, on Archipelago (arca) you cannot use SOES. On Island (ISLD) you can only place limit orders, not market orders.

Prices – the key to the universe

Stocks are all about price, all the more so if you intend to buy and sell them within the day. For that period, what do you care if they sell cement or seaweed? As noted already price is quoted as the bid ask. The quote is shown on a Level I screen, i.e. any disply showing the best bid and ask price.

Each company or ECN posts its bids and asks. The one bid you see on the Level I screen is the highest bid out of all the bids (i.e. the highest price someone is willing to pay you for your stock). Similarly the offer you see is the lowest offer (i.e. the lowest price someone is willing to sell to you at).

In a Level II screen, also called a market-maker screen (provided by software vendors – who we shall list later), you can see all the bids and all the asks. The style of the window is similar to that in Table 27.1, i.e. the bids are on the left in descending order, and the offers are on the right in ascending order.

MSFT	82 5/8	+3/8	1000		
Open	81 7/8	High	83 1/4	Low	82 1/8
Tick	Down	Volume	953 500	Time	14.13
GSCO	82 5/8	10	MSCO	82 3/4	10
ISLD	82 5/8	20	INCA	82 3/4	23
MASH	82 5/8	10	HMQT	82 7/8	10
BTAB	82 1/2	10	MLCO	82 7/8	10
MLCO	82 1/2	10	BTAB	82 7/8	10
RSSF	82 1/2	10	RSSF	83	10
MSCO	82 3/8	10	MSCO	83	10
HMQT	82 3/8	10	GSCO	83	10

Table 27.1 Example of a Level II screen

Screens such as the one shown in Table 27.1 are color coded by each of the same value bids and each of the same value offers, so that it is easier to grasp what is happening. Each bid and offer has the acronym of a market maker or ECN, and the size in hundreds. For instance, someone on the Island (ISLD) ECN is bidding for 2000 shares of Microsoft at 82 5/8.

If someone then bought 1000 shares of Microsoft from MSCO at 82 3/4 and 2300 shares through INCA also at 82 3/4 then the screen may look like Table 27.2.

Note that the offer price has risen due to buying, i.e. the public is willing to pay a higher price at which the ECNs and market makers were willing to sell. They would not sell at a lower price, and the public was willing to pay the higher price, and so the stock price rose.

MSFT	82 7/8	+5/8	1000		
Open	81 7/8	High	83 1/4	Low	82 1/8
Tick	Down	Volume	953 500	Time	14.13
GSCO	82 5/8	10	HMQT	82 7/8	10
ISLD	82 5/8	20	MLCO	82 7/8	10
MASH	82 5/8	10	BTAB	82 7/8	10
BTAB	82 1/2	10	RSSF	83	10
MLCO	82 1/2	10	MSCO	83	10
RSSF	82 1/2	10	GSCO	83	10
MSCO	82 3/8	10	ISLD	83 1/8	10
HMQT	82 3/8	10	RSSF	83 1/8	10

Table 27.2 The same screen minutes later

By the way:

- Island   = ISLD
- Instinet   = INCA
- Terranova Trading   = TNTO
- Bloomberg TradeBook   = BTRD
- All Tech Investment Group   = ATTN
- Spear Leeds and Kellogg   = REDI

We have seen now some of the key jargon terms and acronyms. Now it is time to move to some market action.

Fill me

From a trader on Silicon Investor on 5.6.1999

Any successful momentum trader will tell you that one key to success is the ability to get your orders filled. Virtually anyone can be a successful momentum paper trader. Why? Paper trading is easy. Very easy. Anyone should be able to successfully paper trade after several months of effort. The difficulty is in converting paper success into real success, with real dollars. The sole obstacle to this transition is getting your orders filled.

What is the best way to get your orders filled to buy a momentum stock on the move? I wish I knew. I am aware of a number of options, and will try to discuss my opinions of the strengths/weaknesses of each.

Some people find excellent success by using discount brokers (i.e. those that receive payment for order flow from a market maker). Oftentimes, these brokers can get your order filled instantly, at the inside bid or ask. Sometimes even receiving price improvement on their orders. This is possible, since market makers deal with thousands and thousands of orders per day from the discount brokers. These orders are, on balance, very profitable to the market maker. Therefore, the market maker is willing to lose money on those occasional orders placed by "smart" traders in order to profit from the ongoing order flow from the "dummies." In addition to excellent fills, discount brokers can also offer cheap commissions. What a combination!

Unfortunately, discount brokers also have some weaknesses. In a very active stock, the market maker can turn off their auto-execution system and have all of their orders executed manually. In this case, your order could be filled very slowly, while you are left hanging for a fill report. Also, the discount broker may not offer access to Level II data, and may not have an order entry set-up that is conducive to quick order placement. However, all things considered, using a discount broker for day trading can be very intriguing.

ECNs are the solution many traders employ to execute their trades. Screw the market makers! Who needs them! Well, actually, it can be very difficult for a momentum trader to use ECNs for their order execution. Island orders are filled from the book on a first come first served basis. The challenge is to identify the trade opportunity extremely quickly, and be the first trader to get your order to the ISLD for the fill. Otherwise, you will have to attempt a fill several levels above the ask to get filled, once the stock turns up. Conversely, you might sell your long position several levels below the bid price, once the stock turns. Repeatedly giving up one or more levels on entry and exit is a short path to suicide, in my opinion. Therefore, the key is to be fast, very fast. You must hit the ISLD ask at the moment the stock is turning, and before ISLD leaves the inside ask. This can be very difficult, but it is possible.

Other traders use "smart" order routing systems to fill orders in momentum stocks. Most real tick III firms have access to ARCA order routing, and Cyber Trader uses a similar technology. I have never used either of these systems, but I am skeptical that they could be used indiscriminately to enter momentum stocks. Both order routing systems, I believe, rely on SelectNet order routing to send the order to the "best" market makers that are "most likely" to fill your order. The problem is that all of the market makers are sworn to screw you, and you will only get a fill from them when it is to their advantage (slight sarcasm acknowledged).

I guess the final options for the momentum trader is to attempt order executions using SOES, SelectNet, or by posting an ISLD order. Unfortunately, these methods are all very hazardous to the momentum trader. Although using the SOES or SelectNet systems used to be a quick road to success, rule changes have made using these systems equivalent to simply asking for market maker pity to fill your order. It won't happen, unless the stock is about to reverse. Of course, you can always post an ISLD order to buy at the bid. However, when a momentum stock moves up, how often do you see trades occur at the bid? Virtually never, until the stock reverses, then you're stuck in a losing position.

Once I thought I had the perfect solution to getting all of my orders filled quickly at the inside bid or ask. Unfortunately, I woke up and the dream was shattered.

I don't know the "best" way to fill an order. There are strengths and weaknesses to each method. A successful trader needs to know which methods work best for him. I have probably missed several other methods for filling orders in momentum stocks. For completeness, feel free to add other methods to get orders filled, along with their strengths/weaknesses.

28

Electronic day trading strategies in summary

Online trader problem

■ What are some of the main strategies used by day traders?

In this chapter I am now going to give you a run down of the tactics used by electronic day traders to make money. The thing that you should notice is the complexity and shrewdness of the strategies, the quickness of mind needed to essentially outwit a competitor. If it is something you can do, you should be proud of yourself. But there are easier ways to make money in the markets. A longer term, but still short-term trader may make as much, if not more money, with a fraction of the time and energy expended. Who would be the shrewd one then?

Terminology: Do you speak the lingo?

Bid into
The bid is the price the general public sells the stock to the market maker. To bid into is to buy a stock.

Dealer flip
This is when a dealer flips from the bid to the offer, or vice versa.

Down off
A bearish signal when a market maker was the high bid (i.e. willing to buy at a price) and then no longer is.

Down to ask
Another bearish sign when a market lowers his offer (i.e. the price he is willing to accept for a stock) in hopes of shifting more stock by selling at a lower price.

Fill

When an order is executed, as in "filled at 106."

He drops

When a market maker "drops" his bid from being the best bid to a lower level.

He lifts

This term is used to indicate when a market trader adjusts his offer so it is no longer the lowest offer.

He stays

This term is used when a market maker sells or buys some stock, but remains willing to buy or sell some more at the same price.

Hit the bid

This is when a trader sells stock at the current bid price.

Lift offer

A bullish sign when a market maker moves his offer price up, i.e. is willing to sell only at a higher price.

Low offer

A bearish sign when a market maker lowers the price at which he is willing to sell the stock, so that his is the lowest price in the market at which you can buy the stock.

Offer out

When you "offer out" you are acting as market maker by selling to the public at the offer price.

On the o

This is when you offer your stock at a price higher than the current offer.

Off the offer

The bullish sign where a market maker who was the lowest offer raises his offer, because he is willing to sell at a higher price only.

Track the big boys

Most Level II screens will tell you the number of times a particular market maker has been the best bid and the best offer, i.e. "made the inside bid or ask." So, for example, if Salomons were the best bidder of a stock 120 times, but a seller of the stock 43 times on the inside offer, then we can see that Salomons was a net overall buyer of the stock. That is a bullish indicator, and we can see how the other institutions stand, and place our own position accordingly.

If you follow one stock closely then you should get a very good appreciation of the order flow for that stock and undertake this strategy. The strategy is optimized by also viewing real-time intra-day technical analysis indicators to ensure they are bullish (see Chapter 11).

Other things to look for

- Similarly, if the biggest market makers are all on the offer side then you may not want to sell a stock. If big market makers switch from offer to bid, that may be a signal to buy.

- If a market maker gets his order on the bid filled, but just puts yet another order in on the bid at the same price, then this signals he has more buying to do. This is bullish.

- If the market maker pays the retail price for the stock, then this means he is even willing to buy the stock at the offer price and that is very bullish. Beward, however, since sometimes a market maker will pretend to buy when he actually has a lot to sell, so as to lure in a lot of naive ECNs to take the stock he wants to sell.

Level II rotation strategy

Imagine a day trader sees the Level II screen in Table 28.1.

Now imagine it changes to look like Table 28.2.

The Level I quote is the same (82 5/8 bid and 82 3/4 offered), 2300 shares of MSFT were bought at 82 3/4. A buying opportunity is created when the best-bid tier expands and the best-offer tier contracts. And, similarly, a selling opportunity exists if the best-offer tier expands and the best-bid tier contracts.

In this situation, day traders will buy MSFT at 82 3/4 because there is only one market maker, hoping Morgan Stanley will stop selling at 82 3/4 and raise the offer to a higher price. This act of buying by the day trader is what is meant by "SOESing in." The hope of the SOES bandit is that the momentum continues and the trader can then sell the stock he bought at a higher price (see Table 28.3).

As you can see from Table 28.3, MSCO has raised its offer to 83. Now the day trader can use the ECNs to sell his 1000 shares at 82 7/8 that he bought at 82 3/4. If he uses ISLD and does indeed sell at 82 7/8, he will make $1/8 on his 1000 shares, or $125, less commissions. If the proverbial hits the fan and the momentum slows and the trader could not get out, then he could just sell at the best bid of 32 3/4.

MSFT	82 5/8	+3/8	1000		
Open	81 7/8	High	83 1/4	Low	82 1/8
Tick	Down	Volume	953 500	Time	14.13
GSCO	82 5/8	10	MSCO	82 3/4	10
ISLD	82 5/8	20	INCA	82 3/4	23
MASH	82 5/8	10	HMQT	82 7/8	10
BTAB	82 1/2	10	MLCO	82 7/8	10
MLCO	82 1/2	10	BTAB	82 7/8	10
RSSF	82 1/2	10	RSSF	83	10
MSCO	82 3/8	10	MSCO	83	10
HMQT	82 3/8	10	GSCO	83	10

Table 28.1 Example of a Level II screen

MSFT	82 5/8	+3/8	1000		
Open	81 7/8	High	83 1/4	Low	82 1/8
Tick	Down	Volume	954 500	Time	14.18
GSCO	82 5/8	10	MSCO	82 3/4	10
ISLD	82 5/8	20	INCA	82 7/8	10
MASH	82 5/8	10	HMQT	82 7/8	10
BTAB	82 5/8	10	MLCO	82 7/8	10
MLCO	82 5/8	10	BTAB	82 7/8	10
RSSF	82 5/8	10	RSSF	83	10
MSCO	82 3/8	10	MSCO	83	10
HMQT	82 3/8	10	GSCO	83	10

Table 28.2 The same screen moments later

MSFT	82 5/8	+3/8	1000		
Open	81 7/8	High	83 1/4	Low	82 1/8
Tick	Down	Volume	955 500	Time	14.20
GSCO	82 3/4	10	ISLD	82 7/8	10
ISLD	82 3/4	20	GSCO	82 7/8	10
MASH	82 5/8	10	HMQT	82 7/8	10
BTAB	82 5/8	10	MSCO	83	10
MLCO	82 5/8	10	BTAB	83	10
RSSF	82 5/8	10	RSSF	83	10
MSCO	82 1/2	10	MSCO	83	10
HMQT	82 1/2	10	GSCO	83	10

Table 28.3 The same screen a little later again

If you are planning to do what is essentially "scalping" a small gain many times a day to make a profit, you need to be warned of the following:

- What is the trend? Clearly you want to be trying to make profits on the long side of an upwardly trending market. So, on uptrends, you may wait for a dip and buy that.

- Day time? If you are trying to scalp the market then remember it is the most liquid and active and therefore better for scalping in the middle of the day, when tired (and lazy) traders take a break.

- Getting in and out. You must make sure you exit a scalp before the momentum dries up. That being so, it should not be difficult to sell your stock on upward momentum, because there should be lots of buyers.

- Do not forget technical analysis. Good Level II screens should also plot intra-day price charts with technical analysis so you can use this as an additional dimension in determining what direction to trade. Technical analysis is also very important to determine stock support and resistance levels.

Spread strategy

As you saw from the last example our day trader only made 1/8 of a point, sometimes he makes as little as 1/64 of a point. The spread, i.e. difference between the best bid and best ask, is narrowest on the most liquid, i.e. popular stocks. For this reason, some day traders will focus on stocks with wider spreads. The downside with this is that the stock tends to be less liquid and it may take far longer to exit, and if things go wrong, then the trader may suffer a proportionately larger loss.

Market-maker strategy

This is a very simple strategy; it can be too simple in moving markets. You are basically acting a market maker, posting your offer and your bid and expecting to pocket the spread (see Table 28.4).

In Table 28.4 you would be looking to buy stock at 82 5/8 and sell it at 82 3/4. Sounds easy, but isn't necessarily so. Sometimes, you may end up buying stock only to find that you cannot sell it at a higher price. The sophisticated market-maker strategy maker is trying to buy on the dips in momentum.

MSFT	82 5/8	+3/8	1000		
Open	81 7/8	High	83 1/4	Low	82 1/8
Tick	Down	Volume	953 500	Time	14.13
GSCO	82 5/8	10	MSCO	82 3/4	10
ISLD	82 5/8	20	INCA	82 3/4	23
MASH	82 5/8	10	HMQT	82 7/8	10
BTAB	82 1/2	10	MLCO	82 7/8	10
MLCO	82 1/2	10	BTAB	82 7/8	10
RSSF	82 1/2	10	RSSF	83	10
MSCO	82 3/8	10	MSCO	83	10
HMQT	82 3/8	10	GSCO	83	10

Table 28.4 Level II screen for market-maker strategy

This is complicated

Using Level II to outwit day traders is complex, with its own set of internal pragmatic rules developed through experience. For instance, if in Table 28.4 GSCO bids up the stock, some questions that you need to ask are:

- When the bid changed, how did the other market makers react?
- Where did the other market makers move to and at what price levels?
- If the stock rises up, how does GSCO react?

It is all the many issues and complex, quick thinking and quick reactions needed that mean that day trading is a very particular skill. If you have the concentration of an air traffic controller, and the reactions of a gunslinger, then this may be for you.

That is why no book can teach you how to day trade. The aim of this one is to introduce you to some of the issues, so you can investigate them further through paper trading and further reading.

29

Day trading infrastructure

Online trader problems

- Right then, what hardware and software do I need to get started?
- Where do I get it from, and what kind of bills am I looking at?

In this chapter

This chapter is a brief overview of some of the hardware and software you should have if you want to go ahead and day trade. I have tried to give some indication of costs, but these can fluctuate, of course.

Access

As mentioned before, you should not use an ordinary online broker account, e.g. Waterhouse Securities, Ameritrade, Quick & Reilly, etc. for day trading, because they are not set up for direct access to order books, and whereas a one-second delay may not matter to someone placing two trades a day, it does matter to someone who day trades 30–40 times a day and is looking for profit from the smallest price moves.

You can either try to have everything set up at home, or day trade from the offices of a day trading firm which gives you access to all the set-up you need. The latter is, of course, preferable because of cost savings. You need to deal through specialist day trading firms who tend to be known only by other day traders. For a fee, these firms provide systems that are directly linked to accounts via dedicated phone lines, offering the speed you need which the internet can provide.

As with all accounts you need to know about commission charges, data provision costs, phone charges, what the software offers, e.g. real-time charting as well as Level II screens.

From a trader on Silicon Investor on 5.6.1999

Daytrading with "discount" broker versus direct access electronic brokers

For the sake of this post, I'll define discount brokers as firms that sell their order flow to market makers. This would include firms such as Fidelity, E*trade, Ameritrade, etc. Direct access firms, by contrast, provide direct access to SOES, SelectNet, and one or more ECNs to their traders and do not route any orders through a third party.

Advantages of direct access firms:

1   Typically provide Level II data to allow the trader to "see" the depth and size of the market in the stock

2   Enable extremely fast placement and routing of orders. SOES orders *can* be filled in less than three seconds, and ISLD orders *can* be filled in less than 0.5 seconds

Disadvantages of direct access firms:

1   All orders are placed in the "real world" and are subject to the whims of the marketplace. Fast order placement is useless if not accompanied by subsequent order executions. It can be very difficult to get your orders filled

Advantages of discount brokerage firms:

1   Many traders report better executions through discount brokers than they could have achieved on their own. Your market order or limit order is routed to a market maker. During normal times, the market makers computer is set for "auto-execution," meaning that your order will immediately be filled

2   Often you may be able to get an execution buying (selling) at the inside ask (bid) for 1000 or 2000 shares, even when the size of the inside ask (bid) is only 100 shares. In other words, increased liquidity may be possible

3   Sometimes, discount brokers will give you price improvement at prices in between the inside bid or ask

4   Discount brokers often offer cheaper commissions than day trading firms

Disadvantages of discount brokerage firms:

1   During volatile times, a stock can be taken off "auto-execution." When this happens, all orders in this stock are filled manually, subjecting the investor to much slower fills and the potential for surprisingly adverse fills when the stock is moving in the wrong direction. On the day after Thanksgiving 1998, many discount broker customers placed orders to sell shares of a popular stock at prices of 90–95 as the stock was dropping rapidly. Fifteen minutes later their fills came back at prices as low as 50!

2   Order cancellations may not come back in a timely manner for stocks that are not on "auto-execution"

Quote system

You need price data and software (electronic direct access platform). This will have to be state of the art and you will not be able to skimp on money, because Merrill Lynch do not try to save $10 going for a cheaper option and you are competing against them. To receive quotes over the internet is not enough, it is simply too slow. You must ensure quotes are received via dedicated telephone lines (T1). The cost of these (if you wanted everything at home) would be up to around $600 per month. If you trade from a day trading brokerage firm, this should have its data delivered through this method, or better.

Order execution

The software and quote vendor must provide you direct access to, say, NASDAQ. You do not want your order routed through a broker who then sends it to a third party to fill. Speed is of the essence. So ensure you are getting direct access, an EDAT (electronic direct access) platform will put you in direct contact with either the specialist (NYSE) via SuperDOT or the multiple ECNs and SOES system on NASDAQ.

Software design

Another consideration is to look at the screen of the software you will be using to see if it is well-designed and easy for you to understand and use. You are going to have to make very quick decisions and so want the screen to be readily comprehensible. You do not want your brain to be spending a millisecond longer than need be trying to comprehend the data. Well, you did want to day trade didn't you, and I said it wasn't easy.

Computers

If you are planning to day trade from home, as opposed to a day trading firm, then you need two computers. One as a back-up but on which you can place trades, research, plot graphs, etc. The other for live streaming quotes. CPU speed should be at least 400MHz and 128 RAM. A laptop with fully charged batteries and modem connection is also a good idea in case of power failure. No one said it was going to be cheap.

Customer service

Trading at the offices of a day trading firm means you will want to know how good their customer service is: can you get phone access to them when you are at home, can they give you account status details, can they answer technical difficulties?

Connectivity

From a trader on Silicon Investor on 5.6.1999

Broadband connectivity choices for day traders

1 **Cable modem** – provides a continuous, broadband (200Kbps–3Mbps) connection. The high-speed data signal is delivered on the same cable coax which delivers your cable TV signal, modulated as a high-frequency signal which carries the data stream. Since the same cable is connected to every house, this is a "shared media" technology. Therein lies the potential problem. When too many users are deployed on the same cable coax loop, the system can bog down, resulting in poor performance. You do not have a choice of ISP with cable modem – the ISP comes "bundled" with the high-speed connection, as a package deal. Therein lies another potential problem. For example, I recently tested Cable CoOp's 2Mbps cable modem service in Palo Alto, CA. Although it was great for snappy web access, it was unusable for real-time, Level II quotes and trading. The reason? Trace Route's revealed a 60 percent packet loss in the backbone ISP (Cable & Wireless) routers in San Francisco. This problem recurred repeatedly over a three-week period, so I dropped the service and went back to Frame Relay (the ISP behind the cable modem service was providing sub-standard service). But many traders report excellent results with cable modem hookups. It all depends on your provider, and how many other people are using the service in your area (the fewer, the better).

2 **DSL/ADSL/HDSL "digital subscriber loop"** – This is the phone companies' latest and greatest solution for providing low-cost broadband services to residential and cost-sensitive commercial customers. There are more technology variants than you can count. ADSL is a little more affordable than HDSL, providing "asymmetric" bandwidth (more downlink bandwidth than uplink), and can be very good for traders. Generally, DSL connections are dedicated in nature and not shared media. An ATM aggregator called a "DSLAM" (DSL ATM multiplexer) aggregates your traffic across a high-capacity digital backbone, carrying it across the service provider's network to the ISP. Again, you are usually locked into an ISP. But because DSL is run across a switched network by the service provider (usually the local phone company, or a "CLEC" – competitive local exchange carrier), there is often more choice of ISPs when you go with DSL. Many times, ISPs will partner with DSL providers (Rhythm, Northpoint, etc.) and offer special package deals. AOL is also big on DSL and is cutting a few deals. DSL is more reliable, and the prices are reasonable (generally, $89–$300/mo depending upon the bandwidth).

3 **Frame relay** – is a dedicated data connection, provided with bandwidth and "service level" guarantees. 56Kbps sounds slow, but because of the dedicated nature of frame relay, it actually performs much better than most dial-in 56K modems. The advantage is cost – a 56K frame line is available for $100–$125 in most parts of the country. I run a 128Kbps ("fractional T1") line, which is a bit pricey compared to DSL. However, frame relay service is industrial strength; there is generally a team of technicians assigned full time, dedicated to maintaining your connection/service, 24 hrs x 7 days. Frame relay is usually fixed price, regardless of usage. Another big advantage of frame relay is, you can buy a "PVC" (permanant virtual circuit – a dedicated virtual data "pipe" through the FR network) connection to just about

anywhere; so you can use any ISP you choose. Here in Silicon Valley, we have some excellent high-end, boutique ISPs like www.walltech.com (no affiliation; just my choice), where great service is always less than two rings away when you have to call them. A friendly, competent, high-performance ISP is a wonderful thing, in my experience!

4 **ISDN integrated digital subscriber line** – comes in both "nailed-up" (permanent) connection variety (preferable, usually called "centrex" or PBX ISDN), or dial-up (transient) connection services. I tried it for about six months (three times), and each time went back to frame relay. ISDN hasn't been a real big success, and configuring it can be a headache. The biggest thing to watch out for is usage-based billing – to be avoided unless you're sure about their billing rates, and your usage levels. You want to look for flat billing, regardless of usage. But many traders report good results using ISDN – in certain areas it's the best solution. Generally, it is being surpassed by DSL as the phone company's preferred offering though.

5 **Satellite** – some traders have experimented with high-speed internet connectivity provided by satellite dish, like Hughes "Direct PC." Generally, the problem is not bandwidth (which is very good); it's the latency which is a problem for traders. A geo-synchronous satellite orbits at 22 000 miles, so you're talking big delays to get the signal up there and back, nearly half a second depending upon your location relative to the satellite. And the ISP behind these networks was not designed to optimize service for trading quotes. Generally, to be avoided unless you're trying to trade out of an RV up in the Rockies . . .

6 **Wireless** – here in the Bay Area, I frequently use a battery-powered, thin 8-oz "ricochet wireless modem" to trade from my laptop, in remote locations (such as StarBucks). The service is only $30/month including the ISP, and data rates are ~40Kbps (shared media like cable modems, so mileage may vary depending on network usage conditions). Ricochet (www.metricom.com; no affiliation) works surprisingly well for delivering quotes, and I run RealTick III on top of it, along with Windows on Wall Street, both receiving real-time quotes, no problem. The service is widely deployed in the SF Bay Area, Seattle, large parts of Los Angeles, Washington DC, and there are nodes in many major airports. They are about to deploy a much higher speed service which will quadruple data rates. It's a trip!

Some software and quote providers

Software: The Watcher
- From: Datek www.datek.com
- Firm: Broadway Trading
- Account min: $75 000

Software: TradeCast Pro
- From: TradeCast Ltd www.tcast.com
- Firm: TradeCast Securities
- Account min: $2000

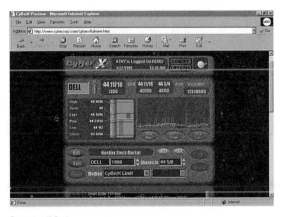

Software: CyberX

- From: CyberCorp www.cybercorp.com
- Firm: CyberBroker
- Account Min: $15 000

Screen 29.1

Software: Attain

- From: All-Tech Investment www.attain.com
- Firm: All-Tech Investment
- Account min: $25 000

Screen 29.2

Screen 29.3

Software: Real Tick III

■ From: Townsend Analytics
   `www.taltrade.com`

■ Firm: Various including MB Trading, AB Watley

■ Account min: $5000 (MB Trading); $20 000 (AB Watley)

30

Best-of-breed day trading sites

Online trader problem

■ I want to visit the top day trading sites to find out more.

In this chapter

I have provided a delectable assortment of day trading web-sites. I have chosen ones which are well-designed, have quality real-life experience information, and are, preferably, free.

Active Traders Network **

www.activetraders.net
Lots of educational material here that is up to date, which is important given the industry-wide changes occurring daily. The site also discusses in some detail day trading strategies, but take care to monitor before you try.

Dynamic daytrader *

www.dynamicdaytrader.com
Some educational stuff here, but you have to pay, however, you are paying to watch the trades of a day trader.

Elite Trader *

www.elitetrader.com
You may be able to glean some tips from the chat rooms and some of the educational materials loitering about the site – and that is why it may be worth visiting – some real down and dirty day trading talk.

IQC ✳✳✳

www.iqc.com

I have mentioned this site before. It has excellent real-time charting tools, so you can monitor the stocks you may be looking to trade real time, and see what the technical indicators look like for them. Remember technicals only really work for liquid stocks.

Momentum Trader

www.mtrader.com

There is some good educational material and a great chat room – but it is darned expensive. $150 a month when I looked. Free one-week trial available.

Trading Systems Network

www.tradingsystems.net

The free tools in here are useful, and the list of stocks that are moving can be useful for you to then look into. Design could do with some improvement.

Trading Tactics

www.tradingtactics.com

Lots of freebies here, chat site which is okay, Java charts, and then some not so useful stuff. It is worth looking at to see if the chat is on topics of interest.

Lots of sites for day traders, and check out the megasites and directories chapter (39) to search for more, as new ones are always springing up and old ones vanish into the internet ether.

E-brokers

31

Finding a good broker: What you need to ask

Online trader problems

- What are the things I should look for in a broker?
- How do I choose a broker suitable for me?
- Who are the best brokers?

In this chapter

What are all the issues we should be concerned about and aware of when choosing an online broker? In this chapter we look at some of the key and lesser known issues concerning broker selection, and also some sites that monitor brokers.

Benefits of an online broker

- **Cost.** Internet services tend to cost less than comparable off-line services with the lower costs being passed on, in part, to the consumer, in the form of lower commissions and margin rates and competitive rates of interest on credit balances.
- **Convenience.** You can enter an order at any time, night or day, and so suit your own timetable. Useful if like me you do your analysis late at night.
- **Quick confirmation.** Your trade is usually confirmed electronically, saving you the time to hang around on the phone, or call back busy brokers.
- **Total account keeping and monitoring.** Because everything is done electronically, most online brokers have a facility to permit users to access their accounts and positions on the net. This again is another minor convenience.

So who are the best?

There are sites that rank brokers according to different criteria. For instance on www.gomez.com, at the time of writing, the ranking for overall score were:

Firm

1. E*Trade
2. NDB
3. AB Watley
4. TD Waterhouse
5. Datek
6. Web Street
7. Charles Schwab
8. ScoTTrade
9. DLJdirect
10. Wang
11. Firstrade
12. Suretrade
13. Fidelity Investments
14. Trading Direct
15. Discover Brokerage
16. Ameritrade
17. My Discount Broker
18. AFTrader
19. Bidwell
20. Brown

Smart Money (www.smartmoney.com) produced the following (Table 31.1), just to prove no two broker watch sites are the same.

Rank	Firm	Toll-free no	Trading costs	Breadth of products	Mutual funds	Online trading	Extra services	Staying out of trouble	Responsive- ness	Web reliability
1	Muriel Siebert	800-872-0711	14	8	8	4	5	7	1	1
2	Waterhouse Securities	800-934-4410	11	1	3	3	1	14	14	12
3	Quick & Reilly	800-262-2688	16	5	11	2	3	7	19	14
4	Bidwell	800-547-6337	4	12	5	15	8	14	4	8
5	Charles Schwab	800-435-4000	21	3	16	1	4	7	15	6
6	National Discount Brokers	800-417-7423	3	5	6	8	13	19	5	5
7	Accutrade	800-882-4887	13	14	2	13	13	1	3	15
8	T. Rowe Price	800-225-5132	20	8	15	17	11	1	1	3
9	Ameritrade	800-454-9272	2	16	1	14	17	7	13	9
10	Jack White	800-233-3411	9	1	6	10	2	14	20	12
11	Vanguard	800-992-8327	15	13	14	18	9	1	10	7
12	DLJdirect	800-825-5723	6	10	4	8	12	1	15	17
13	Discover	800-584-6837	5	14	12	7	6	7	11	19
14	American Express	800-297-8800	17	3	19	6	19	1	7	9
15	USAA	800-531-8343	17	16	10	21	10	1	17	4
16	Fidelity	800-544-8888	19	5	9	11	7	7	9	18
17	E*Trade	800-387-2331	8	11	13	5	15	14	21	20
18	Brown & Co.	800-822-2021	1	18	20	20	18	14	11	1
19	Sottsdale	800-619-7283	6	19	20	15	16	7	6	16
20	Dreyfus	800-896-8284	12	20	18	19	20	21	17	11
21	Datek	888-463-2835	10	21	17	12	21	19	8	21

Table 31.1 Complete rankings

Broker comparison

Some sites offer a comparison of other brokers. Table 31.2 is from ScoTTrade.

Pssst . . . Security: How safe is the process?

The site

All the major online brokers assure their clients that they have unbreachable security in terms of someone placing rogue trades or transferring money out of their account. Security is usually assured through several procedures:

■ The broker will have audit trails of all trades and cancellations which are available for you to inspect.

	ScoTTrade®	E*Trade	Ameritrade	DLJ Direct	Schwab
Personal broker Branch offices nationwide NASDAQ	Yes 101	No 0	No 0	No 0	Yes 300
Market orders NYSE and AMEX	$7	$19.95	$8	$20.00 + $0.02/share over 1000	$29.95 up to 1000 or $0.03/share for orders over shares
Market orders NYSE, AMEX, and NASDAQ	$7	$14.95	$8	$20.00 + $0.02/share over 1000	$29.95 up to 1000 or $0.03/share for orders over 1000 shares
Limit orders	$12	$19.95	$13	$20.00 + $0.02/share over 1000	$29.95 up to 1000 or $0.03/share for orders over 1000 shares
Margin interest rate with $7500 debit balance	7.50%	9.25%	9.00%	8.50%	9.25%
Credit interest	4%	2.00%	2.50% over $1000 0 % under $1000	3.50%	4.70% $100 min. Money Mkt.
Real-time account updates	Yes	No	No	No	Yes

Table 31.2 ScoTTrade's broker comparison chart

- In addition to this, all firms listed in this book have some form of insurance protection (usually SIPC, Securities Investor Protection Corporation) ensuring client funds are either segregated or protected, should the firm have financial difficulties. However, as E*Trade points out in its small print "Protection does not cover the market risks associated with investing." Pity!

- Use of firewalls, these are like, well, walls of fire, that prevent access from the outside through links, etc.

- Use of account numbers, user names, and passwords.

The browser

If you are using Internet Explorer 4 or 5 or Netscape Navigator 4 or higher then you are using a secure browser. Data passing through your browser to and from your broker will be encrypted. You can tell you are in a secure site because:

1 The URL changes from http: to https:.

2 A pop-up window informs you that you are about to enter a secure site.

3 In Internet Explorer, a lock icon appears in the bottom left-hand corner.

4 In Netscape Navigator, an unbroken key icon appears in the bottom left-hand corner of the browser.

---

hot tip! **Things to do when placing an online order**

1 Double-check and read the order carefully.

2 If in doubt, check by phone.

3 Do be careful when clicking on the **submit order** button. Do not send a duplicate order.

You

The most important thing you can do to help yourself is guard your personal identification number, account number, and username. The PIN is the most important of these.

What to look for

At a glance

- Competitive commissions:
  - Check for what size trade the advertised "low" commission applies.
  - Any maintenance or handling charges (i.e. hidden costs)?
  - Commissions sometimes vary on the price of the stock, e.g. extra charges for a stock trading less than 50c.
- Account details:
  - Minimum initial deposit.
  - Minimum account balance.
  - Interest rates for idle funds.
  - Good brokers ought to automatically sweep excess funds to a high interest account.
  - Margin and checking accounts:
    1 A margin account will allow you to borrow – what are the rates?
    2 It will be convenient to be able to write checks.

3 Is there a cost for wiring funds from the account?

- Availability of account data online.
- How often is the account updated? Intra-daily may be important for the day trader.

■ Established on the net, not new – with potential teething problems.

■ Price quotes.

■ Methods of confirming orders (an online screen, and an e-mail at least).

■ Emergency back-up.

■ Types of orders accepted (see appendix on orders).

■ Portfolio monitoring:
- How often is your portfolio updated?
- Is a tax summary available?
- Is an automatic performance measure calculated?
- Is a transaction summary available?

■ News.

■ Research available:
- What is available, is it free, is it online, or posted?

■ Customer support:
- Phone, fax, e-mail is ideal.

Factors in choosing a broker

Of course, price is of primary concern. Online trading is popular partly because it offers discount commissions for investors who do not want to pay a full-fee broker for advice they could have discovered themselves on the internet, or for trades where they do not want advice. But even among online brokers, the commissions can vary greatly and comparison is near impossible with each calculating commissions on a different basis – some using the value of your trade, others the number of shares bought, and others the frequency with which you trade.

But there is more to online broker selection than price, if there wasn't then Schwab in the USA, which is one of the most expensive online brokers, would not have the largest market share. The most important factor in selecting an online broker is customer service, according to a recent study by JD Power and Associates. The same study, based only on US brokers and traders, found Schwab topped the list for offering greatest customer satisfaction.

Reliability

Reliability in service is an essential pre-requisite for any online trader. There is no point saving £20 in commission on buying a stock, only to find you can't sell it because your online broker has broken down. Such "downtime" by online brokers is becoming increasingly frequent in the USA, and only recently even the mighty Schwab had one full hour where trades could not be placed. In a survey by the TheStreet.Com, again a survey of US brokers by US clients, DLJ Direct came top in the category of reliability.

Execution

Poor execution, too, can override price as a concern for an online trader. The price at which your trade is "executed" should be as close as possible to the real-time price quote you see on the screen before you trade. Poor execution can often end up swamping any commission savings. In the TheStreet.Com survey just mentioned, Schwab came above DLJ Direct, which in turn narrowly beat E*Trade on the issue of execution prices.

Design

Site design is an important consideration for me. There is nothing worse when you are trying to find a quote, do some research, or quickly place a trade, than to find navigation around the site as difficult as up the Amazon (the river, not the site). I want my online broker easy and intuitive to use. There is only one way to see what suits you – and that is to visit the sites themselves. I am sorry to report I find the purely UK online brokers, unlike US brokers with UK sites, too often competing for the title of most off-putting site and most turned-away potential customers, that's when they are not racing to see who can be the most expensive. Did these site designers speak to a single online trader?

Free pickings

Online trading is about more than placing a trade through an online broker instead of phoning a traditional broker. Trading online profitably still requires research to arrive at stock picks, and the internet is an excellent resource to offer this. I always check to see what research the online brokers offer. Do they provide free portfolio monitoring, charting, news from major wires, research from renowned institutions, commentary, or are they just a web-site appended to a traditional brokerage?

Broker watch

In this section we take a run through sites which rate and rank brokers according to different criteria such as performance, speed, commissions, etc.

Gomez ***

www.gomez.com

An excellent site covering rankings of many different things, not just brokers. A clear and easy-to-navigate site that is up to date.

Internet Investing **

www.internetinvesting.com

Gives quite a detailed list of commission rates for all major online brokers, but has a semi-professional feel to it.

Keynote Web Brokerage Index *

www.keynote.com

Most useful for its rankings of speed of access. Design not too bad either.

Smart Money Broker Ratings ***

www.smartmoney.com

An excellent site (and an excellent magazine). I could spend hours on this one playing on the broker speedometer! Lots of rankings for different criteria. A lesson in how to present information.

Brokers

To help you gauge the sites, I have provided a rough-and-ready rating for the sites, based on general impressions of the services from inspecting their sites and the charges they inflict.

*key

*** Good value for money, appear on the ball and client oriented

** Worth investigating, good rates and fair information on the site

* A little expensive but potentially a good service provider

E*Trade UK ***

www.etrade.co.uk

The UK version of the US site is among the very best of all the sites open to UK investors. The charting section is especially good. Offers portfolios, message boards (which could be better organized, but are the one of the most active in the UK for stock chat), news, and research. Well-designed and organized. Did I mention the commissions are among the UK's cheapest?

E*Trade ***

www.etrade.com
E*Trade Securities
4 Embarcadero Pl
2400 Geng Road
Palo Alto, CA 94303
Tel: 1 800 786 2575

A site with a lot of features, some free before you register, others for account holders. The site is easy to navigate and the information is very easy to find. On the Gomez rankings they have been the Number 1 overall broker for some time. As brokers, they have a lot of awards and positive reviews making them a must-consider broker.

Message boards and financial services are also available from the site.

Datek ***

www.datek.com
Datek
50 Broad Street, 6th Floor
New York, NY 10004
Tel: 212 514 7531

Datek is not only cheap, but I do keep on hearing good things about it from chat boards, e-mails, and press comment. Either it has a very good CIA-like undercover publicity machine, or it is, in fact, very good. The site also has a reassuring number of positive press reviews. I always find that comforting when considering a site marketing itself on the basis of having a very low cost base.

Charles Schwab ***

www.eschwab.com
Charles Schwab
101 Montgomery Street
San Francisco, CA 94104
Tel: 415 627 7000 / 1 800 435 4000

Charles Schwab is not the cheapest broker, and it doesn't care because it is the largest. Very experienced at what it does, and has an enormous number of positive press comments. If you are a little concerned about trading on the net then a broker such as Schwab provides some added security in that you are dealing with an old hand in internet broking. I wish they would use their size to do even more strategic alliances and offer their clients even more free stuff.

Ameritrade ***

www.ameritrade.com
Ameritrade
PO Box 2209
Omaha, NE 68103 2209
Tel: 1 800 454 9272

A very good site. The home page is a lesson in simplicity coupled with professionalism. The site is quick; research is not as good as others but then again the broker is one of the cheapest around. Very easy to navigate, and designed very well and less cluttered than other sites.

ScoTTrade **

www.scottrade.com
Nationwide

The site seems to be extremely slow. It is supposed to be cheap however, and I liked the design and lay-out of the site.

Charles Schwab Europe ***

www.schwab-worldwide.com/worldwide/europe

www.sharelink.com

Charles Schwab
Cannon House
24 The Priory Queensway
Birmingham B4 6BS
UK
Tel: +44 121 200 7788

An increasingly impressive site, with free research, easy navigability, and good design. There is also a phone brokerage service for those not quite ready to jump onto the cybertrain. Site also offers UK investors the opportunity to buy US securities.

Xest **

www.xest.com

A much improved site, but still needs some improvement to assist download speeds. Some of the graphics did not seem to download, and knowing where to start or open an account was not as easy as on some other sites. Seems to have been designed by IT specialists without consultation with an online trader.

Redmayne Bentley **

www.redm.co.uk
Tel: 01870 241 0138

Now a pretty good home page showing some free price charts and news. Easy to see how you would open an account, but someone forgot to tell us why we would *want* to open an account; whatever happened to explaining what you get by way of research, portfolios, and what about showing some demos?

Discover **

www.discoverbrokerage.com

Owned by Morgan Stanley, but the site does not come in as having the cheapest commission, or the best design, or the most research. It sort of does a bit of everything without excelling at any one, or indeed all. However, given who owns it, it provides the security you may want in an online broker.

DLJ Direct UK ✳✳✳

www.dljdirect.co.uk

A relatively new entrant to the UK market, and the site is well-contructed with good research available. It is fast and slick. Liked it.

DLJ Direct ✳✳✳

www.dljdirect.com

The US site is very nice and well-organized. It gives you reasons to open an account, and makes it easy to find commission rates. DLJ realize it has to offer added value through research and does so. The only thing is that it is not the very cheapest.

Money and risk management for e-trading

32

Money management: The road to riches is paved with boring old concrete

Online trader problems

■ How much of my money should I risk on a single trade?

■ How much money do I need to start online trading?

■ What sums have other successful online traders started with?

Money management is about as exciting as a date with an actuary. Unfortunately for online traders, it is also essential to understand if we are to play the game, and make money. Consider the simple fact that if you suffer a 50 percent loss, it will then take a 100 percent return just to break even. Not a nice prospect is it? That's why you shouldn't leave home without money management.

In this chapter

In this chapter we run through some of the mathematics of money management. It complements the later chapter on the psychology of risk and money management. Don't worry, you won't need a calculator.

Intermediate

Calculating how much to risk

Now, this may seem a bit detailed and tedious, at least that is what I thought when I first realized years ago that it was important. However, if you are serious about making money from trading then you just have to take another sip of the gin and tonic, and read on.

Whether a trade is worth making depends on the risk to reward levels, not just on the signals your system provides. By risk I do not mean the size of your position, but the size of your potential loss.

Imagine you are trading one contract of the FTSE future. The same principles apply whatever product and time frame you are trading. Each point equals £10 per contract (£10 = $16 approximately). Imagine you also have £10 000 to trade with in total capital. Your reasoning should run like this:

■ How much of my total equity should I be willing to risk? Most experts would advise anything from 0.5–5 percent of your total equity per trade.

■ In this case since you have £10 000 in total equity, the most you should be willing to risk in one trade is £500.

■ £500 is 50 points movement (remember each point is £10).

■ So, the maximum number of aggregate points I can afford to lose is 50. (I have said aggregate because if you trade one contract it would be 50 points, but if you trade two it would be 25 points on each, and so on).

■ Now imagine that the contract is at 6580, you expect a move to 6610. That is a profit of 30 points per contract (see Fig 32.1). There are now two considerations: For a good trading system your downside should be determined by your expected upside. So, if you are expecting 30 points on the upside, you should *not* be willing to risk 50 points on the downside to achieve it. What should the upside to downside ratio be? Well, 2:1 at least. So the most you should be willing to risk, given an upside of 30 points, is 15 points on the downside, i.e. downside stop of 6565. That is good risk and money management. So your risk to reward ratio is 1:2. But how many contracts should you have?

■ You can afford to have three contracts because even if you lost 15 points on each that would total 45 points, which is less than 50. So in that situation you would buy three contracts, and still limit your downside risk to 5 percent of total equity on the trade with a 2:1 reward to risk ratio. Wasn't too painful, was it? Now, how about a whisky?

Let us just run through that again:

1 Five percent of your total equity determines the most loss in aggregate you can allow yourself to suffer on a trade. In this case it is 50 points in aggregate. Of course, you could limit it to 3 percent.

2 Your downside risk has to be at least half that of your projected upside reward. Upside points gain is estimated to be 30 points, so your downside can only be 15 points.

3 You can afford to have three contracts each losing 15 points and still have maintained your equity loss to under 5 percent.

So, what happens? See Fig 32.2.

As you can see, from our entry point the future did move down a little bit, but not so as to activate our exit, and then moved towards 6610 just as we anticipated and hey,

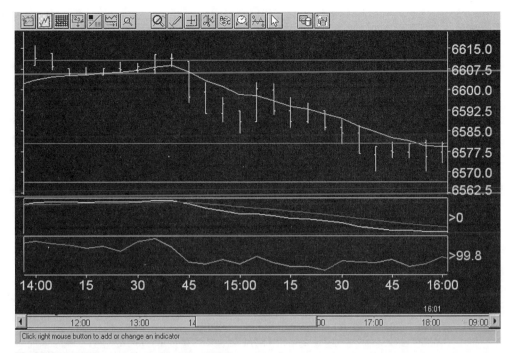

Fig 32.1 FTSE future contract with price at 6580

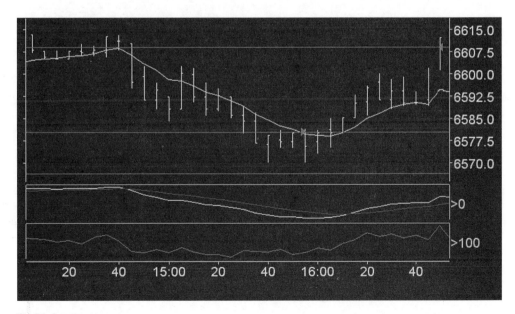

Fig 32.2 FTSE 100 future

presto! – 30 points per contract, three contracts, that's £900 pounds total profit or 9 percent return on total equity, in a few minutes. Remember we had limited calculated risk. Don't you just love it?

expert ✓ advice **Bernard Oppetit, Global Head of Equity Derivatives, Paribas**

You have to have good money management. You have to ensure you are not going to be hopelessly underwater. You can have rules like maximum drawdown, or value at risk ,or limits. You can also have your own internal rules like "this is too much money to lose." You must have that in your mind and that you are not going to risk more than that at any one time. You have to make sure you are left in the game. That is very important. Once this is clearly established, you need fear, you need to feel that things can very quickly go wrong.

chat box 32.1 *From a trader on Silicon Investor on 6.6.1999*

The figure of merit is how much of your equity is at risk for each consecutive trade. The book suggests that 1 percent is a reasonable figure. This applies to the amount at risk, not the gross amount of the trade. For instance, if you could relatively expect to scalp a reasonably liquid stock without ever having a loss worse than $3/4 per share, then in order to trade 1000 shares, you would need to have $0.75 * 1000/0.01 = $75000 in your account.

What if you limit the most equity you are willing to lose on a trade from 5 percent to 3 percent?

In this case you would reduce your overall risk to 3 percent, but you also reduce the number of contracts you would be trading, so if the trade were profitable your rewards would be reduced. By reducing your risk, you protect your downside more.

example **It is not necessarily a risky business**

Imagine you risk 2 percent of your equity in any one trade. Allowing for the fact that your account size drops on each occasion, your initial equity would be down 50 percent after 34 consecutive losses. What are the chances of 34 consecutive losses? Well, if there is a 50–50 chance of profit on any one trade then the chances of 34 consecutive losses would be 0.5^{34} or one in 17 billion. Makes you wanna trade doesn't it?

What if I am willing to accept a 1:1 reward to risk ratio?

The upside would be that you would give the price more room for maneuvre, i.e. allow the trade more space to prove itself; the price could drop further before you had to exit.

But the downside is that if the price just kept falling you would suffer a bigger loss when you exited. Another risk is that you are not playing the odds and if you got a string of losers you could be wiped out.

expert advice ✓

Bill Lipschutz, former Global Head of Foreign Exchange, Salomon Brothers

With a trade you always look at a multiple upside to downside. But how much greater? A good rule of thumb for a short-term trade – 48 hours or less – is a ratio of three to one. For longer term trades, especially when multiple leg option structures are involved and some capital may have to be employed, I look for a profit to loss ratio of at least five to one.

chat box 32.2

The loser's spiral – the dark side of trading

From a trader on Silicon Investor on 9.6.1999

All of us, as traders, normally sense that trading can become "dangerous," if you let it get out of control when it's not going well. It can indeed be a rather dangerous (risky) endeavor, financially speaking. A friend of mine, after trading marginally successfully for a few months, said to me "Man, I sense this is really dangerous – I could get into a lot of trouble here." He was right. There is one basic process that destroys almost everyone that "blows out" of trading; I call it "the loser's spiral." I know all about it, as I went through it myself several times, in the process of really learning how to trade more consistently. Only extreme interest in trading, and perseverance through travails got me through this one! I've never met a good trader who hasn't been through grappling with this, either. As they say, "You must learn how to lose, before you can win." It is "the filter" which keeps most away from full-time, long-term trading success.

It goes something like this (simplified, for brevity). Trader makes a little bit of money. Skills develop. Trader makes a lot of money. Takes bigger risks. Things going well. Then . . . Wham! Big loss. Wham! Bigger loss. Trader tries to "make back" loss by taking bigger risks . . . and so on. The spiral is self-perpetuating.

Think that won't happen to you? Well, it happens to 80 percent+ of beginning traders within six to nine months (mileage varies, depending upon prevailing market conditions). It happens to a lot of intermediate traders, and experienced traders. It happens to world-class traders who run huge hedge funds, and it happens to people that have written scholarly books (Victor N.) and who are geniuses. So don't think it can't happen to you – it will, unless you study the mathematics of money management, and carefully calculate how much you can risk, versus your total tradeable capital. The statistics are overwhelmingly against you, if you violate the cardinal rules (generally, if you are risking more than 1–5 percent per trade, depending upon your trading style). For those with higher net worth, more tolerance for risk, or a longer time frame (usually a combination of these factors), the parameters are different. But the basic idea is, if you are trading too "large" (of risk on each trade), sooner or later it will destroy you and blow you out of the game – probably, sooner rather than later.

Other factors to consider

Market volatility

The price could be moving about so greatly that the place where you have to put your stop to prevent your losing more than 5 percent of your equity is just too tight, and is likely to be hit. In that case you cannot place the trade. It is too risky.

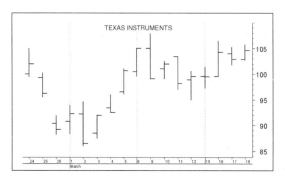

Fig 32.3 Lone Star Instruments

The upside might also be so small that you have to have a tight stop-loss, and again it may have to be so tight that it would be easily hit and would not be worth your time (see Fig 32.3).

If you anticipated a price move from 105 to 110, i.e. a 4.8 percent upside, your downside protection would have to be at most 2.4 percent i.e. at 102.5. As you can see, such a tight stop would be hit in normal daily volatility. The trade is just not worth it. This is actually an extreme example, but the principle is the same.

---

expert advice ✓ **Bill Lipschutz, former Global Head of Forex, Salomon Brothers**

With a trade you always look at a multiple upside to downside. You can look at the percentage probability of a rise or a fall. The problem with that is that you may have many trades that are 50–50. So you are trying to set something up which may have a 8:1 pay-off. The fact of the matter is that if you put on a lot of 14:1 structural ratio spreads, you are going to make money, because you have to be wrong 14 times in a row to lose, for every once you are right.

I think risk is asymmetrical. To achieve successful longevity, you have to focus on your losses, or drawdowns, or whatever you call them. It's very simple. Just know what you are prepared to lose. It doesn't matter how big, little, right or wrong your position is. You have to know what you are prepared to lose, I don't mean mentally prepared, I mean mathematically what can be lost when you enter a trade. You must not put yourself out of business. You have to be back. You have to be there tomorrow, the next day and the day after. If you manage the downside, the upside will take care of itself.

Of course, when you first put on a trade you do have target levels, levels at which you think you are wrong. The price levels of those targets should be determined as a result of your trade idea analysis. The size should be determined as a result of your absolute dollar loss constraints. For example, let's assume that the current price level of dollar yen is 125 yen per dollar. Let's further assume that your analysis of the latest round of trade negotiations between Japan and the United States leads you to believe that the yen may weaken to 130, but due to technical considerations should not strengthen beyond 122.50.

Further analysis of the pricing of yen options leads you to determine that the optimal trade structure will be to simply sell the yen against the dollar in the spot market. How large should the position be? The answer lies in the asset size of the account you are doing the trade for and its loss limit. If you are only prepared to take a three percent loss on a ten million dollar account, then it follows that you should buy $15 000 000 against the yen. If you are wrong on the trade, your loss will be $300 000 and if your analysis was correct and you sell the position at 130, your profit will be $600 000.

Probabilities

Strictly speaking you should calculate your reward to risk ratio based not just on absolute figures but expected profit and expected loss. What does that mean? Well, let me give you some (painless) probability theory first.

Your expected gain is the probability of the gain occurring multiplied by the value of the gain. Trust me, this is relevant to trading. So, imagine there is a die. If it shows 1–5 I will lose $5, but if it shows 6, I will win $30. Should I take the bet? Trading the markets is a little like this.

In this example, my expected gain is $1/6 \times \$30$ i.e. £5. (i.e. the probability of a 6 on a die is 1/6). My expected loss is $5/6 \times \$5$, that is $4.17. So, since my expected reward is greater than my expected loss, I should take the bet.

Of course, I will lose more times than I win, but when I win, I should wipe out my accumulated losses. You could have a trading system that produces $30 profits one-sixth of the time and $5 profits five-sixths of the time. But note that your reward:risk ratio would not be 30:5. This is very important. If you forget the probabilities of your system, then you will think you are placing more favorable a trade then you actually are.

So how do you calculate the probability? You could use sophisticated computers, or back-test your system and estimate. Remember, even in a game of dice, there are no guarantees, only theory and reality, and they seldom converge. Large price moves have a lower probability of occurring than smaller ones. My suggestion is not necessarily to be hyper-scientific, but to take probabilities into your calculations.

expert advice **Bernard Oppetit, Global Head of Equity Derivatives, Paribas**

Even though I know I will get out after a certain loss, I consider the amount I have risked as the whole amount invested. Also, I look to see what percentage probability there is of a certain percentage rise and I compare that to the risk I am taking. I would look at some kind of distribution of possible outcomes, such as a 50 percent chance of doing something special, or a 50 percent chance of doing nothing in particular, or a 50 percent chance of a small loss against a 50 percent chance of a great gain. There has to be some idea of the distribution of outcomes.

| chat box 32.3 | # When should I quit? |

From a trader on Silicon Investor on 6.6.1999

Successful day trading is very difficult. The vast majority of those who try day trading end up losing money. However, the few successful day traders make huge sums of money – once they gain the knowledge and experience to be successful.

During the inevitable "learning curve" virtually all traders lose money. The tough decision is when to "pull the plug" and give up day trading if you are not successful. The following ideas may be worth considering:

1 Are you financially secure enough to trade without the anxiety of needing a "paycheck" at the end of every day?

2 Does day trading still interest you? Do you look forward to the open of the market every day? In short, do you enjoy trading. If not, you are likely not committed to the extent that is required. Most people cannot excel at something they don't enjoy. The most successful people are virtually immersed in their fields.

3 Is your trading improving? If you have made several hundred trades, you should be seeing some improvement in your trading results. Keep detailed records of your trades in a spreadsheet. This will give you irrefutable data that show your results in black and white. Don't argue with the facts.

4 In addition to the statistical data, do you feel you are avoiding many of the dumb mistakes that you made when you first began trading?

5 Are you trying to trade with some kind of plan, or are you just trading from the seat of your pants? Hopefully, after several weeks or months of trading, you are beginning to formulate some ideas on a personal trading strategy to guide your trading. Even if not successful with a particular strategy, you will gain knowledge by *learning* that the strategy was not successful. Then you can modify or refine your system to improve performance. If you trade by the seat of your pants, you have no reference point to *what* you were doing that was unsuccessful.

The decision to quit trading is a very difficult one. Over 90 percent of day traders wish they had made this decision sooner. Do not let your ego prevent you from giving up trading. The odds are stacked extremely heavily against success. People who lose money are in very good company. Not being a successful day trader should be nothing to cause embarrassment or to be ashamed of.

In the end, it is a personal decision of when to stop day trading if you cannot find success. I think an individual needs to very honestly review their situation and make their best decision.

Note: Don't decide during market hours!

expert advice ✓ **Jon Najarian, CEO, Mercury Trading**

I believe discipline could be a learned response. You could teach somebody to do it, but you really have to hammer it into them to if they have got a problem – you cannot let them ride it at all. You have to be very, very honest with yourself. The single biggest thing is that they need to have a goal for every trade that they make. So if I do a trade and, say, I am buying a stock at $30 because I think it is going to $35, then I know what my downside limit is; it is $25, because if I am going to make $5, if I am right, then I do not want to have to lose more than $5 if I am wrong. So if I have a goal which I think the stock is going to reach, then as a minimum I set my loss at where I think the gain could be if I am right.

Beginner ▷▷

How much money to start with?

A very popular question raised by many new traders is how much money they should start trading with. Well, the answer is not as simple as giving a figure. You didn't think it would be, did you? Consider the rich trader and the poor trader.

Rich trader

This trader has oodles of cash, let's say $1 000 000 for argument's sake. His problem is not whether he has the minimum needed to trade, but rather: "What is the minimum he should trade with?"

Just because you have a small fortune does not mean you should look to use it all in your trading. It is advisable to paper trade first, then trade small, and gradually build your way up as your confidence rises. The issue of how much the rich trader should start trading with depends on his answers to the following:

- How confident do you feel?
- How much trading experience do you have?
- Have you traded this product or time frame before?
- How profitable have you been so far with the system you plan to use?

The other problem the rich trader has is one of opportunity cost. Does he really want to use all $1million trading a system producing 20 percent return a year? He may be better placing some money into other ventures.

Poor trader

This trader is more like the most of us. He does not have a silver spoon in his mouth, or any other orifice for that matter. Consequently, he is wondering whether he has enough money to trade with at all. The first thing to bear in mind is that if you trade with money that is needed for other more pressing things, such as school fees, mortgage, clothing, food, then pretty soon you will lose it. You would simply be putting to great a strain on yourself to "perform" to succeed. You should be trading with "uncommitted" funds.

The minimum needed to trade with depends on the following factors:

■ Those listed in the "rich trader" section you've just read.

■ Broker account minimums:

– These are so low nowadays they are not too large a hurdle.

■ The volume of trading you are intending to do:

– If you are planning to day trade, that means you will be expecting to make a lot of small profits daily. So you will be trading high volume each day, and incurring commission for each trade.

Of course, the optimist will argue that he will reinvest all the profits he intends making back into his trading account. In which case, he may calculate a shorter time frame than a year as a benchmark for profits. For instance, commissions for a month of day trading on the trading in our example is $3333.

Whatever happens you would have to have enough money to make $3333 profit a month, just to break even.

The key point is that the lower the volume of trading, the less trading capital you need.

■ Profits to make the endeavour worthwhile: If your system was likely to produce 100 percent a year return before commissions, then in the first month you may expect 9 percent return before commissions.

■ To improve your profit, you can either: increase your trading capital, or your system's return, or reduce commission costs by trading less while maintaining returns.

example If you trade 10 times a day, and pay $8 to open and $8 to close a position and trade 250 days a year, then you will pay $40 000 in commissions.

example If you had trading capital of $50 000 then at the end of the first month you would have 2.3 percent return for the first month after commissions (using our previous example of 10 trades daily at $8 to open and to close).

That would equate to 28 percent annualized *after* commissions *without* reinvestment of profits, or $14 000 in profit for the year (before tax).

That is not much of a return for a lot of work, and that was with a system producing 100 percent a year.

chat box 32.4

Minimum trading money for day trading

From Eric P. on Silicon Investor on 6.6.1999

While different traders may disagree on this point, I believe that $50k is about the right minimum size for a day trading account. Anything less can reduce your likelihood of success . . . and the odds are not great to begin with.

chat box 32.5

Minimum trading money for day trading

From Palo Alto Trader on Silicon Investor on 17.6.1999

I would say $50 000 is rock bottom to have decent odds. $75k is OK, $100k is a good number, not too big, not too small. I've day traded and swing traded $25k and $50k accounts at time in the past myself.

Below $25k, I'd recommend instead of trying to day trade, swing trading positions to build up the account. It can be done! You just have to be really cautious, since there is less margin for error.

Summary

If there were just one essential secret to trading then money management and limiting the amount you risk on any particular trade would be it. It is a question of getting the numbers on your side. Pay great heed to this chapter.

33

Stop it right there: Using trading stops to finesse a trading system

Online trader problems

- Should I use stops or not?
- I have a system, how can I improve it with stops?
- What types of stops should I use and when?
- How do other online traders improve their performance with stops?

In this chapter

An understanding of stops is essential for the online trader in the profitable execution of a trading system. In less pompous language that means: "You had better read this chapter." A stop is a delicate balancing act which is part of the art of trading. It limits risk and is the point of contact between a theoretical trading system and the real markets. Clever use of stops can make the difference between a good system and an outstanding system. Our aim in this chapter is to fully get to grips with the stop, pitfalls to be aware of in its use and how to use it to increase profits.

One important thing to bear in mind is that a stop is used as a "override" mechanism to a trading system. In other words, if the stop is hit, we override the system's signal. In this way if the system's signal is too premature or too tardy, the stop acts as a finessing mechanism to improve entry and exit times. We are also going to see what other online traders think of stops and how they use them.

Buy and sell stop orders

Normally a trader wants a price to rise *after* he is long the security. Not so when using buy and sell stop orders. Trading stops are a means of managing a trade so as to maximize profits, and avoid losses. Most traders think of stops as "stop-losses," that is, a point at which they will exit the market. However, they can be useful as means of entering a trade. You would effectively be buying at a higher price than the current price. What's that? Buying more expensive? Intrigued? Enraged? Read on.

A buy stop order is placed above the current market price, and becomes a "buy at the market" order. The reason a trader might use it is if he thinks the security is worth buying only if it rises to a particular level first. You want to buy at a higher price (buy stop) because you reason that if the price moves to that higher level the market will have told you something (e.g. that your buy signal from your system was valid). However, you are not sure if the price will move to that higher level and that is why you wait and see what the price does.

Price is king

Whatever your trading system, you will almost always want the price level to be the final determiner of whether you enter or exit the trade. For instance, would you buy a stock on a signal despite the price continuing to fall? You might, but you would probably be better off waiting for the price to move up, thereby confirming your buy signal.

Look at Fig 33.1. A buy signal occurs (stochastic indicator moves up tick) on the 19th of the month. You would only see this at the close of trading, because that is when the price bar chart would be completed and then the indicator would be plotted. Therefore the earliest you could act on that buy signal would be the next morning, i.e. the 20th of the month.

But the next day (the 20th), the price falls, as illustrated by the down arrow. Actually, it rises a little above the opening price at some point during the day. This "false" move, where the price moves into positive territory in the immediate period after a buy signal, suggests that buying right at the open before seeing how far the price moves in a direction confirming your signal is not a good idea. Neither is it a good idea to buy after a very small move up from the open, because, as seen in this example, the price continued to fall after the small "false" move.

Here, then, you should not have entered at the open on the 20th. Instead you would be much better having placed a stop order to enter the market if the price broke the preceding day's high, i.e. the price went higher. The reason you wanted the price to go up on the 20th *before* you bought, was to make sure the "buy signal" you got on the 19th was valid and confirmed on the 20th. So you used the stop to

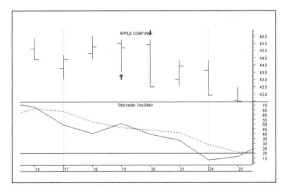

Fig 33.1 A buy signal occurs

buy at a higher price! But for good reason; you wanted proof positive about your trading signal.

Whatever your system, and here we just used a simple one to illustrate a point, watch out in your historical tests to see what the price does the period after a signal. That would be your first opportunity to enter the market.

The purposes of the illustration is to show that what the price does after a buy or sell signal from our system is more important than the signal itself. (In fact, what the price does is the only truly important thing.) Since what the price does is so important, and stops are activated on such price action, stops, too, become very important.

That is where stops come in. When the market price hits your stop price, the stop becomes an order to either close or enter the market. In our example as part of your system you could have required the price on the 20th to break the preceding day's high price before you entered the trade. So, you may have placed your stop at one tick above the high price of the 19th. That way you could have had enough price confirmation on the 20th that the buy signal indicated on the 19th was valid and worth acting on.

Price prove it

Another reason why a trader may want a price to move higher *before* entering a trade is because there are price resistances he is unsure whether the price will overcome. Here the trader is asking the price to prove it can overcome the resistance before the traders puts his faith in it and buys some stock.

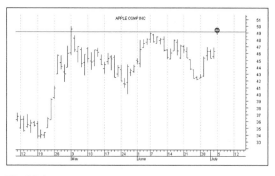

Fig 33.2 Set a buy stop

Look at Fig 33.2. The trader in Apple stock sees that there appears to be a resistance level (as marked by the horizontal line) and he is unsure whether the price will break through that level. He wants to buy Apple stock if the price does break the resistance, but if it fails to break he does not. So can set a buy stop as shown in the figure.

Sell stop orders are below the market price and, yes, you guessed it, sell at the market price when the stop price is hit.

Hitting stops

Ever feel the market is out to get you? This is often the feeling a trader has when he does everything according to plan and the market does just enough to stop him out, and then moves in the right direction with our trader watching from the sidelines. The usual reason for this is that the market has hit his stops, and knowing where best to place your stops is an art.

If you better understand this phenomenon and what the floor trader is trying to do, it may not only save you hours of frustration, but save you money by ensuring your system performs in reality to how it did in theory.

Examine Fig 33.3 of Cisco. The parallel horizontal lines show where there is a degree of price resistance and likely stops. Imagine the price is at $56.5 on 22 May and you are short the market. You want the price to fall. Fearful it may rise, you place a stop to limit your loss. You place the stop at $59.5.

However, other traders who may have bought the stock at, say, $55, know that when the price is $58.5, if they offer $59.5, you will have to buy it from them, because you have a stop order. They are guaranteed a fill. They can sell the security to you at a relatively high price. After that the price falls back down, which you as a shorter of the stock wanted to happen, but are now helplessly out of the market.

Fig 33.3 Cisco and accumulated stops

---

expert advice ✓ **Bernard Oppetit, Global Head of Equity Derivatives, Paribas**

"Before entering a trade I will decide what to do if one thing happens, and what to do if another thing happens. Sometimes that will involve setting stop-losses; which are mental – I would never place a stop-loss for real. I know the best game in time is trying to hurt the stops. I also plan in terms of a target, but not always."

Everyone knows the public places stop-orders at the most obvious places; round numbers, such as 10. Imagine a stock is trading at 11–13, that is, it is 11 bid and 13 offer. A market maker would buy at 11 and sell at 13. Conversely a member of the public is willing to sell at 11 and buy at 13. Assume a member of the public has a stop-loss at 10 bid. A market maker is likely to figure out there is going to be a stop at that price. The market maker will therefore force the price down to 10–13, buy from the stop-loss for 10 and then immediately offer it at 13. This is why Bernard Oppetit avoids stops.

"In some markets having stop-losses is a very good rule I am sure. If it is a liquid market. Once in a while you will be hurt because of whipsaw." In other words, what Oppetit is discussing is that if you do not have an actual stop, it is for you to enforce the discipline of the stop. It is up to you to honestly analyze whether you should exit the trade.

How do the other traders know where the stops are? By examining price charts, and getting a feel for the ebb and flow of the market. What is more, stops are often near round numbers, e.g. $60.

Stop placement: Drawing the thin red line

So, how can you counter the uncanny traders who seem almost psychic at times? To avoid having your stop hit you can either place it further away, e.g. $62, but the danger is you risk suffering a bigger loss if the price does move to $62 than if your stop had been at $59.5. Alternatively, you could have a mental stop rather than an actual one. The problem with this is that since you would have to act on your mental stop if it is to be at stop a all, then it does not help you.

In placing stops we, therefore, have to perform a balancing act. On the one hand, stops cannot be too tight. That is, at a position that does not allow the market to move before your stop is hit and you are out of the market. If you do that, your stops will be hit very often before you can benefit from what may have been correct analysis. Your system may give you good signals, but your stops confound the system.

On the other hand, if a stop is too wide, then you could be wrong in your analysis and not be out of the market until you have suffered an unnecessarily hefty loss.

Consider Fig 33.4. Imagine you enter the market at the first up arrow at $31. The higher of the parallel lines represents your "too tight" stop-loss. Why is is too tight? Because it knocks you out of the market, leaving you on the sidelines, when the market moves from the position marked 1 to the position marked 2.

The second of the two parallel horizontal lines represents a "too lax" stop. It is too lax because you have lost a very significant amount of your initial equity before you are out of the market.

The chapter on money and risk management (boy, doesn't that sound like a tempting read, but I assure you it is worth it) will further expand on the issue of how you decide where to stop.

Fig 33.4 Cisco Systems and tight and lax stops

I trade AMZN on a daily basis . . . Obviously I am not scalping 1/8s.

I try for a minimum of 3/4 pt per trade. When I first started it was difficult to achieve on a regular basis, however I noticed that most of my losing trades were not due to faulty analysis or terrible entry points, it was due more to placing too tight stops.

As my goal was 3/4 pt, I used a 3/4 point stop This was way too tight for a volatile stock like AMZN. I then experimented with various stops and settled on 1 1/2. While this does expose me to a greater loss when my entry points are incorrect, it has significantly improved the percentage of winning trades especially when timing reversals.

I suppose the lesson here is that stops cannot be simply a percentage of the dollar amt of trade – the normal price fluctuation of an issue needs to be factored in. I'm sure this is old news for most of the thread but for me it as a revelation.

More stops: When will all this stop?

There are several types of stops used in trading systems to improve performance. Think of them as the trading equivalent of tailfins and nitro, or Viagra if you prefer – they all help to produce superior performance!

Trailing stops

The purpose of the trailing stop is to protect your profits. As the trade moves in your direction so does the stop. Fig 33.5 shows the workings of a trailing stop.

As you can see from the figure, the stop protects profit by exiting us from the trade, as the price falls and irradicates our profits. Our system could use such a stop to override the system's usual exit.

Fig 33.5 Trailing stops

There are lots of different ways of trailing your stops.

High low stop

For when you are long the market the stop today is the price low x periods away. The low of the previous day may be too tight, but the low of 300 days when you are trading short term is too far away. So, once again, we are left to a balancing act. When you are balancing this act these are some factors to consider:

■ Since the purpose of the stop is to protect profit (except at the very beginning of the trade when there is, of course, no profit), the trailing stop cannot be so far from the current price that it would take a very long time to enter profitable territory.

■ The trailing stop is a stop. As with all stops, if it is too tight it may lead to premature exits.

Moving average stop

With such a stop you use a moving average as the place for the stop. You will have to use the tried and trusted method of trial and error to determine the best values. Try, five, seven, 12 periods.

Breakeven stops

This stop makes sure you get out at breakeven, thereby losing only your commission. You bring it in once you have some profit, the danger is you could lose all your profit, but you would not be taking a loss. I prefer trailing stops.

---

chat box 33.2

The breakeven stop: One of a short-term stock trader's best friends

A trader on Silicon Investor on 10.6.1999

I would like to address a technique that I've found to be one of the most useful available, for the short-term stock trader's arsenal: the breakeven stop. Simply put, once you enter a stock, long or short (set-ups/entries are another topic) with a breakeven stop philosophy you are looking to "work" your stop (whether a mental, or an actual stop; another topic) to the "breakeven" (entry) point as quickly as possible. Not too quickly – the trade needs time to move in your favor. Instead, at just the correct (proper) time, which you can gain a sense for.

Typically, depending upon the volatility of the security you're trading, your initial entry stop might be 1 pt away or less. To apply a breakeven stop, once you enter and the position moves in your favor 1 pt, your stop moves up or down 1 pt to the "breakeven" (entry) price. At that time, you have essentially created a zero-risk situation, a "free trade." You are free to take your profits wherever, all at once, in pieces, etc. – but the main thing is, even if you're stopped out, you haven't lost – at most, you've suffered a tiny nick. There are many ways to manage the position once you're in at breakeven or better, a state that I always covet upon entering a trade!

Which makes this a good time to introduce my first three rules of stock trading, which I've developed after careful thought and reflection, during my first five years of trading:

1   *Don't lose money!*

2   *Don't lose money!*

3   *Don't lose money!*

Get it? This all ties in to the "equity curve tracking" concept. If you can consistently keep your losses small, which is what the breakeven stop is all about, you set yourself up for success.

When you lose money, you set back your equity curve – you go backwards. Then, you have to make that back, to get back where you were. This is all wasted time. The only thing that is necessary is small losses. That is why it is so much more lucrative, over time, to trade with small losses. Common sense, right? But, for most traders (myself included), it takes a long time to fully "get" (believe and internalize) this simple, powerful concept, and to apply it consistently.

There are many ways you can apply or refine the breakeven stop. I like to set the breakeven stop an eighth or a sixteenth above (longs) (or below, for shorts) the entry point, so if I'm stopped out, I've covered commissions (I hate losing, and psychologically I find this better to take a micro-profit). If you start using this technique, you may at first be uncomfortable with it, finding yourself stopped out at breakeven as much as half the time (or more). Get used to it – those are trades you previously would have lost money on! Many top-drawer stock traders trade that way – it takes some getting used to. And remember, you can always re-enter. Think nimble.

As for taking profits, I like to leave that discretionary. I am always trying to gauge the true strength of the stock (another topic), and exit into strength or at least as the issue plateaus into resistance (encounters mild selling pressure), vs on a pullback where you must "give back" more. Often it's as simple as (preferably) offering the stock out or (if you're a little too slow) "hitting the bid" when an issue stops trending and starts to consolidate sideways. At other times, you might want to hold a stock that moves sideways, because strong stocks often consolidate by going sideways (instead of pulling back), before they move up again.

Many of the most skilled, seasoned pros recommend taking your profits in pieces, using a trailing stop on the final lot. I don't like using trailing stocks because you have to give too much back (I try to be gone before they're needed), but they can be a very good idea, if you're not nimble enough to get out sooner – which still happens to me all the time.

Although selling a piece once the position moves in your favor requires multiple (exit) commissions, I've found it very psychologically helpful, in managing the trade, to take off at least a third of the shares once the position runs in your favor. Depending upon market conditions, the stock, the chart, etc. this could occur anywhere from 1/4 point away from your entry point, to a point or two. The point is, you've "locked in" a profit. With that profit "booked," you'll find that you're quicker to obey your breakeven stop, since you won't want to give back the booked profit. Again, all positive self-imposed "trade psychology," working in your favor.

Which brings us to another frequently cited rule: "Never let a winner turn into a loser" (in other words, "use break-even stops"). This is a great piece of wisdom for stock trading, which can prevent a lot of losses. This is what the breakeven stop is all about. I suggest, for those inclined to try this, to try trading stocks with the objective of "getting into a breakeven position" once you enter; make that the objective, not so much your profits – they will come naturally. You'll find the downside evaporates a lot of times. Remember, many of the best stock traders are stopped out at breakeven on half (or even more) of their trades. That is a victory! On the bad entries that go strongly against them, they might typically lose 3/8 or 5/8, up to a point, but those are rare. So, by applying this you can have a lot of small losers, and a number of potential winners. And, that's the formula for trading success.

Profit objective stops

This is a predetermined, premeditated stop level at which you will take your profit. The thinking behind it is that if the market is choppy, then it will sooner or later move in your favor and you get out at that point. It makes most sense when you compare it to a trailing or moving average stop in such choppy markets. The last two are likely to produce more losses. The profit objective stops (as long as the objective is not too optimistic) produces lots of small gains. I prefer not to trade such markets.

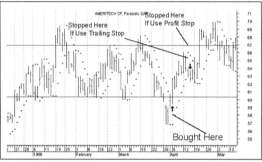

Fig 33.6 Battle of the stops: trailing versus profit

See Fig 33.6. Here, a trader, seeing the market moving in a trading channel, buys at the point marked, which is the bottom of the channel. He sets a profit stop near the top of the channel, knowing the price has reached that level on several occasions before. He is stopped out at a greater level than if he had used a trailing stop.

Time stops

This type of stop places a time limit on the trade after which you exit, and is especially important for the short-term trader. The thinking behind it is that sometimes your stop-loss may not be hit, and your system does not signal an exit. In this unusual circumstance, your capital is tied up and the longer time progresses from your initial buy signal, the riskier the trade becomes. That is when you need to set a time limit.

High risk

Stops strategies: Reverse and double up

If you are stopped out with a loss, you double the position in the opposite direction in an attempt to recoup your losses. Since your position size is doubled, the market only has top move half as far for you to recoup your loss. While the strategy works best in volatile markets and markets prone to false breakouts, it is risky because you are doubling up your position.

I do not recommend this strategy, because you are focussing on being right or wrong and not on maximizing profits. Double position size and send your risk–reward ratios out of the window and into the flight path of a passing bird. So, why do I make note of the strategy? Well, one day, sooner or later you would have come across it, or worse still, have dreamt it up yourself as a brilliant idea. It is my duty to steer you away from such reckless acts of irresponsibility.

chat
box 33.3 *A trader on Silicon Investor on 10.6.1999*

Knowing when to buy is only half the battle of becoming a successful trader. Knowing when to exit a trade is equally important.

One of the hardest things to realize as a new trader is to never, never, *never* get emotionally attached to a stock.

After you enter a trade, always place a stop-loss order. Place your original stop-loss at ¢ basis point from your entry price. You can put your stop-loss any place you feel comfortable with but never lose more than 5 percent on any one trade. This strategy will help you avoid losing your shirt.

Never let a trade languish for more than five trading days. If you enter a trade and the trade does not develop after five trading days, exit the trade. There are too many good trades out there to get stuck in a none-mover. Low commission rates, especially those offered by online brokers, have made this technique possible.

Place a breakeven stop-loss once you have attained a ¢ basis point profit on your trade. Make sure you use the bid price on stocks you are long and the ask price on stocks you are short to determine where to place your breakeven stop-loss. This step can help reduce your number of losing trades dramatically.

Consider taking some money off the table once your trade has produced more than a one basis point profit. Sell ¢ your position at this point in your trade. Also, place a breakeven stop-loss on the remaining ¢ of the trade. If your trade makes it to this point, you are guaranteed a profit. This one little step guarantees you of not letting a winning trade turn into a losing trade.

At this point, the pressure is off, and the trading becomes fun. If the trade continues to move in your favor, simply adjust your stop-loss for every ¢ basis point move in the stock. Some brokers will place a trailing stop-loss on the trade for you. Others will require you to do this step manually. Now just sit back and watch your profits grow and grow and grow. This step will help maximize your returns.

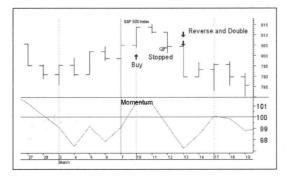

Fig 33.7 How the stop strategy is supposed to work

Instead, I say unto you: Focus on your system as a whole, if you suffer a loss, take it on the chin, and move to your next buy or sell signal. Fig 33.7 shows how the stop strategy is supposed to work: upon receiving a buy signal from the momentum indicator, our trader buys and goes long the next day. However, the day after that the market drops and hits his loss. At this point, our foolhardy trader reverses his position and doubles up. As the market goes lower he makes a healthy profit.

Stops strategies: Multi-position stops

This is a strategy especially for those in two minds about whether to be in or out of a

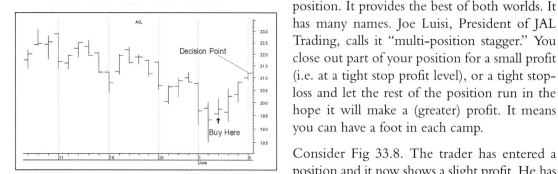

position. It provides the best of both worlds. It has many names. Joe Luisi, President of JAL Trading, calls it "multi-position stagger." You close out part of your position for a small profit (i.e. at a tight stop profit level), or a tight stop-loss and let the rest of the position run in the hope it will make a (greater) profit. It means you can have a foot in each camp.

Fig 33.8 Showing a profit and faced with some choices

Consider Fig 33.8. The trader has entered a position and it now shows a slight profit. He has three choices:

1 Take part of the profits by closing, say, half the position.

2 Take none of the profits, and leave the whole position intact in the market.

3 Take all the profits, and close out the entire position.

These three choices are analyzed in Table 33.1.

	Positive aspects	Negative aspects
Choice 1	If the price now moves down, then at least the trader will have some profits	If the price moves up, then the half of the position we closed out does not earn us any profits
Choice 2	If the price rises, then we have the whole of our position in the market and it all benefits from being in the market	If the price moves down, we have fewer profits to show for it than if we had chosen Choice #1 or #3
Choice 3	If the price moves down then we have maximum profits intact	If the price goes up then we are sitting on the sidelines looking pretty stupid

Table 33.1 How you pays yer money and takes yer choice

If your first stop takes you out at a loss, then you of course are hoping that the market turns and you can be part of the run–up into a profit. The danger is the market continues against you and you lose more by not getting your whole position out at the first stop.

If your first stop takes you out at a profit, then you have some profit for sure, against which to hope the market continues upward. If it turns down, then at least you have some profit.

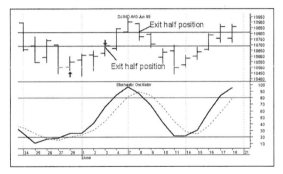

Fig 33.9 **Dow Jones Industrial Average June 1999 futures contract**

In Fig 33.9 our intrepid trader has been trading futures and bought after a buy signal on the stochastic indicator (stochastic crosses its own moving average.) He has a first stop profit at the lower of the parallel horizontal lines. His second stop profit is at "where the price breaks the preceding day's low"). This then exits him at where the higher of the parallel lines is.

The downside for the trader is that after a small profit, if the price continues upward, he loses out on having *both* parts of his position profiting from the price rise. On the other side of the coin, since half his position is still in the market, at least he is getting some profits compared to what would have happened if he had closed out completely at the first stop.

What I particularly like about this strategy, which I use regularly, is that it is psychologically comforting to know you can delay committing to being out or in. Typical male: fear of commitment. The counter-argument is that your system should either be followed, and you are out or in.

Summary

Imagine you have only a 50–50 chance of calling the market right. In theory, if you then stop losses after a certain point and let profits go up to a higher corresponding but opposite point – you should make money. That (oversimple) theory is part of the attraction of stops. You will hear over and over again the addage about letting your profits run and cutting you losses short. Stops are the means to help you do that.

More best-of-breed online trading sites

34

Chats and boards: Come join our community

Online trader problems

- How best to use online chat sites, if at all?
- Which are the key sites online traders use to talk trading?

The aim of this book, as with all good trading books is to impart more than information. Its aim is also to impart knowledge and wisdom. The experience of others besides your humble, yet omnipotent, author is essential to such a task. In trying to maintain a community feel boards and chat rooms are an essential source of information, making this an important chapter in the book.

A top chat room or board will create a genuine community feel with intelligent conversation, inclusive of all experience level users. Unfortunately, such chat rooms are as rare as a Democrat president who doesn't philander (my lawyers inform me I have to add "and whose name is not Carter, and who was president since 1960"!).

With a chat room you can talk real time by typing, posting, and seeing instant replies (if anyone is in the room and deigns to reply). With boards you post a message and wait for a reply at some future time. In this chapter we shall see some of the "best" ones, what "best" means, and how to use them.

Why and how they are used

- To pose questions about issues you are unsure of.
- To get ideas about what to trade. Be very wary of using them for this. A lot of posters put the "bull" into "bulletin board." Be especially concerned if anyone offers insider information: it is usually the last cry of someone stuck in a bad losing position.
- As an educational tool by learning from the experiences of others, for instance in which orders to use at what time of day.

chat box 34.1

From Sam on Silicon Investor on 6.6.1999

1 Getting a read on general market perception.

2 Getting a heads-up on stock movements you are not following that day (i.e. momentum trades).

3 Feeling out others' thoughts on particular stocks, sectors, news releases, etc.

4 Companionship.

But it is not good for getting picks in real-time imo.

That said, know your fellow posters. There will be those you trust, and those you don't. Most, unfortunately, are not to be trusted. Not that they are looking to screw you, but more likely (as with SI) they will only admit selective info. Thus, it goes without saying, don't ever follow the hype. Remember, if someone has made a move, you are already late to the party. Don't allow yourself to buy their shares as they corral you into a foolish move. You are not in business to bail them out. But, if you can trust them, you can see what they are playing on any given day and why. But don't let it rule your day. That's just plain lazy. It is a learning tool – that's all. There's work to be done all day long. Research and analysis (as well as actual trading). Getting other people's picks should never be a priority.

■ As a review of online trading sites. By this I mean many postings may review who are the best brokers, or the cheapest sites, etc.

■ Just to "chill" and bond!

Glossary

You will need to know the first terms just so you too can appear dead cool by knowing what the board's hippest in-crowd is talking about. It's a sociological thing.

B4	before
BBL	be back later
BCNU	be seeing you
BFN	bye for now
BRB	be right back
BTW	by the way
CUL8R	see you later
F2F	face to face
FAQ	frequently asked questions

Screen 34.1

FWIW	for what it's worth
GBH&K	great big hug and kiss
HHOK	ha ha, only kidding!
IMHO	in my humble opinion
IRL	in real life
J/K	just kidding!
LOL	laughing out loud
NT	no text
NTR	not trading related
OIC	oh, I see!
OTOH	on the other hand
OTT	over the top
ROTFL	rolling on the floor laughing
TIA	thanks in advance
TTFN	ta-ta for now

Before I set you loose, you will also want to know the following.

Flaming

A nasty or rude response to someone who breaches netiquette, e.g. by posting adverts, thereby treating the board members like buffoons.

Posting

The act of placing a comment on a board, done by a poster.

Thread

This is a line of discussion on a board with one person making a posting, the replies being the threads. Also, a thin piece of material used to keep garments together.

What to look for and watch out for on chats and boards sites

When considering which chats and boards sites to make your regular hangouts, you should consider the following issues.

Size

When it comes to boards, size matters. You obviously want a board with lots of subject matter and members to ensure you get the broadest views, and are not sharing the site with a sad lonely broker from Florida.

Quality of postings

Some sites just have poor-quality postings for several reasons. It may have been taken over by a few "bully" posters who cajole, intimidate or just try to poke fun at anyone who may not know as much as the bullies think they themselves do. Sometimes postings are poor because the people posting on them are simply not that good, and postings degenerate into slanging matches and challenges to settle matters outside the board. Sometimes you get an invasion of ramping postings: those morons who inform you something is about to sky-rocket because they know a man, who works for this woman, whose husband's mistress's cousin's niece's stepmother's alien dog told her the stock was a good purchase.

Topics

As well as a wide range of topics the boards should be divided into sub-groups so you can get into a relevant topic in enough detail and quickly.

Design and navigability

It can sometimes seem there are millions of messages on billions of topics posted every nanosecond. In fact, it is worse than that. All this makes design and navigation especially important otherwise you will never get to read about what you want to know or post questions or replies.

Price

Ideally, you want a free site. Failing that a free trial period followed by a cheap subscription will have to do.

Screen 34.2

The Silicon Investor ✳✳✳

www.techstocks.com

Despite having a name that does not match its web address, this is probably one of the most famous online trading board sites. These are the stats they proudly proclaim to all visitors.

Size

140 000+ messages posted per week, and 580 000 messages posted per month

10 769 922 searchable messages stored in the SI database

29 788 discussion threads have been created by SI members

More than 120 000 people have become active members of Silicon Investor

Quality of postings

Quite high, not much "noise."

Topics

Topics include the following (with sub-topics within) (see Table 34.1).

- Aerospace and defense
- Banking and finance
- Brokerages/investment resources
- Canadian stocks
- Casinos/gaming
- Coffee shop
- Five dollars and under
- Food processing and agriculture
- Futures and commodities
- Gold, mining, and natural resources
- Initial public offerings
- International
- Internet financial connection
- Iomega (IOM) and IMP (IMPX)

- Market trends and strategies
- Miscellaneous (biotech/medical)
- Miscellaneous (general)
- Miscellaneous (technology)
- Mutual funds
- Overvalued stocks
- Puts, calls, and other options
- Real estate/REITs
- Short-term traders
- Specialty retail
- Transportation
- Web/information stocks
- Welcome to SI
- Year 2000 stocks and discussion

Table 34.1 Silicon Investor topics

Design and navigability

Its design is probably what a web-site may have looked like in the 70s if they had had the modern internet then. Nevertheless, it is relatively easy to find topics, and some helpful chaps collect the best postings for a particular topic and archive them. I love that idea.

Price

Reading is free, posting costs. There is a free trial membership plan for a fortnight and also a subscription fee of $100 for a year and $200 for life (best not take out the latter if you're 101 years old, then).

Screen 34.3

Investorville ***

www.investorville.com

This site reeks of good ideas. It is easily one the best chat sites on the web, here's why.

Size

Lots of members and postings – no worries there.

Quality of postings

A very quality content. Editing by the Mayor of Investorville ensures that adverts and bad posting are deleted. In fact, I could not find one poor-quality posting!

Topics

As well as covering topics by stocks, there is also a "user created" forum section which ensures relevance to the online trader, discussing the issues of most relevance to them. There is an "ask and question" forum for all those questions which may not be answered elsewhere but also ensures there is a welcoming place for the novice. Now, that is my kind of community.

An excellent "overheard" section lists and links to all the best most perceptive and intelligent postings. Yet another good idea. Another section worth a mention is "Hot Boards" which lists the most popular boards so you can instantly get a feel for where the most vibrant discussion and latest issues may be being discussed. The "new posts" section lets you quickly keep up to date with the most recent new discussion.

Design and navigability

Very easy to read and navigate. I cannot think how it could be simpler. Yeah, I know I am heaping praise on it, but when I see something I like, I just gotta let ya know. There are no annoying reference codes as on so many other sites which clutter threads.

Price

Free as air, and twice as sweet.

Screen 34.4

Topics

Stocks are covered in alphabetical order, and can be searched by industry group which is helpful. But they should have industry-based discussion, too.

Design and navigability

The design and navigability are fine. Not too bad, not too great. Since they focus on particular stock talk, there is very little you could do to improve it. They could have a hot boards section which lists those stocks with the most postings.

Price

Free, but you have to become a member even to read, let alone post messages.

The Stock Club **

www.stockclub.com

The site offers real-time chat as well as boards. Specializes in stocks alone.

Size

I got the impression that there are a few people there, but not as many as on, say, Silicon Investor.

Quality of postings

About average.

Screen 34.5

Marketforum **

www.marketforum.com

This caters for futures and options, and not stocks traders.

Size

The site claimed 3676 messages in the past two days when I did a search under "online."

Quality of postings

A very high-quality site with "serious" talk.

Topics

Topics are restricted to talk about commodities at an intermediate level.

Design and navigability

Not too bad a design, navigation was a bit difficult and could have been easier to see a long list of articles than having to search by topic.

Price

Free.

Summary

There are few very good sites which can be used for some restricted purposes as outlined here, such as getting the "word on the street" from those who have been there, done that. Do not use them for stock tips – ever. In the next chapter I highlight one of the ways chat rooms can excel: in providing good-quality real-life trading advice.

35

Technical analysis sites: Charting on the web

Online trader problem

■ Which are the best web-sites for doing technical analysis online if I don't want to buy technical analysis software?

You can look at price charts, and perform technical analysis in two ways: you can buy software, load it onto your computer and subscribe to a price feed over the internet, cable, satellite, FM, or you can go to one of the free web-sites listed in this chapter. They do not allow as much functionality compared to the software, but are a good place to test the waters.

Educational sites

Table 35.1 shows good places to learn more about technical analysis, and don't forget the recommended reading.

Name	Address	Comment
DecisionPoint	www.decisionpoint.com	A good educational site – lots of free educational material
Equis	www.equis.com	The specialist software company, that does a neat line in online education
Market Technicians Society	www.mta-usa.com	The site for the society of Technical Analysts
Technical Analysis of Stocks and Commodities Magazine	www.traders.com	The special magazine for technical analysts
Trading Tactics	www.tradingtactics.com	Each major indicator is hyperlinked and explained. Quite good

Table 35.1 Technical analysis sites

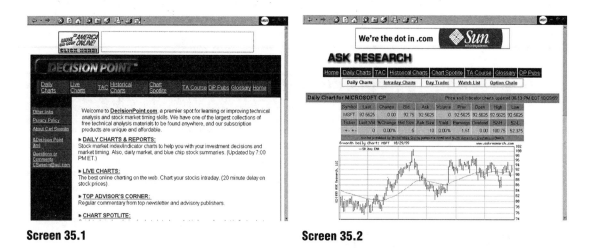

Screen 35.1   **Screen 35.2**

Charting web-sites

The next section contains some of the best online charting web-sites. Performing technical analysis on an online web-site is not as easy as on dedicated software, but they are a good starting point before you invest in software. The best sites tend to be one with "Java" charting. Essentially, this makes them more interactive because a small amount of software is downloaded onto your browser. Other things to look out for are sites that:

■ display multiple windows so you can look at more than chart at a time

■ permit the display of several indicators at once

■ have intra-day charts (an especial bonus)

■ have least 2 years' history.

---

*key   *** An excellent charting site, lots of indicators and clear displays. Java charts

** Quite good with some good features

No sites below ** listed

Big Charts ***

www.bigcharts.com

Charting is not an add-on feature to this site. Big Charts does charts first and foremost. A very good, easy-to-use online charting site. It allows a good range of indicators to be displayed and is crisp and clear in design.

Equis ✱✱✱

www.equis.com

The company that produces the best-selling charting software, Metastock, also runs this very good Java-based site. Unfortunately, my browser has difficulty running their latest Java site. Fortunately, you can still access the previous Java-version site – and this is phenomenal. It is very quick and, again, easy to use.

Prophet Charts ✱✱

www.prophetfinance.com/charts

This is another Java-based site. It is good quality and some users may prefer its lay-out.

Alpha Chart ✱✱

www.alphachart.com

A very good charting site, allowing multiple windows. Could be a little easier to use. It is one of the original internet charting sites.

Ask Research ✱✱

www.askresearch.com

This one is a good site for real-time charts. Again, one of the first internet sites to provide charting and still going strong with pretty good design and ease-of-use features.

E✱Trade UK ✱✱✱

www.etrade.co.uk

Now, I know this is a brokerage site, but a lot of effort has gone into making the charting aspect of it best of breed. Charts that blow up a new screen on the browser permit multiple screening, plus all the main indicators are covered. Not Java based, but the design means it is still very user friendly.

Wall Street City ✱✱✱

www.wallstreetcity.com

An excellent site, crisp and clear, just like I like it. Not Java, though.

IQ Charts ✱✱✱

www.iqc.com

An excellent, free, Java-based real-time charts site. The minimum frequency of updates for intra-day charts is five-minute bars. Covers most of the major indicators. A very useful site for monitoring intra-day prices.

Summary

If you do not have or do not want to invest in state of the art technical analysis software plus price data feeds over the internet, cable, satellite or FM then the technical analysis web-sites offer a very good FREE alternative. I do love that word free.

36

Prices for software daily and historical: Feed me

Online trader problem

■ Where do online traders get their daily and historical prices for charting software?

Having seen, in the last chapter, some of leading software for charting, and for creating and testing software, we, of course, need historical and daily updates of prices. In this chapter we examine what you should be looking for in price providers and details of some leading ones.

Prices for your software

The software needs price data, of course, for charting. We need historical and daily data. Any company we use has to meet the following standards:

■ The price feeds have to be compatible with our software.

■ The company should preferably be a well-known name.

■ The data have to be known as good quality and error free.

■ The daily download should be available as soon as possible after market close.

BMI (Bonneville Market Information) ✱✱✱

www.bmiquotes.com

3 Triad Center
Suite 100
Salt Lake City
UT 84180
Tel: 800 255 7374
Fax: 801 532 3202

Exchange and data coverage

■ Stocks, bonds, options, futures, foreign exchanges, indices statistics, mutual funds, and more.

■ Futures exchanges: All leading world exchanges.

■ Equity exchanges: All major and many minor international exchanges.

Market data transmitted

■ General: Open, high, low, close, last trade, total volume, statistics, official volume.

■ Futures: Nominal open, open ranges, close ranges, open interest, tick volume, cabinet prices, spreads, settlement.

■ Equities: P/E ratios, dividends, earnings, yields, x dividend date, 52-week high/low, stock name, full bid/ask time (on NYSE and AMEX), best bid/ask time (on regional exchanges), bid/ask size, incremental volume.

Compatible with which software?

MarketCenter Platinum, SuperCharts RT, Aspen Graphics, Ensign Windows, Ticker Watcher, TradeStation, TradeWind, Vista RT, DollarLink, First Alert. Contact BMI regarding others.

Broadcast methods

Cable

BMI broadcasts over Superstation TBS and American Movie Classics (AMC) cable networks. BMI states it is the fastest and most accurate cable quote provider in the industry! The financial information comes through cable TV, so installation is relatively simple and easy.

Satellite (KU Band)

KU Band satellite covers the continental USA plus Northern Mexico and Southern Canada. Although it is small and unobtrusive, the KU is nevertheless powerful. With a versatile mount, the dish can be placed on a roof, a patio, or a wall.

Other features

- Fast quotes: Price quotes based on ticker symbols entered by the user.
- International online quotes: ADRS, major forex, international stock indexes, international markets, foreign stock quotes.
- CMS bond quotes: US treasuries, corporate bonds, mortgage bonds, CMO bonds.
- Mutual fund quotes.
- News: News alerts, headlines and full news stories. Apparently, during the typical business day, over 12 000 stories are broadcast. Respected equity and futures services such as Dow Jones, Futures World News, S&P MarketScope, Zacks, and many others are available.
- Portfolio monitoring: The web-site permits users to create and edit up to four portfolios with up to 10 stocks each.
- Historical charting: Web-site permits downloading of charts based on type of chart (e.g. bar) and time frame. Charts for all international/foreign equities as well as the usual, e.g. mutual funds and index charts.
- Fundamental data, news, research: Based upon ticker symbol.
- Trial software download from web-site.

Comment

BMI is best known for its delivery of quotes and data. It has an 18-year pedigree and is one of the market leaders. Their business is the business of quote and historical information delivery, and therefore perhaps we should not expect too much else besides. However, I was impressed by their news service and all the freebies.

First, their news service was up to date and of direct importance to the trader. It is clearly written by people who know and care about trading and not just journalists trying their hand at finance.

Second, the freebies were impressive. Even if you don't subscribe to BMI their web-site was very easy to navigate and not cluttered. From the same single page you could monitor your portfolio, download a historical chart, obtain fundamental data, and get fast quotes. Very well-designed.

I was very impressed at the fact that I could download the one year candlestick chart of several Vietnamese stocks! For free.

The only complaint I had was the lack of more technical information on the web-site. That would have rounded off a very good and straight-to-the-point site.

Prestel Online ***

www.prestel.co.uk

Knightsbridge House
197 Knightsbridge
London SW7 1RB
Tel: 0207 591 9000
Fax: 0207 591 9001

Exchange and data coverage

■ Stocks, options, futures, foreign exchanges, indices.

■ Futures exchanges: LIFFE.

■ Equity exchanges: London Stock Exchange.

Market data transmitted

■ General: Open, high, low, close, last trade, total volume, statistics, official volume.

Compatible with which software?

All major formats.

Broadcast methods

Internet (dial-up).

Comment

Prestel shook up the market for UK-listed company and derivatives quotes a couple of years ago when it started delivering data at phenomenally low prices. I use it myself. No problems to report.

DBC (Data Broadcasting Corporation) **

www.dbc.com

Data Broadcasting Corporation
1900 S. Norfolk Street
Suite 150
San Mateo, CA 94403
Tel: 800 527 7521/415 571 1800
Fax: 415 571 8507

Lincoln House
Kennington Park
Oval
London SW9 6EJ
Tel: 0207 793 3100
Fax: 0207 793 3101

Exchanges and data coverage

- Stocks, bonds, options, futures, foreign exchanges, indices statistics, mutual funds, and more

- Futures and options exchanges: All leading worldwide exchanges.

- Stock exchanges: New York Stock Exchange, American Stock Exchange, NASDAQ, Options Price Reporting Authority, London Stock Exchange.

Market data transmitted

- General: Open, high, low, close, last trade, total volume, statistics, volume.

- Futures: Open, close, open interest, cabinet prices, last, spreads, settlement.

- Equities: P/E ratios, dividends, earnings, yields, x dividend date, 52-week high/low, stock name, bid/ask, bid/ask size.

Compatible with which software?

A very wide selection of popular software.

Broadcast methods

Satellite
Most conventional satellite receivers should work satisfactorily, with a footprint serving North America, Europe, Middle East, and North Africa. A satellite dish is needed!

Cable
Via CNBC, WGN or AMC.

FM
Available in most metropolitan areas in the USA and Canada.

Also, via the internet.

Other features – premium/optional

- News and commentary services: Including Dow Jones Online News, ONE Headline Service, Elliot Wave Neowave Report, Hot Stocks Report, Instant Advisor, Vickers Stock Research Corporate, Insider Trading Report, Zacks Earnings Surprises report, Jake Bernstein Futures report, MarketLine.

- Historical charts and analytics.

- Pager, cell phone, e-mail and desktop alerts on price and volume.

Other features

- Fast quotes: Price quotes based on ticker symbols entered by the user.
- International online quotes: ADRs, major forex, international stock indexes, international markets, foreign stock quotes.
- Bond quotes US treasuries, corporate bonds, mortgage bonds, CMO bonds.
- Mutual fund quotes.
- News: News alerts, headlines, and full news stories using CBS MarketWatch.
- Portfolio monitoring.
- Trial software download from website: Error! Bookmark not defined.

Comment

DBC provides a very thorough and comprehensive quote delivery service; comprehensive in both methods of delivery and geographical outreach. You can obtain quotes, using one method or another, throughout Europe, the Middle East, and even North Africa, as well as, of course, North America and Canada.

The FM and cable methods are likely to be most popular since they require the least hardware. Unfortunately, delayed prices are not available online and so the online option is restricted to those with free internet access.

The company is very much geared toward the international as well as the American client and consequently a non-American will feel relatively at ease using this service since the company is likely to know the ins and outs of the user's country.

The premium packages provide an impressive array of news reports and tips, but it's impossible to judge how good these are. They were all individually priced and some appeared rather expensive. The free news service was more than adequate, and had excellent interviews and content.

Dial/Data ✳✳✳

www.tdc.com/dialdata

Track Data Corp.
56 Pine St
New York
NY 10005
Tel: 800 275 5544/212 422 1600
Fax: 212 612 2242

Exchanges and data coverage

- Exchanges: All major world exchanges.

Market data transmitted

- Stocks: Open, high, low, close, volume.
- Mutual funds: Net asset value.
- Money market: Yield, average days to maturity.
- Government agencies: Bid, ask, yield.
- Treasuries: Bid, ask, yield equity options, open, high, low, close, bid/ask volume, open interest.
- Index options: Open, high, low, close, bid/ask volume, open interest.
- Market indices: Open, high, low, close, volume.
- Market statistics: Varied.
- Futures: Open, high, low, close, volume, open interest.
- Futures options: Open, high, low, close.
- S&P industry groups: Weekly, index value, rank.

Compatible with which software?

All major popular software.

Broadcast methods

Internet

If you have the latest downloading (stock price retrieval) from either Omega, Equis, or AIQ, you can access Dial/Data through the internet. If you use software from other analysis programs you will have to check with them on availability of Dial/Data internet access.

Other features – premium/optional

- Company profiles: The unique company profiles:
  - Summarize fundamental data, investment performance, earnings estimates, and more for 7000 publicly traded companies.
  - Include technical data as one-year and three-year relative beta, relative strength index, and moving averages.
  - Provide earnings estimates and analysts' summaries from a respected institutional reporting service.

■ The news feature:

  – Displays up-to-the-second headlines and complete text on more than 5000 daily news stories from Dow Jones Online News and Comtex.

  – Retrieves news from any company/ticker symbol.

  – Presents insights into the forces moving stocks that are important to investors.

Other features

■ Trial software download from web-site.

Comment

Although the site is disappointing, functional and informative – lacking the freebies of other sites – Dial/Data is one of the most reliable and ubiquitous data providers around. You can be assured the data provided will be screened for errors, and will be timely. The international coverage is excellent.

Bridgefeed **

www.bridge.com

Bridge
3 World Financial Center
New York
NY 10281
Tel: 212 372 7100/
800 600 rely

78 Fleet Street
London EC4Y 1HY
England
Tel: 0207 842 4000
Fax: 0207 782 0964

Unicom Electronic
Publishing
4F, No.12, Sec.2
King-San Road
Taipei
Tel: 2 321 9209
Fax: 2 341 6188

Earlthorn Investment
Room 802
Dominion Centre
43–59 Queen's Road East
Wanchai
Tel: 2529 1211
Fax: 2866 2796

50 Raffles Place
19–02 Shell Tower
Singapore 0104
Tel: 222 9992
Fax: 222 4930

Exchange and data coverage

■ Stocks, bonds, options, futures, foreign exchanges, indices statistics, mutual funds, and more.

■ Futures exchanges: All leading world futures exchanges.

■ Equity exchanges: All major and many minor international exchanges.

Market data transmitted

- General: Open, high, low, close, last trade, total volume, statistics, official volume.
- Futures: Nominal open, open ranges, close ranges, open interest, cabinet prices, spreads, settlement.
- Equities: P/E ratios, dividends, earnings, yields, x dividend date, 52-week high/low, stock name, full bid/ask, bid/ask size, incremental volume.

And for markets that use local market pricing conventions, such as Australia, Germany, Hong Kong, Italy, and Japan, special valuation prices are available.

Compatible with which software?

Virtually all major file formats; check with Bridge, including MegaTech, Metastock, SuperCharts, Reuters Triarch, TIBCO TIB, CSK Software InVision, Telerate TTRS, Bridge MV Link, Midas-Kapiti FIST, and Syntegra OTS.

Broadcast methods

Internet (direct dial-up).

Other features – premium/optional

- News: BridgeFeed provides breaking news and timely, accurate analysis of financial, commodity, and economic markets worldwide, including easy-to-use category codes and key words that expedite search and cross-reference.
- Reports and commentary.

Comment

Again, a web-site light on information. However, it is recommended for the quality of its quotes and its service, not its web-site. Because it is so light on information, the best thing to do is contact them with details of what you need and ask for a quote.

This company is definitely one of the big boys and has just acquired Dow Jones Telerate. It has an international reach and feel. So, whether you are based in America, Africa, or Afghanistan, it can reach you.

Quote.Com

www.quote.com

3375 Scott Blvd
Suite 300
Santa Clara
CA 95054
Tel: 800 498 8068/408 327 0700
Fax: 408 327 0707

Exchange and data coverage

■ Stocks, bonds, options, futures, foreign exchanges, indices statistics, mutual funds, and more.

■ Exchanges.

Market data transmitted

■ General: Open, high, low, last, net, volume, ask, best ask, size, best bid.

Compatible with which software?

Provided as ASCII, so almost all software should be able to handle. Displayed on website.

Broadcast methods

Internet.

Other features – premium/optional

■ News: Reuters, Marketscope, Businesswire, PR Newswire, S&P News, Newsbytes, Edgar Online, nightly business report.

■ Historical charting: Web-site permits downloading of charts based on type of chart (e.g. bar) and time frame. Charts for all international/foreign equities as well as the usual e.g. mutual funds and index charts.

■ Live charts.

■ Live portfolio.

Other features

- Fast quotes: Price quotes based on ticker symbols entered by the user.
- Mutual fund quotes.
- Portfolio monitoring.

Comment

Another sturdy quote site from a specialist in the business. Quote.com often receives commendations in the press for its services. It concentrates on behind-the-scenes screening to ensure data are "clean'; a thankless task, which many quote vendors ignore to save costs.

It is a mystery why the site does not give more details about Quote.com. Don't they want more business?

Summary

For the more serious investor who knows he may well be using more sophisticated charting than that available on web-sites software mentioned in the previous chapter, a good-quality provider of daily and historical data is essential. The sites discussed in this chapter consistently get mentioned as the most popular ones.

37

The future and its options: Futures and options sites

Fewer and fewer traders trade by the seat of their pants and the traders that do tend to be futures traders.

Jon Najarian, Chairman and CEO, Mercury Trading

In this chapter

In this chapter are listed and described some sites that will be helpful for futures and options traders. As before, they are placed in a separate chapter to help the reader navigate the book a tiny bit more easily. Of course, futures and options exist in relation to underlying products and these sites deal not only with the futures and options, but also with the many underlying products, e.g. equities, commodities. However their emphasis tends to be on the nature of futures and options.

The mark of quality

A good futures and options site will have the following features.

Quotes

Given the vast number of futures and options contracts available on just one underlying asset, quotes and "chains" can be very useful. Real time would be most helpful since we're talking leverage, and want to keep a close eye on prices.

Market commentary

Market commentary: the more frequent the better. A good site will be quite detailed and be produced by a competent trader.

Charts

Again, preferably intra-day, although we would probably just go to the specialist charting sites anyway, listed in Chapter 41.

Educational material

A peculiarity of futures and options sites is the wealth of educational material. This is where the internet comes into its own: free education, 24 hours a day! A good site will have well-designed and easy-to-understand articles and essays.

Discussion groups

Always useful for bouncing ideas.

---

*key I have awarded the sites stars based on the following criteria:

*** A very good, model site that is easy to navigate and has a large selection of high-quality information

** A good site with much information of use provided in a readily accessible manner

* Some useful bits of information and worth a visit. Could come in useful

---

Table 37.1 provides a summary of the sites listed in this chapter.

Name and web address	Ranking	Quotes	Market commentary	Charts	Education	Discussion forum
Alaron www.alaron.com	***	✓	✓	✓	✓	
Options Industry Council www.optionscentral.com	**				✓	
OptionSource www.optionsource.com	**	✓	✓	✓	✓	
1010 Wall Street www.1010wallstreet.com	***		✓		✓	
Commodity Futures Trading Commission www.cftc.com	*		✓		✓	
Futures Net Www.futures.net	***	✓	✓	✓	✓	✓
Futures Online www.futuresmag.com	***	✓	✓	✓	✓	✓
Futures Source www.futuresource.com	***	✓	✓		✓	✓
INO Global www.inoglobal.com	***	✓	✓	✓	✓	✓
Market Plex www.cbot.com/mplex	***	✓	✓	✓	✓	
Options Direct www.options-direct.co.uk	*		✓	✓	✓	

Table 37.1 Futures and options sites

Alaron ***

www.alaron.com

Alaron is a Chicago-based brokerage, with a strong internet strategy. The content is very good and reveals a lot about the knowledge of the staff working at the firm. Lots of functionality here, and educational materials.

Options Industry Council **

www.optionscentral.com

I have recommended this site for educational materials. You can get just about as much free information as your heart desires, but it is not written by traders and so is more theoretical than practical.

OptionSource **

www.optionsource.com

Lots of different material here for options traders, but check out the wealth of educational material.

1010 Wall Street ***

www.1010wallstreet.com

Jon Najarian, profiled in *The Mind of a Trader*, is a director of the Chicago Board Options Exchange and a leading options trader as well as chairman of Mercury Trading, and he founded this site. The commentary is excellent, because it is provided by him and not only is he phenomenally successful at what he does, he is experienced and actually trades, doesn't just stand on the sidelines. The downside is that all the commentary is subscription only. But you would not expect it for free when it's that good, would you?

Commodity Futures Trading Commission *

www.cftc.gov

This regulatory body is mainly useful for industry news and legal matters concerning futures. Your aim in visiting it is mainly to keep half an eye on the future of futures.

Futures Net ***

www.futures.net

The main attraction of this site, which claims to be "the world's biggest and best community for futures traders," is its discussion group. While it will not be useful for all futures traders, it is a dedicated and focussed area.

Futures Online ***

www.futuresmag.com

This online version of the off-line magazine has useful and professionally written market commentary, and full articles of the magazine.

Futures Source ***

www.futuresource.com

Futures World News provides the news and market commentary for this site, which is its key feature. Worth a visit if you are looking for market commentary to see how it ties in with your needs compared to the other sites.

INO Global ***

www.ino.com

Global is correct. This is an umbrella site with ample links and its own content which taken together provide comprehensive coverage of futures and options-related materials.

Market Plex ***

www.cbot.com/mplex

This site is part of the Chicago Board of Trade's excellent web-site. Market Plex is another umbrella site and an excellent resource of information for the futures and options trader.

Options Direct *

www.options-direct.co.uk

Options Direct is actually a brokerage firm, but it provides useful information and analysis for the UK options trader. While anemic compared to US sites, if you're trading LIFFE products this site is actually one of the best!

Summary

Futures and options sites cover a wide range of underlying products because there is a wide range of products on which futures and options are available. The choice and coverage of markets is diverse for the trader and the individual considering derivatives. Because most derivatives traders tend to be more experienced than stock traders, sites tend to be more professional. There is certainly no shortage of quality information.

38

News sites: The news, and nothing but

In this chapter

Keeping up to the minute with the latest news and analysis is essential for any trader. There are some excellent sites out there to make sure you can make even Henry Kissinger seem dumb. Access to good news is especially important for the shorter term trader because we will be looking to exit at short notice. So pay close attention.

The mark of quality

A news site will have certain features, as follows:

Well-designed
Oh boy, there will be hell to pay if I can't find my way to the news quickly!

Categorized
News is a lot easier to find when it is divided into categories, e.g. technology.

Prioritized
Sites which dump every single useless bit of news are just padding out. News items need to be prioritized as to what is the most important.

Archives
A good site should let you search through archives easily, so you can conduct deeper research on a security to see, for example, if it has had good news flow for a long period.

*key   I have awarded the sites stars based on the following criteria:

*** A very good, model site that is easy to navigate and has a large selection of high-quality information

** A good site with much information of use provided in a readily accessible manner

* Some useful bits of information and worth a visit. Could come in useful

Any site below * is not listed as it is simply not recommended or the sites that are listed cover the same material better.

UK Invest ***

www.ukinvest.com/freeserve/

Great site for concise UK news and commentary. Good UK news sites that are easy to navigate are thin on the ground, so I really like this one. What is better is that it is owned, produced, designed by GlobalNet – a US company, and the Yanks do make the best sites.

BBC News **

www.news.bbc.co.uk/hi/English/business

You just cannot beat the BBC for news. Well, you can equal them if you are CNN. A well-designed, quick site for UK news. But can have a journalistic feel, as opposed to a "by traders for traders" feel.

CBS MarketWatch ***

www.marketwatch.com

Talk about information overload! Can they cram more into this site? Very detailed up-to-the millisecond news. Very well categorized.

CNNfn **

www.cnnfn.com

Relies on the the brilliance of the parent company. A very good site with good business and stocks coverage. Does cover broader business issues and that can sometimes mean wading through those to get to the meat of tradeable ideas.

Financial Times **

www.ft.com

This site seems to get better each week as Pearson pours the necessary resources into it and grows to realize it has the mother of all brands on its hands. The archive is second to none, and I highly recommend it even though you have to pay a small fee to download articles.

Reuters MoneyNet ***

www.moneynet.com

Another site by a major newswire, and, again, a great site. Good site to get a good quick feel of the news. Sometimes difficult to get older stories.

TheStreet.com ***

www.thestreet.com

The great thing about this site is that a lot of content is by traders and so has that hard insight. Even the content by journalists is very much focussed on trading for traders unlike other sites which focus on business and not the business of trading.

Bloomberg **

www.bloomberg.com

www.bloomberg.co.uk

Bloomberg provides proprietary screens for traders worldwide, and is also a very well-respected newswire, as well as TV company, and god knows what else. Focus is on worldwide news, business in particular. The site is good, with a growing number of categories. News tends to be detailed and of a very high quality. Just could do without the constant banner ad for Mike Bloomberg's book on every single page – the site is better than that.

Summary

The quality of news sites is truly tremendous. I would love to just sit in front of them and read news item after news item. Time for the Betty Ford Clinic for me, I think. But, seriously, the designs are so good that they do turn you into a news junky.

39

Online financial megasites:
Big just ain't the word

Online trader problems

- Where should I go for some quick online research about trading?
- How do I keep up to date with the latest, newest site?
- How do I get a feel for the types of sites out there for the online trader?

In this chapter

With the massive rate of growth of the internet, one problem all online traders face is knowing what new sites are popping up. This is especially important because the new sites often have valuable free information to lure traders, or are simply doing things better. Fortunately, there are a number of financial megasites that organize lots of top finance web-sites by category. They are a virtual financial *Yellow Pages* – but ecologically superior, as they don't use any yellow-dyed paper. In this chapter some of this top sites are listed and reviewed.

Which ones then?

I have listed some of the top ones in Table 39.1. They tend to be the ones many online traders and people I spoke to on bulletin boards and chat rooms congregate to according to personal experience.

Megasite	Address	Ranking	Special sections for day and short-term traders
Dow Jones Business Directory	bd.dowjones.com	**	✗
Invest-o-Rama	www.investorama.com	***	✓
Yahoo!Finance	quote.yahoo.com and country-specific sites	**	Upgrade/downgrades and earning surprises pages

Table 39.1 Top financial megasites and directories

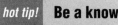 *key

I have awarded the sites stars based on the following criteria:

*** An excellent site with lots of categories and links. Very well-designed, easy to navigate and up to date

** A good site with a good selection. May have some very good features

hot tip! **Be a know-all**

Since megasites can be a great source of specialist knowledge, very quickly acquired, you should definitely bookmark them on your browser as one of your favorite sites. If anyone asks you anything about anything financial then you will be able to say, "Get back to you," scurry to the megasite and direct them to the top sites.

Dow Jones Business Directory **

`bd.dowjones.com`

A nice, slick and pretty site. What I especially like is that it rates each site according to content, speed, navigation, design, and overall score. They also kindly tell you the key reasons you may have for using the site, and provide hyperlinks to that site's key pages. Some of the categories could be more detailed, and it could do with a few more sites. Although there are sites which a day trader or short-term trader would find useful, they are not specially categorized.

Invest-o-Rama ***

www.investorama.com

Bills itself as "the most complete directory of investing sites on the web, with more than 11 754 links in 141 categories, each with a brief description." It certainly is big, and easy to navigate because of extensive sub-categories. Unfortunately, it does not have the good looks of Dow Jones Directory, or the useful reviews. The brief comments are often not independent reviews, and sometimes there ends up being effectively just a list of sites. Quite a few ads as well. Don't get me wrong, I am not trashing it – it is just so extensive that it's useful. What is more, it has a special day trading directory.

Yahoo!Finance ***

quote.yahoo.com

While being a directory is Yahoo!'s business, the links on this site do not provide enough information about the sites, which you then have to visit to make your own mind up. Nevertheless, it is comprehensive, which is what we expect from Yahoo! What is also great is that there are country-specific sites for the global short-term trader with ambitions to rule the world.

Summary

The number of very good sites a trader can turn to that offer a wide range of links appears to have decreased of late. It appears more sites want to give you proprietary content, and keep you all to themselves. A trend leading Yahoo!, which was originally a directory, of course, to spin off specialist sites such as Yahoo!Finance. The reasoning is, of course, that there is more money in proprietary content, and they may not be too bad for the viewer as long as that content is everything the links would have provided. This, however, is rarely the case.

40

Newsletters: Let me be your guru

Online trader problems

- Should I use a newsletter?
- Where do I find them, how do I know if they are any good?
- What do other online traders have to say about using newsletters?

In this chapter

Right, you've got your own strategy, but maybe you want to follow, or just observe from afar how others are doing it (a kind of trading voyeurism). In this chapter we highlight some of the benefits and disbenefits of following a newsletter. Also, if we are going to use a newsletter, how can we use it to maximum benefit, what we should be aware and beware of and which sites are best for getting hold of some good 'uns. As well as expert advice from yours truly, also included is advice from the online trading community, so you can use their cunning ideas to get the most out of newsletters.

Why should I bother?

Don't get me wrong. I am not saying you absolutely positively should use a newsletter, just that sometimes they may be a useful supplement to your own trading strategies. Newsletters can be a good source of trading strategies and ideas. A newsletter may be useful if you fall into any of the following categories:

- You're a little unsure if you are doing things right, and it would be nice to see how others are doing it.
- You are about to start trading a new product or time frame and want to get a feel for "best practice."

- You just can't come up with strategies you like, and would prefer to follow someone else's.

- You just want to see if there are better strategies than your own.

- You need an "assistant" to draw certain opportunities to your attention, but you'll decide on your own analysis whether you'll follow them or not.

- You're pretty sure of yourself, but it would be nice to get confirmation that the way your outlook on a stock or the market ties up with that of a full-time gun-totin' swaggering guru.

Warnings: Things your Mom should have told you about newsletters

Before you start giving away your hard-earned trading cash in subscription fees, here are some pointers of things to watch out for.

Published since

All other things being equal you would obviously prefer a newsletter that has been going for a few years than one which has your and the editor's mother as its first-ever subscribers.

Pages per issue

This might seem a bit extreme, but I would calculate how many dollars I am paying for each page of info. Of course, the real test is quality, not quantity, but still. . .

Delivery methods

For day traders and short-term traders, time is of the essence. Any newsletter worth its salt will know this. But just double-check how quickly you can get your grubby little paws on it after the ink has dried. In order of preference for speed: net access by password, e-mail, fax, snail mail.

Editor biography

The trading tips in the newsletter are one thing, but how qualified and experienced is the writer? (I just know you are about to flick to the "About the author" page of this book. Did the publisher leave out the details about my Nobel Prize?)

Sample issues

If you are not offered more than one free sample back issue, be very wary. Do, of course, go back over the recommendations the newsletter made and calculate how much you would have made or lost had you followed the newsletters' advice in those back issues.

hot tip!   Sample back issues should preferably be sequential, otherwise the publishers of the newsletter may just have picked out one or two of the issues which had the most accurate, best predictions where they got lucky.

Price

It's astounding how expensive some newsletters can be. Remember to add the cost of your newsletter to your trading expenses.

Trial period

Before taking out the annual subscription and after viewing the sample back issues, you will want to know if there is a trial period (e.g. 1–3 months) for which you can subscribe – just to make totally sure the newsletter is for you. Of course, there are those who would say "Stop being a wimp and just buy the darn thing." My view is that trading is about dollars, pounds, ringgit (or whatever your local mullah is), and so I will watch every penny when it comes to earning trading profits.

Periodicity

How often does the newsletter come out? Even day trading and short-term trading newsletters vary in the frequency of publication; some come out daily, with hourly phone updates, others are weekly!

Two things to watch here are how often the newsletter comes out, and how often updates (and their cost) are released.

Strategy

Probably one of the most important things to watch – does the strategies the newletter advocates and uses make sense to me and are they something I would be comfortable doing?

chat box 40.1

Goldfinger on www.dskjhf.com

Do not just accept blindly the tips presented to you. If you do that then just give all your cash to the editor and let him trade with it. Instead you should confirm what the newsletter suggests with your own independent objective analysis.

expert advice ✓ ## Jon Najarian, CEO, Mercury Trading

In the United States you see a huge number of people who subscribe to newsletters. Internet chat rooms seem to be a pretty great way for people to talk with each other to see if they find something they mesh with. Not every great trader is going to have a personality like your personality, your investment goals. So getting into these chat rooms is one way to do it.

Another way to do it is reading books and reading magazine articles to see which trader seems to have a style that would work for you. I think that an awful lot of us have a difficult time seeing how one guy makes a lot of money and applying it to ourselves. But when you finally find a guy or woman that manages money the way that you manage money and who deals with risk the way you feel comfortable with then you have got a better fit. You can't fit a round block into a square hole. I would tend to trade with someone who had a style I was comfortable with because then I am going to like coming to work every day.

Some sites where gurus exhibit their wares

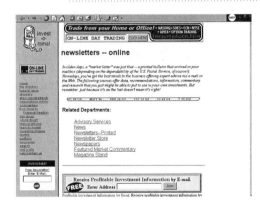

Take a look at the Invest-o-rama site (http://www.investorama.com/newsletter_online.html) for a list of newsletters and a brief description of each.

Summary

We have seen that newsletters are best used as a means of getting trading ideas which you will investigate further yourself, and as a tool for education on how the more experienced trader trades.

41

Be an online bookworm

Online trader problems

■ Thinking of entering a new market, or trading a new product (e.g. futures), or trading a new time frame?

■ Need lots of information from experts to build on your experience?

In this chapter

One of the major problems we traders face is accumulating a lot of knowledge about a topic, without having the luxury of being taught it at our merchant bank – unlike the institutional traders! I always advise online traders to read as much as possible about a subject before ploughing their ill-gotten gains into the market. When you want to research a trading topic a little deeper sometimes it is worth considering non-internet resources, namely books. Online bookstores can very often undercut normal bookstores, because of lower operating costs. In this chapter we examine looking for and buying books online.

Online stores

The best sites have several features.

Search

All the sites permit you to search for books. The better sites permit searches based on:

■ author

■ title

- subject
- publication date
- publisher
- ISBN.

Categories

Many of the online bookstores have books listed according to categories, which can help surfing if you are not quite sure what you want.

Jacket picture

I always find this helpful.

Reviews

Reviews of the book from either online readers or taken from the jacket is a useful feature.

Table of contents

Sadly, few include this, but many should, given that in a bookstore this is probably the first thing you will examine.

Synopsis

Vital, unless you know what the book is about.

E-mail notification

Some sites monitor titles similar to ones that you tell them interest you and notify you of new releases. This can be useful, or, sometimes, tedious.

Other

Since some internet bookstores are massive businesses they will often have lots of other features: guest speakers, best-seller guides, reviews from magazines, "books in the news," etc. With other sites you can pay in several different currencies. Most deliver anywhere in the world.

Things to bear in mind

When buying books online there are several pieces of advice worth bearing in mind.

Check out several sites

The price of a book between online stores can vary significantly. Bookmark or add to favorites all the bookstores listed in this chapter and check them out if you are making a purchase. Another reason to check out different stores is because the amount of information varies from site to site.

hot tip! **Mix and match**

Since the prices of books and information about a book varies between sites, why not get all you want to know from one site and place the order with another site?

Beware P&P

Prices quoted exclude postage and packaging. Some sites only tell you those charges after you have placed a provisional order. Remember to factor in the cost. Most sites offer a variety of delivery times, and if you are not in a hurry, take the slow and cheap option.

Delivery

Find out what the delivery times are. Sometimes online books can take up to three months to be delivered.

Worried about giving credit card details online?

All the sites listed in Table 41.1 should, if viewed through Internet Explorer or Netscape Navigator, encrypt and keep secure your credit card details. You can also visit the sites and view their reassurances on online security if not convinced. Some sites provide a phone number for phoning or faxing orders. Alternatively, if you are still unhappy, look for the book online and ask your local bookstore to order it from its supplier – of course, it won't be as cheap as the online order.

Name and address	Ranking	Price of *Trading Online*	Search	Categories	Jacket picture	Reviews	Table of contents	Synopsis	e-mail notification
Global Investor www.global-investor/bookshop	*** (Recommended)	$39.36	✓	✓	✓	✓	✓	✓	✓
Amazon www.amazon.com	***	$21.56	✓	✓	✓	✓	✓	✓	✓
Barnes and Noble www.barnesandnoble.com	***	$21.56	✓	✓	✓	✓	✓		✓
Internet Bookshop www.bookshop.co.uk	**	$22 (£13.81)	✓	✓	✓	✓	✓		✓
Traders Library www.traderslibrary.com	***	$26.95	✓	✓	✓	✓		✓	✓
Shopping.com www.shopping.com	** (Recommended on price)	$20.97	✓	✓	✓	✓		✓	

Table 41.1 Table of online stores

Comparisons

As you can see the price of a book can vary greatly between sites, some offering the same book at double the price. This led me to recommend Shopping.Com for price. However, the cheaper giants, such as Shopping.com and Amazon.com, may not have as many titles on trading as the more specialist stores. Many a time have I found the title I have been looking for on Global Investor when I failed to find it elsewhere.

Global Investor ***

A specialist site concentrating on trading books. Lots of innovative ideas, such as book bundles that complement each other, comments from prominent people on books they recommend, competitions. The site also gives you as much information as possible, short of giving you the book. I would like to see extracts and customer comments, however. An excellent site from which to buy your books. A useful currency converter ensures they have clients in over 100 countries worldwide. Use them myself.

Amazon.com ***

A small book company based in Seattle. You may have heard of them. They cannot provide some of the specialist content a specialist site such as Traders Library or Global Investor can, but provide cheap books, customer comments, and star ratings from readers.

Barnes and Noble ***

Another small bookstore gone online. They have one or two real bookstores, too, I believe. Price is the key attraction here, again. Somehow always seems one step behind Amazon in features.

Internet Bookshop **

One of the earliest online bookstores outside the USA. Medium sized, not a specialist trading bookstore, but useful for UK book buyers.

Traders Library ***

This site has come a very long way in the past year. Like Global Investor, seeks a competitive advantage to the big stores like Amazon on the basis it has specialist expertise in its field. This strategy works, and I get the feeling with the site that it is provided by people with a lot of knowledge about trading.

Shopping.com **

This is an AltaVista company that provides very cheap books on trading, but with limited information about them. If price is king then this store sits on the throne. However, often lacks some of the titles to be found at Global Investor and Traders Library, and the advance notice of new trading books to be found at those sites.

Summary

Thankfully, there are some excellent specialist trading sites on the web. It seems that there will continue to be a division between the supersites, such as Amazon, which have to try hard to add specialist content, and the more specialist sites like Global Investor. The latter live and breathe trading books, and so, as well as offering individual titles, they can anticipate trader needs and offer bundles of books, competitions, newsletters, software, etc. Unfortunately, the bigger sites with their clout with the publishers and distributors can offer lower prices. Hopefully, this will change soon.

42

Exchanges for e-trading information

Nobody ever achieved greatness by doing nothing. You have got to step
out and do something and take a chance and get your teeth kicked in.

Pat Arbor, Chairman of the Chicago Board of Trade,
the world's largest derivatives exchange

Online trader problem

■ Want more background on a particular trading security, e.g. futures?

In this chapter

This chapter contains all the internet sites operated by the exchanges. The best thing
about them is that they are all free.

An exchange is basically a market which trades in financial products in place of fruit, veg-
etables, meat, and fish. The financial product may well relate to those more traditional
market products, however, for instance, the Chicago Mercantile Exchange trades in
frozen concentrated orange juice futures.

Top exchange sites will have . . .

Exchanges can be a good source of free or heavily subsidized educational and background material. A good exchange site should have the following characteristics.

Exchange history/working

A section in the site where you can learn more about how the exchange came into being and why, and also how it works today, how orders are routed, the main products it deals in, etc.

Publications list

A good site should have a list of recommended reading, for both beginners and more advanced traders. It should also provide a wide variety of free educational materials, including videos and printed matter which can be ordered from the site. Where possible, I have ordered a selection of free publications to gauge their value.

Data download/quotes

Exchanges are, of course, the source for all commercial data providers and sometimes, if the exchange is on a sufficiently commercial and experienced footing, the exchange itself can be a good and efficient source of historical and daily price quotes.

hot tip! Remember the product you are interested in may be traded on several different exchanges, so if you want to know more about it, check for free information available from each of the exchanges, that way if there is something you do not understand from one of the exchange's free publications, you may understand it from another.

Market reports

Although these tend to be a little bland on exchange sites, often reporting only volume and describing chronological price changes, they can be a good way to get a better feel of what actually happened that day. Exchanges rarely attempt to place a journalistic spin on a day's market activities, leaving you to make your own mind up.

Rules

Some exchanges list their membership rules, for most readers this will be of intrigue value only.

Others

Some exchanges are beginning to realize that there is nothing stopping them developing internet sites similar to those provided by commercial financial sites, and so including charts, fundamental research, news, listing of the most active products, etc.

hot tip! Try and visit an exchange near you, and get on the mailing list. It is a great way to learn and keep abreast of developments. Also, many exchanges provide educational courses, check your nearest one – these are usually heavily subsidized by the exchange and so can be great value for money.

*key I have awarded the exchanges stars based on the following criteria:

*** A very informative site with ample free educational material, easy to navigate and a model exchange site

** A very good site with some free material. Should be informative

* Worth a visit and most traders should end up learning something about the exchange or the products it trades.

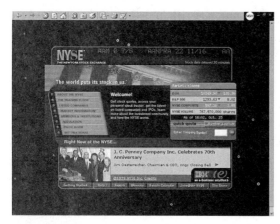

Screen 42.1

Screen 42.2

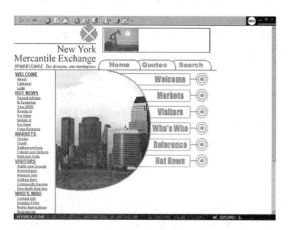

Screen 42.3

Name and web address	Rating	Products	Exchange history/ workings	Publications list	Data download quotes	Market reports	Additional comments
American Stock Exchange www.amex.com	**	Stocks and derivatives	✓	✓	✓	✗	
Arizona Stock Exchange www.azx.com	*	Stocks	✓	✗	✓	✗	
Chicago Board of Trade www.cbot.com	***	Bonds, financial futures and options, commodities	✓	✓	✓	✓	The world's largest futures and options exchange
Chicago Board Options Exchange www.cboe.com	***	Options on stocks and all futures	✓	✓	✓	✓	
Chicago Mercantile Exchange www.cme.com	***	Futures and options on financial products and commodities	✓	✓	✓	✓	The world's third largest futures and options exchange
Chicago Stock Exchange www.chicagostockex.com	**	Stocks, warrants, notes, bonds	✓	✗	✓	✗	The second largest stock exchange in the USA. A good source of free stock research information
Coffee, Sugar, and Cocoa Exchange www.csce.com	**	Futures and options on milk and coffee, sugar, cocoa	✓	✓	✓	✗	
Kansas City Board of Trade www.kcbt.com	**	Futures and options on wheat, gas, value-line stock indices	✓	✓	✓	✓	
Mid-America Exchange www.midam.com	**	Liquid futures contracts	✓	✓	✓	✗	
Minneapolis Grain Exchange www.mgex.com	*	Grain and fish futures and options	✓	✓	✓	✗	
Nasdaq Exchange www.nasdaq.com	**	Mainly technology stocks	✓	✓	✓	✓	Good basics for stock investors
New York Cotton Exchange www.nyce.com	**	Futures and options on cotton, oranges, potatoes, financials	✗	✗	✓	✓	
New York Mercantile Exchange www.nymex.com	***	Futures and options on energy, eurotop, metals	✓	✓	✓	✓	
New York Stock Exchange www.nyse.com	**	Over 2500 stocks	✓	✓	✓	✓	The largest stock exchange in the USA
Pacific Exchange www.pacificex.com	**	Stocks and options	✓	✗	✓	✗	
Philadelphia Stock Exchange www.liffe.com	***	Stocks and options on sectors, stocks, currencies	✓	✓	✓	✓	A good site for educational materials

Table 42.1 US exchanges

Name and web address	Rating	Products	Exchange history/ workings	Publications list	Data download quotes	Market reports	Additional comments
Australian Stock Exchange www.asx.com.au	**	Stocks and bonds	✓	✓	✓	✓	
Bombay Stock Exchange www.bseindia.com	**	Stocks	✗	✗	✓	✓	Portfolio manager
Deutsche Terminbörse www.exchange.de	**	Futures and options	✓	✓	✓	✗	
Hong Kong Futures Exchange www.hkfe.com	**	Futures and options on financial products	✓	✓	✓	✓	
Italian Stock Exchange www.robot1.textnet.it/finanza	*	Stocks	✗	✗	✓	✗	
Kuala Lumpur Options and Financial Futures Exchange www.kloffe.com.my	*	Financial futures and options	✓	✓	✓	✗	One of the world's newest exchanges
Kuala Lumpur Stock Exchange www.klse.com.my	**	Stocks	✓	✓	✓	✓	
Lisbon Stock Exchange www.bvl.pt	*	Stocks	✗	✗	✓	✗	
London International Financial Futures, Options and Commodites Exchange www.liffe.com	***	Futures and options on most products	✓	✓	✓	✓	The world's second largest futures exchange
London Stock Exchange www.stockex.co.uk	*	Stocks	✓	✓	✗	✗	
London Metal Exchange www.lme.co.uk	**	Metal futures and options	✓	✗	✓	✗	
Madrid Stock Exchange www.bolsamadrid.es	**	Futures and options	✓	✓	✓	✓	
MATIF www.matif.fr	**	Financial futures and options	✓	✓	✓	✗	Based in Paris
MEFF www.meff.es	**	Fixed income futures and options	✓	✓	✓	✗	Based in Barcelona. Some excellent internships
Montreal Exchange www.me.org	**	Stocks, options, and futures	✓	✓	✓	✗	
OM Stockholm www.omgroup.com	**	Futures and options	✓	✓	✓	✗	Some information in Swedish only

Table 42.2 Main exchanges from around the world

cont.

Name and web address	Rating	Products	Exchange history/ workings	Publications list	Data download quotes	Market reports	Additional comments
Paris Stock Exchange www.bourse-de-paris.fr	**	Stocks	✓	✓	✓	✗	
South African Futures Exchange www.safex.co.za	**	Futures and options	✓	✓	✓	✗	
Santiago Stock Exchange www.bolsantiago.cl/ingles	**	Stocks, futures and options	✓	✓	✓	✗	
Singapore International Monetary Exchange www.simex.com.sg	***	Futures and options	✓	✓	✓	✓	
Sydney Futures Exchange www.sfe.com.au	*	Futures and options	✓	✓	✓	✗	
Tokyo Grain Exchange www.tge.or.jp	**	Commodity futures and options	✓	✓	✓	✓	
TIFFE www.tiffe.or.jp	**	Futures and options	✓	✓	✓	✗	
Tokyo Stock Exchange www.tse.or.jp	**	Stocks, options, futures	✓	✗	✓	✗	
Vancouver Stock Exchange www.vse.com	*	Stocks	✓	✓	✓	✓	
Warsaw Stock Exchange yogi.ippt.gov.pl/gielda/gielda	*	Stocks	✗	✗	✓	✗	

Table 42.2 *cont.*

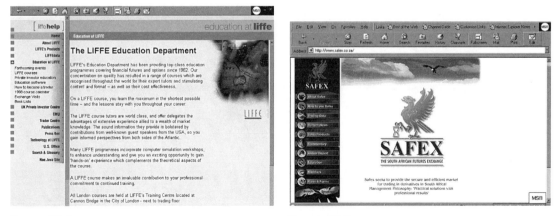

Screen 42.4

Screen 42.5

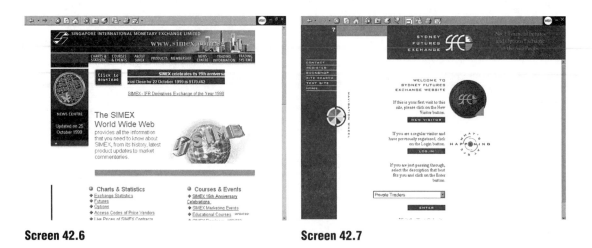

Screen 42.6   **Screen 42.7**

Summary

In many respects, the world's exchanges are an often forgotten source of top-notch information. They are improving all the time, and beginning to recognize their unique position and role on the financial internet. Unlike commercial sites, these sites are funded with the non-profit motive of encouraging trading. I feel added comfort when using these sites.

Essential trading psychology for online trading

43

The trading psychology of risk and money management

Bernard Oppetit and risk aversion

As part of my endeavors to discover the traits of the leading traders in the world and what they can teach the rest of us, I interviewed **Bernard Oppetit**, Global Head of Equity Derivatives at Paribas. This part of the interview focusses on risk and money management – two essential components to trading success.

Paribas, part of Groupe Paribas, is an international wholesale bank with a presence in over 60 countries. Groupe Paribas has total assets exceeding $269 billion. Bernard Oppetit is a slim, tall, and pensive Frenchman.

Bernard Oppetit deals mainly with equity derivatives, options, and index options, in all developed markets, and a selected number of emerging markets such as Brazil, Argentina, Mexico, most of South East Asia, and now Hungary and Poland. He specializes in risk arbitrage, which involves trading stocks which are likely to be active due to special situations such as litigation, etc.

However, what Oppetit has to teach on trading applies to all instruments.

Great traders tend to be risk-averse

The public perception of traders, propagated by trading scandals, is that they are attracted to wild risks and take massive gambles. Of all the traders I interviewed for this book, not one claimed to be risk loving.

Oppetit details the contrary view:

I am very risk-averse. I would definitely take the certainty of making $10 000 dollars than the 10 percent chance of making $100 000. In terms of economics, my personal utility function is very much concave.

When we speak of risk in trading we are, of course, discussing price volatility. Price volatility cannot be discussed without an idea of probability. The probability of a stock's price reaching your target can be derived from the historic price volatility of the particular stock. Consequently, risk, price volatility, and probability go hand in hand. Good traders wait until the probability of a favorable move is the greatest and the risk of an unfavorable move the lowest. Moreover, unlike non-professional traders, the great trader knows that risk and reward are not always directly proportional. There are very low risk and yet high reward trades.

Oppetit continues:

The important thing is to look at risk in a rational way, and an imaginative way. A good trader knows how and when to take risk and how and when to avoid risk. There are risks which should be taken and risks which should not be taken. The game is to distinguish between the two. You do not need to risk a lot to profit a lot. There are a lot of trades where you can make a lot of money which are not particularly risky. You may have to invest a lot of your time to do research and discover what is going on, but the actual money you invest may not be at much risk.

There is a joke about an economics professor who is walking in New York with a friend. His friend notices a $100 bill on the sidewalk and points to the bill and says, "Look professor, a $100 bill." The economics professor replies, "No that can not be so, if that was a $100 bill somebody would have picked it up already." Still I believe there are opportunities to make money with very little risk.

Analyzing risk and probability

So, how does Bernard Oppetit analyze risk and probability when he examines a position?

Even though I know I will get out after a certain loss, I consider the amount I have risked as the whole amount invested. Also, I look to see what percentage probability there is of a certain percentage rise and I compare that to the risk I am taking. I would look at some kind of distribution of possible outcomes, such as a 50 percent chance of doing something special, or a 50 percent chance of doing nothing in particular, or a 50 percent chance of a small loss against a 50 percent chance of a great gain. There has to be some idea of the distribution of outcomes.

What Bernard Oppetit does when analyzing a potential trade is to consider at risk the whole amount he is trading with. This is even if he knows that he will exit the position if the price falls by, say, 15 percent and, therefore, he would only risk losing 15 percent of his stake.

He then examines the reward. He measures reward by examining the probabilities of various outcomes. You can only gain an idea of the reward if you examine the probability of it occurring.

Bernard Oppetit would then compare the risk with the reward. For instance, an options position opened with $10 000 would place $10 000 at risk. To get an idea of his risk and reward ratio, Bernard Oppetit would then examine the likely outcomes and their probabilities. This would give him some idea of the reward he may get for the risk he is taking. (If he were being very mathematical he would sum the products of all the outcomes and their corresponding probabilities, and compare this figure to the amount risked.)

Money management

Good risk analysis and management is not only about volatility and probability, it is also about good money management.

As Oppetit explains:

You have to have good money management. You have to ensure you are not going to be hopelessly underwater. You can have rules like maximum drawdown or value at risk or limits. You can also have your own internal rules like "this is too much money to lose." You must have that in your mind and that you are not going to risk more than that at any one time. You have to make sure you are left in the game. That is very important. Once this is clearly established you need fear, you need to feel that things can very quickly go wrong.

In devising a money management plan, you should consider the following:

■ What is the most money I will risk on any single trade at any one time, i.e. what is too much to be lost?

■ What amount must I avoid losing on a trade, given that I might lose on a consecutive number of trades, so that I do not become in serious danger of being out of the game?

■ Once in the trade, what is the maximum percentage I am prepared to lose before exiting? Some decide this based on "value at risk," i.e. a mathematical calculation based upon the probabilities of various outcomes of all open positions, and hence the value of money at risk of the positions.

Facing a loss

When sitting on a paper loss a trader will indubitably experience immense pressure and fear.

Oppetit continues:

It is very important to experience this fear to ensure you do not end up in that situation again. Fear is also a bad thing in that it will affect your judgment, in the same way elation would affect your judgment. You have to take a very neutral approach.

So, experience the fear when faced with a loss, do not deny it. But use the fear as a means of loss prevention in future, not as a cause of ever-increasing losses. When looking at a new price you do not focus on the fear of how much you have lost, or the hope it may turn around:

You have to ask, if you are a buyer at this new price, if you didn't own it already, would you buy it? If the answer is no, then I sell it. You have to look at the position with an open mind, and ask if you would put it on today if you did not already have it. If new information came in while I had an open position, I would change my expectations. But you have to be honest with yourself. It is a question of attitude. It is an easy trap to fall into to kid yourself that you are holding onto something because you believe things have changed and it will now rise. It comes back to being honest with yourself.

Handling a profit

As well as hope, another damaging emotion surrounding open positions which prevents an honest analysis, is that an unrealized profit may vanish:

It is a cliché that you cut your losers and ride your winners – but it is very true. Most people and many traders do the opposite. There is a desire to take profits, sometimes encouraged by accounting rules. Many people look at their unrealized gains as non-existent. They think taking profit is making real profit and it is unreal before then. They feel taking a loss is an admission of being wrong.

Again, this emotional attitude to profits has to be eradicated.

Instead of focussing on whether he was right or wrong, Bernard Oppetit focusses on his expectations regarding a position, in order to maintain objectivity:

If what I had expected to happen does not happen then I know to get out. Whether I get out at a profit or loss does not matter. As soon as I realize my scenario was wrong I get out. Another easy case is when everything I expected happened, so I take my profits. Those are the two easy case, and everything in between is difficult.

What Bernard Oppetit is discussing is that all open positions have to be viewed objectively. That means you have to focus on certain questions and reasons and ignore others.

You need to focus on these points:

■ Has what you expected to happen happened?
■ Are you a buyer or a seller at this price?
■ Is the probability of what you expected to occur still the same as when you placed the trade?

You have to ignore:

- How much of a loss you are sitting on.
- How much of a profit you are sitting on.
- How much you paid for the position.
- The fact that the position may turn around.

Risk advice from Pat Arbor

Risk taking is older than literature. As far back as 3500 BC the Mahabharat, the holy scriptures of the world's oldest religion, Hinduism, describes a game of chance played with dice on which kingdoms were wagered. Little wonder then, as Peter Bernstein states in *Against the Gods* (Wiley, 1998): "The modern conception of risk is rooted in the Hindu-Arabic numbering system that reached the West seven to eight hundred years ago."

Dealing with risk is part and parcel of being a trader, and many traders great and small will have their own ideas about risk management. But what precisely is the relationship of the great trader to risk? What would an experienced trader such as **Pat Arbor**, former chairman of the Chicago Board of Trade, the world's largest derivatives exchange, have to say about risk?

Risk: Why take it?

"Nobody ever achieved greatness by doing nothing. You have got to step out and do something and take a chance and get your teeth kicked in. A good trader has to engage in some acts which are considered risky," says Arbor.

As Pat Arbor explains great traders take risks and manage risks:

I think a great trader certainly has to have a psychological stability about themselves, but not too much stability, because one has to have a certain flair for risk. It is a fine psychological blend you have got to look for in a trader; the ability to take risk, the ability to have some courage, coupled with stability in the psychological make-up. I think the great traders have to have a greater appetite for risk than the normal person or the poorer traders. Then the question is how they manage that risk, the discipline they impose on themselves to manage that risk.

In most cases the risk is balanced. In my own trading I have always tried to be a spreader or arbitrageur. If I am long one month soybeans then I am generally short another month soybeans. And I generally do soybeans or bond spreads. If I am long bonds then I am short 10-year notes. Sometimes if I am long a commodity outright, then I might be long corn and short soybeans or long soybeans and short corn.

You also spread because you may not be prepared for the straight position. You may like the position, you may be bullish on the position, and it may not be going well. You would like to maintain your position, possibly moderate it a little, by selling something against it. You may be long soybeans outright, and you can neutralize it a little by selling soybean meal, or soybean oil or some corn against it. Your S&P position may not be going so well and you may want to sell bonds against it. You are keeping your position but cutting your profit potential. Of course, you could just take the loss. But where you may not do that and have a spread instead is where you think you are right and like the position then you tend to neutralize it a little bit to mitigate the loss.

Spreading or hedging as a form of risk management is not necessarily suited to everyone, as Pat Arbor explains.

Finding a style to fit

As a trader you must decide what you are. You are either a speculator, spreader, or local scalper. You have to fit into one of those categories. Me, I am suited to spreading.

To find what suits his personality, he just has to see whether or not he makes money at what he's doing. I have had people come into the office, saying, "I am a great trader," I say, "You're right," they say, "Know how to trade." I say again, "You're right" and they say, "I predicted that the market was going to go up or down," and I say again, "You are right. But the bottom line is whether you make any money."

So, while hedging can be a good way to manage risk, whether or not you wish to be a hedger depends on what trading style makes money for you given the type of trading personality you are.

From small acorns: progressive trading

Progressive trading is the name I have given to the idea that the best trading results and long-term profitability are assured through a "slow and steady" style of trading. I have yet to meet a great trader that advocates wild risks in order to make spectacular home runs.

As Pat Arbor continues:

The best traders I think are those who try to make a little bit every day. You surely have your success stories; those that hit home runs, but if you take a record or study of the home run hitters against those that try to hit singles every day, the success rate of the former is a lot less than the latter. So a good trader ends up being one who accumulates capital over a period of time.

I remember once explaining this to a young Italian trader and I said to him, it's una fagiola (one bean) a day. If you try to put one bean in a bag per day, then at the end of the month you are going to have 31 beans in the bag. But if you try to put all 31 beans through the mouth of the bag you will spill a few, and in some cases you will not get any of them in. So, it is better to build it up one day at a time, in a small manner, slowly. It's tempting not to do that when you see the George Soros, but if you live by the trading sword, you die by the trading sword.

Implicit in Pat Arbor's advice about "progressive trading" is the idea that it is all right to be out of the market:

The discipline not to trade, that's a big one. A lot of people don't realize that. A lot of people think you should stand there all day long and be in the market all day long. There are times when the market is so dead or so illiquid that you should not be trading. There are times when the market is terribly volatile and makes no sense and you should not be trading. It is generally the former, though. I have seen people stand there all day long when there is nothing going on, just a few locals in the pit. They will put a position on out of boredom. Then they can't get out of it easily. I say to them, "Well, you shouldn't be trading. There's nothing going on. Take it easy. Take a walk. Go off to the coffee shop."

I think I'll go for a coffee now.

Risk aversion: Risk not thine whole wad

Trading is about risk. Risk can be bought and sold like any other commodity. Derivatives are one instrument through which risk is transferred. The great trader has a deep understanding of the nature of risk, but, perhaps most surprisingly, is risk-averse; he takes out insurance against being wrong. Moreover, he balances risk with his own personality to produce a harmony between the two; never being so exposed as to feel uncomfortable and let it affect his trading.

Six feet tall, a muscular physique and bald save for a pony tail – that is **Jon Najarian** by appearance. In 1989 Jon Najarian formed Mercury Trading, a designated primary market maker, responsible for maintaining a market in stocks for which it had been designated. Two years later, it reported a return on capital of 415 percent. Today it is the second most active market maker on the CBOE.

As he is a highly profitable trader, I wanted to know what he would have to advise other traders about risk.

Perceptions of trading risks

As Najarian explains:

I am very risk-averse. You have probably seen on people's walls, "Risk not thine whole wad." We always try to position ourselves so that we can always trade tomorrow. That is the single most important thing. Not making money today, making money today is not more important than being able to come back tomorrow. If I want to be short the market, because I think they are going to raise rates and that will pressure the market, will I be naked short? No, we are long puts and every day that goes by and the market drops, we buy a ton of calls so that if the market turns and goes up we do not lose all the money that we made by being right. You only get so many times a year to be right. But we always want to lock in the profits so we are constantly rolling down out hedge and never just one way long or short.

Many days when placing a spread or a hedge, we think, "god, if someone had tied me up in a closet we would have made a fortune, because as the stock was falling we were taking profits all the way down." Well that is just the curse of being a hedger. It is also the reason why we sleep the way we sleep every night.

Because Najarian knows he has disaster protection insurance, he can be more at ease:

When you come in after a weekend where the market was down 148 points, it looks ugly, they were having trouble finding buyers all day, then if I am stuck in a position I could be very panicked. But we sleep like babies.

Any temptation to go for home runs?

It is comforting to know that the top traders have the same bad trading temptations as the rest of us:

Sure, there are times when we wished that we were not as disciplined. But more times than not we were glad that we were disciplined. We see so many people bet for home runs by putting all their marbles on a big shot. When we bet on a big move we do it with a controlled amount of risk even though we are betting for a home run. We are buying a lot of out-of-the money puts and we are selling out-of-the money puts as well as a hedge against the puts we are buying. If we say we are buying some puts for $4 and selling other puts for $2 then we only have $2 worth of risk. So I can stay at the table twice as long. The other guy, who is unhedged, is starting to gag when the market is going against him, but we can stay with the trade longer.

Since the hedge provides Jon Najarian with a comfort zone, he can be free to exercise clearer judgment. Imagine the last time you were panicked by an adverse price move. Did it ruin your day? Did it plague your mind? Did it affect other trading decisions? If so, have you considered hedging you position? You will, of course, have to examine the cost elements of hedging and the extent you may wish to be hedged. Risk is a beautiful thing, with ingenuity you can purchase or sell just the precise amount of risk:

The other thing we look at is the buyers and sellers. Again, on the derivatives side we see Salomon, Morgan Stanley, Lehman, NatWest buying, buying, buying a certain stock and we know they are betting on the upside, too. So, we are reading all these tea leaves as well. We see that the chart pattern looks good, institutional buyers are coming in – is there anything in the news? Are there earnings coming up, has anybody commented on it favorably, is there a new product coming out, is there a lawsuit pending? We look at all those things so that by the time we actually place the bet we probably have a huge edge because of all those factors we looked at, that our winning percentage is off the charts. Most people do not have the benefit of seeing all that information so what they have to do is give themselves the chance of being as right as possible.

It follows from this that when Jon Najarian does enter a trade he wants the upside to be far greater than the downside, even if the downside move is highly improbable:

The worst I do is a 1:1 risk reward ratio. Most of the time I want a 2:1 or 3:1 reward to risk ratio. So if I think it could go to $35 then I sell at a loss, if I am wrong at $29 or $28 so that I have a multiple risk reward ratio on the upside. If I am wrong I cut the trade and move on.

You cannot be willing to say I am going to ride this stock down to $20 if I am wrong, but I am going to make $5 if I am right. If you do that kind of thing you are just not going to be in business very long.

I would never put a multiplier on the risk to the downside. I would never say that although there is $5 on the upside, I am so confident that I am willing to take a $10 risk to the down side. It would not be acceptable risk.

Few people would associate such a risk-averse, belt and braces approach with a trader, let alone a great trader. However, risk aversion and caution are the hallmarks of great traders. While many of us may have a strong appreciation of this, it can never hurt to be reminded.

The equation using other people's funds

Many traders dream of going it alone and managing money. So what are the pitfalls that a private trader working for himself should be aware of when competing against the institutions?

Bill Lipschutz is an institutional investor who went it alone and set up his own company. Lipschutz was Global Head of Currency Trading at Salomon Brothers at the end of the 1980s. If ever there were a right time and a right place for a trader, that was it — then and there.

Over the eight years he was there, Bill Lipschitz earned for his employer an average of $250 000 profit each and every trading day. Here is a man who knows his trading.

It's not all the same money: source and effect

Bill left Salomon in 1990 and currently has a company called Hathersage Capital Management, focussing on FX Trading.

It is often not realized that the source of trading funds can affect one's trading style and performance. As Bill Lipschutz explains, this fact is something even the most able traders do not appreciate until they experience it:

I was unaware that there were these differences. Seven years ago, I had a naive view that you get the money from here, or from Salomon Brothers" proprietary capital, whether it is ten high net worth individuals or a fund of funds I felt it was all the same; let me see how much I can extract from the market.

The whole money management game is a difficult game. It has not only to do with how well you perform, but what kinds of results people are looking for in their portfolios. Absolute performance is a real misleading thing. I can say to you, "We were up 600 percent" over five years in our most aggressive program, and you might say, "Wow, 600 percent." But that does not necessarily mean that much in and of itself, without knowing how well other currency-only managers performed. For example, say a guy is managing $200 million, and $120 million of it is a fund that he runs with a very specific mandate. If he made 600 percent over four years in that particular fund, he may have people pulling money out from that particular fund, because they are nervous, because that really was not the kind of variance they were looking for. So, it is very complicated.

As Lipschutz explains, one way the source of funding can affect your trading style is through the motivation of the lender and the terms on which the funds were granted. We all, as traders, seek more capital with which to trade. Whatever the source of money, you must be aware that since it can affect your trading style it may also affect your trading performance. The worst time to have a deterioration in your trading performance is when the money is not your own:

But, now when you have to charge clients, the client says to you, "I know you are a speculative guy, or you can be a speculative guy, I am willing to lose 20 percent." I have sat with clients, and we try to talk with our clients and really understand what they want. If a guy looks me in the eye and says, "I can be down 20 percent, no problem," I know he really means 5 percent, because if you call him in three days and say, "You know what, you're down 18 percent, I just wanna know how you feel, so we can discuss what to do from here," he's going to forget he ever said he was comfortable with a 20 percent loss.

Regardless of what they say, because they are not traders, they don't understand, they certainly do intellectually, I am not trying to take anything from them, but they don't understand it emotionally, necessarily, what they are getting into. When you are charged with other people's money you have to help them and not let them get into something they are not emotionally ready for yet.

Sometimes, being wrong, even if there is a 5 percent chance of that happening, is a whole lot worse than being right, even if there is a 95 percent chance of that. It's the old, "Gee, if I make 25 percent for these guys, they'll be really happy, and they'll think I am a great trader and I'll earn big fees." "But you know what, if I lose 5 percent for these guys they're going to pull that money out and I am going to be close to being out of business." But that is not the probability of the trade succeeding or failing. So you have to lay this on top of the probability of the trade succeeding or failing. It is very complicated. It's a whole set of simultaneous constraints that you have to solve at once.

Therefore, trading with other people's money becomes far more complicated than with one's own. You have to consider both the likely outcome of the trade and the likely reaction of the investor to a positive and a negative trading outcome. The decisions you can make are restricted by the likely responses of your client. That, in turn, could impinge upon your trading performance.

A checklist

So, before taking on new funds, ask yourself the following questions:

1 What does the lender *say* he expects?

2 What does he *really* expect?

3 Have I traded successfully in the past *in the manner required* by the lender's expectations?

4 Can I *deliver* what the lender really expects?

5 What are the consequences for me if I *fail* to deliver?

6 How much *control* does the lender want?

7 How *frequently* is the lender going to inquire about the performance?

8 What type of *personality* has the lender? Is he likely to pester and aggravate?

9 Can some *ground rules* be set?

44

Top trading psychology tips from leading traders of the world

In this chapter

This chapter contains a list and summary of the main traits my interviewing the leading traders exemplified.

Opportunity knocks the door down

Since kindergarten each of us is taught to grab our opportunities for they do not knock twice. It is precisely that type of advice, which is so useful in other walks of life, that is detrimental in trading.

Many traders, armed with their trading plan or strategy, will often hastily and prematurely enter a trade. Their decision is often driven by fear; the fear of the missed opportunity. Their mind will be screaming, "Quick get on the trade, you're going to miss it, so what if all your criteria for entering a trade have not been met? Most of them have, so get on, the big traders wouldn't hang around."

The inevitable result is that the trade will not be profitable or not as profitable as it would have been had the trader waited for the precise moment to strike.

In trading the fear of the missed opportunity leads to many avoidable losses. And the game of trading is as much about avoiding losses as about capturing profits. The leading traders have a different perspective on opportunity. Counter-intuitively, they know opportunity knocks once, twice, and then kicks the door down. They know that if this trade does not feel absolutely perfect, there will be another one along in a short while that will. That knowledge alleviates and overrides any fear. That knowledge is the key to unlocking greater profits by waiting for all the trade entry criteria to be met, and not cutting corners.

Bill Lipschutz summed it up when he said:

Out of 250 trades in a year, it comes down to five, three of those will be wrong and you will lose a fortune and two will be right and you will make a fortune; for the other 245 trades – you should have been sitting on your hands.

Great traders tend to be risk-averse

There is a general perception, once again more propagated by life than trading experiences, that one needs to risk a lot to profit a lot. Every one of the traders I interviewed stated unequivocally that he was risk-averse. As Bernard Oppetit, Global Head of Equity Derivatives at Banque Paribas put it: "You do not need to risk a lot to profit a lot." Jon Najarian, CBOE Director and the Chairman of Mercury Trading put it similarly: "Making money today is not more important than being able to come back tomorrow."

Pat Arbor, Chairman of the Chicago Board of Trade, warned against going for the "home run." His trading philosophy is based on "*una fagiola*"; one bean at a time into the bag. As one of the most experienced and successful traders on CBOT, he insists that trying to put lots of "beans into the bag" at once will result in most not going in. He counsels that the steady approach will result in far more profits in the longer run.

The message is to wait, and wait for a high-probability trade in the knowledge that they do exist and can lead to as great a profit as more risky trades. Moreover, the danger of riskier trades is not only a loss, but also such a loss that you have no funds left.

Luck: Stacking the odds

Following on from the nature of traders as being risk-averse, they have a knack for stacking the odds. As Lipschutz puts it: "I happen to believe that by far the biggest component of trading success is luck, it's not the rolling the dice type of luck, but stacking the odds." These top traders practice their risk aversion by ensuring the odds of a successful outcome are heavily stacked in their favor.

This is not only done by ample research and planning, but also recognizing, when they are in a good trade to "push their luck." As David Kyte, Chairman of the Kyte Group and the largest local on LIFFE put it: "You do not step in the way of a train that's going at full steam." Najarian and Kyte both said: "You make your own luck in this game," meaning that you stack the odds of making a profitable trade by planning and waiting until all your trade entry criteria are satisfied, if then the trade does prove to be as lucrative as it promised you "push your luck" by perhaps adding to the position and riding it for all it is worth.

The emotional problem

Traders' attitude to their potential and existing positions is often a great determinant of success. As every trader knows, the moment a trade is executed, everything is different. That is the point at which it becomes real, no longer digits on a screen and numbers in an account. Now expectation is joined by anticipation. The brain is joined by the heart. Reason is joined by emotion. You exchange detachment for attachment.

When you have an open position and you are looking to close it, you will either have a profit or a loss. The emotions relating to each are quite different. For instance, when sitting on a loss many traders experience hope that the position will turn around because they fear and deny that it may not. It is for you to recognize these emotions and to discard them. Your judgment has to be based on detached reason relating to your analysis of the company.

How you behave once you have an open position is all important. Without clear thinking, you could exit too soon or too late. Your key concern with an open position is timing your exit. Of course, there are times when you are deciding whether to add to a position, but generally you are concerned with exit. With an open position you are concerned with closing the position. In order to do that an open position requires an open mind.

As Oppetit puts it:

The key is to be intellectually honest. You have to think of every day as a clean slate. You've got to forget about your loss or how much you paid you have to treat each day as a completely new day. You have to start everyday with a blank page. Mark to market should be the rule so you start each day afresh. There is no expected profit or loss on the book so you have to start from scratch each morning.

P**s poor planning produces pathetic performance

Although an SAS motto, this statement is equally applicable to trading. Top traders do not trade "by the seat of their pants." Planning and its benefits are a key aspect to the way they view the markets. The top traders plan "what if" scenarios and think about their response to each probable outcome. The main benefits are that with plan in hand or in mind the trader's confidence is enhanced, fear of loss reduced and that in turn assists clear thinking and removal of hope so ensuring the trader stays focussed on his original reason for entering the trade.

Oppetit summed this up well when he said: "Whether I get out at a profit or loss does not matter." Martin Burton, founder and Managing Director of Monument Derivatives and former director of NatWest Markets was talking about the same thing when he said:

"It is not a 90-minute game." They both know that sticking to their plan is far more important than temporary blips in their profit and loss accounts.

Losses: A curious view

The top traders are totally at ease with losing. This is not something one expects from those at the top of their profession. Although true in other walks of life, that perfection is to be striven for, in trading perfection is not an option. Paul RT Johnson, Vice President at ING Securities and a Director on CBOT said bluntly: "You are going to be wrong. You are not perfect."

The top traders cut their loss and move on. The issue is not whether the market may turn around if they hang in there. They cut their loss if it is what they say they will do in their plan. They get out at the predetermined level. The discipline of sticking to the plan is primary and the real issue. To say "cut your losses short" misses the whole point and is of no help to anyone. By cutting their loss they can free up capital to place in more profitable positions elsewhere, and free up mental energy to focus on new opportunities. Pat Arbor summed it up by saying: "Your first loss is your best loss." Jon Najarian has a saying as to why cutting losses was so important: "You can't eat like a bird and s**t like an elephant."

Conclusion

It is not possible to do justice to the wisdom and accumulated experiences of the world's leading traders in a short chapter. However, I have tried to convey how their minds work in a way that apparently runs against common intuition. These differing perspectives ensure that with the same tools and products to trade with as anyone else they make far more in profits because their minds are different.

Section 9

Appendices

The basics of futures: Meet the Dow Jones and the S&P 500s

Online trader problem

■ Would like a broad overview about futures before finding out more and considering further whether to trade them online.

In this appendix

Many people are intrigued by futures; this is a painless guide to those derivatives. Remember to see the recommended reading, the exchanges sites in Chapter 48, and the futures and options sites in Chapter 43.

Objective

■ A thorough basic understanding of futures for future study.

What is a futures contract?

A futures contract has several features:

■ It is a legally binding contract.

■ It is usually traded through a recognized exchange (e.g. Chicago Mercantile Exchange).

■ One party agrees to *take* delivery and the other party agrees to *make* delivery of the underlying asset.

■ The specific *quality* and *quantity* of the underlying asset to be delivered is agreed in advance.

- The *date* of delivery is fixed in advance.
- The *price* of delivery is fixed in advance.
- The *place* of delivery is fixed in advance.

In other words, a futures contract is simply an agreement to deliver a specific quantity and quality of an asset at a predetermined price, place, and date. If you are "long" a futures contract then you have bought a futures contract and so are the party that will take delivery. You may already have entered into very similar contracts; ever bought something and asked for it to be delivered? If you are "short" a futures contract then you have sold a futures contract, and so are the party that will make delivery.

The product range

Today futures are available on:

Metals: silver, gold, copper, platinum

Energy: crude oil, heating oil, natural gas, unleaded gasoline

Wood: lumber

Index futures: NYSE Index, S&P 500 Stock Index, US dollar Index, CRB Futures Index, Municipal Bond Index

Currencies: British pound, dollar, French franc, Eurodollars, Swiss franc, Deutschmark, Japanese yen, Canadian dollar

Interest rates: treasury bonds, treasury bills, treasury notes, Eurodollars

Foods and fibers: coffee, cocoa, sugar, cotton, orange juice

Meats: live cattle, feeder cattle, hogs, pork bellies

Grains: wheat, corn, oats, soybean complex

For every futures contract the most important information is:

- minimum contract size, e.g. 100 troy ounces of gold per contract
- how the price is expressed, e.g. $ per ounce
- effect of minimum tick movement, e.g. a $1 move in the contract price equals $100 difference in profit/loss per contract.

So, for example, a typical futures contract might look like this:

Cattle (CME); 40 000 pounds; cents per pound,
quoted at 72 for December delivery.

What this means is that each cattle futures contract on the Chicago Mercantile Exchange is for 40 000 pounds of live cattle, and prices are expressed in cents per pound. The price of 72 means 72 cents per pound. Therefore, a 1 cent price move causes a $400 change in equity (i.e. 1 cent × 40 000).

Note, however, that only about 1 percent of all futures contracts are held until delivery; they are usually "closed" before then. That is, an equal and opposite futures trade is made which cancels out your delivery obligations. The reasons vary as to why most futures contracts are not held to delivery, but the major reason is that the futures contract is used for speculation and one does not care about the underlying asset, and also because the future is used as a hedge (see glossary).

Futures contracts are available in hard and soft commodities, such as various types of grain and metals. There are also futures in financial products, such as interest rates, currencies and indices.

---

example

Gold futures contracts are traded on the New York Commodity Exchange (COMEX).

Minimum contract size is 100 troy ounces.

Price expressed in $/oz.

Therefore, a $1 change in the contract is worth $100.

		$/oz	Contract value	Margin
May 2	Bought one contract COMEX gold June delivery	342	$34 200	$2000
May 23	Sold one contract COMEX gold June delivery	352	$35 200	

Profit is $1000 on an initial margin of $2000. That is, $10 per oz across 100 ounces that a contract consists of.

Futures on the Dow Jones Industrial Average

Probably the most widely recognised index in the world is the Dow Jones Industrial Average. Moreover, it is very easy to track, given that every newspaper, TV and radio station in the world that carries financial news carries news about the Dow, with the possible exception of the *All-Baghdad Finance Show*. Yet until quite recently you could not trade the futures on the index – they did not exist. Now for everyone who has an opinion on the future direction of the Dow Jones, and let's face it, who doesn't, you can put you mullah where your opinion is.

The DJIA

The Dow Jones Industrial Average represents a portfolio of 30 large cap blue-chip stocks traded on the New York Stock Exchange. It includes companies such as Microsoft and GE. They represent about one-fifth of the market value of all US stocks!

DJIA futures – salient features

Unit of trading
$10 times the DJIA. So with the index at say 11 500, holding one futures contract is the same as investing $115 000 in the DJIA portfolio. So, for every point it rises the long, holder makes $10.

Minimum price fluctuation
One point ($10).

Trading hours
8.15am to 3.15pm Chicago time.

Contract months
March, June, September, December.

Last trading day
The trading day preceding the third Friday of the contract month.

Ticker
DJ.

S&P 500 Futures

Like the Dow, the S&P is also a very widely recognized, and well-reported index. On this index, too, you can buy options. The S&P 500 Index is based on the stock prices of 500 different companies. The market value of these companies represents around 80 percent of the value of all stocks on the New York Stock Exchange.

One S&P 500 futures contract is the same as owning $250 multiplied by the futures price. So, with the index at 1100, the value of the contract is $275 000. A change in the price by the minimum tick possible, $0.1, would change the value of the contract by 0.1 x $250 = $25.

Why are there futures contracts?

In the USA, between the Great Lakes, and the grain-growing, livestock-rearing Great Plains, lies Chicago. A natural port for access to the world's markets for most American farmers. Chicago soon became and remains the home of the largest commodities exchanges in the world.

Picture Chicago in the 1850s: As a farmer growing wheat in rural America each harvest I reap the rewards of my annual toils. I sell most of my wheat to a few farmers who use it to feed their livestock. Each year I pray for wheat prices to rise, so that I may make greater profits when it comes to sell my wheat, and each year I worry that the prices might fall. Each year, the farmers pray for bumper crops so that the price might fall and their costs drop, and each year they worry that the price might rise. Then, while in our respective fields it occurs to us to fix our prices several months in advance so that we may plan ahead. While we are at it, we should also fix when, where, and what quality our wheat should be. What we have stumbled across is the futures contract.

Essentially, the futures contract was created to meet a business need. That need still exists today: the need for certainty in an uncertain world. The futures contract permitted hedges (i.e. protection) against adverse price movements by fixing the sale price today. Of course, it soon occurred to some non-farmers in stripey shirts, braces, slicked back hair and fast red Italian and German sports cars that futures could also be used to speculate.

How are futures prices fixed?

A future is a derivative. That is, its price is derived from the price of the underlying asset it refers to. A gold future's price is derived from the price of gold. The cash or spot price of the underlying asset is the price at which the underlying asset is currently being bought and sold in the market. The price of the cash asset changes with supply and demand. The futures price responds to changes in the spot price.

Obviously, at delivery, the futures price and the spot price are the same. If they were not then you could buy one and sell the other for instant profit (arbitrage). Before delivery, the futures price equals the cash price plus the cost of holding the cash commodity until delivery. A little thought makes it clear why this must be so. If it were not so, suppose the futures price of wheat is high relative to the cash price of wheat, you could buy the cash wheat – store it, and pay interest on the money you borrowed to pay for it – and sell ("go short") the future (i.e. promise to deliver the wheat in the future). Basically your costs (of buying and storing the wheat) would be less than your receipts (from selling the wheat) and you would make a profit:

Price, above cash wheat price, of wheat future per bushel for delivery in 1 month	20¢
Costs of holding cash wheat per bushel for 1 month	13¢

Therefore, sell the future and buy the cash stock. Deliver the cash stock against the future in one month. Locked in profit = 7¢ per bushel

What is margin?

Initial margin is a small fraction of the contracts value paid at the time the position is opened. For example, to trade a futures contract worth $20 000 may require initial margin of $2000, just 10 percent of contract value. A 5 percent movement in the contract value, i.e. $1000, would result in a gain or loss of 50 percent of the sum invested. This is what is meant by leverage. Margin requirements are set by the exchange.

Variation margin is the further payments that need to be made if the price moves adversely.

Speculation

A futures speculator is like a speculator in any other asset. He seeks to profit from price changes. How he comes to decide what price changes are likely is his business; there as many different methods as traders. A trader may think that the UN is about to relax oil sanctions against Iraq and so the price of oil likely to fall. As we saw earlier, all other things being equal, if the price of the cash commodity falls then the price of the future is also likely to fall. Consequently, our trader may short oil futures. However, he will have to be careful that there are not counter-vailing price-raising forces which may swamp the effects of the UN decision. The trader will also have to ensure that the expectation of an imminent fall in oil prices is not already discounted in the price, in which case when the event eventually occurs the price will be unaffected.

example **A successful speculation**

			Margin
April 10	Buy one December copper contract at	97.25	$1250
May 31	Sell one December copper contract at	102.25	

Here the speculator made a profit of 5¢ per pound or 5 x $250 = $1250. That is a 100 percent profit on the original margin from a 5¢ move. But losses can be equally spectacular.

Speculators also use spread positions. A simple spread involves a long and short position so that a gain on the long position is offset partly by a loss on the short position or vice-versa. The spreader desires a net gain.

<table>
<tr><td>example</td><td>March</td><td>Buy one May wheat contract at $2.85 per bushel, sell one July wheat contract at $2.80 per bushel</td></tr>
<tr><td></td><td>April</td><td>Sell one May wheat contract at $3.20 per bushel, buy one July wheat contract at $2.90 per bushel</td></tr>
</table>

The net result is a gain of $.25 per bushel. Gain of $.35 on the long position and loss of $.10 on the short position.

Why spread?

The major benefit of spreading is that the downside risk is reduced considerably compared to a net long or short position. Consequently margin is also reduced.

The hedge

A hedge is a futures position that is roughly opposite and equal to the position the hedger has in the cash market. If you are long (own) the cash commodity, your hedge would be to short futures. The hedge is an insurance contract, in effect.

example A farmer notes that the price of wheat is $2.85 per bushel in the cash market. He wants to ensure he can get that price in seven months when it comes to harvest.

	Cash market	Futures market
October	$2.85	Sell wheat future at $2.90
May	$2.44	Buy wheat future at $2.49

In May the farmer sells his crop in the cash market for $2.44. He also got a gain of $.41 per bushel from the futures hedge, i.e. he received $2.85 per bushel. Had he not hedged, he would only have received $2.44.

Summary

The most basic thing to remember about futures is that you buy them (go long) if you think the price will rise, and sell them (go short) if you think it will fall. There is unlimited risk with futures and they should not be traded without a substantial period of paper trading for a full appreciation of the monetary risks.

The basics of options trading and strategies

In this appendix

For those who are interested in options or have just started out, this appendix explains some of the fundamentals. The recommended reading and educational sites listed in other chapters will augment your knowledge.

Objective

- A thorough, basic comprehension of options as the basis of further study.

What is an option?

An option is a contract between the holder and the grantor (called writer of the option). A holder pays the writer a premium for entering into the contract. There are basically two types: call options and put options.

*key terms	Writer
	Strike price or exercise price
	Exercise period or expiry date premium

A call gives the holder the right, but not the obligation, to buy from the writer:

1 within a fixed period of time (the exercise period)
2 a fixed quantity of the underlying security
3 at a fixed price (being the exercise price or strike price).

In the UK, "one contract of the Barclays July 1100 calls priced at 67p" would give the holder the right to buy, any time before a fixed date in July, from the writer 1000 shares in Barclays Bank at a price of 1100 pence (or £11) each. To purchase the option in the first place the holder would have to pay the writer £670 (1000 x 67 pence) as premium.

In the USA equity options relate to the right to buy or sell 100 shares, and in the UK to 1000 shares.

ABC Corp. July 80 calls entitle the holder to purchase 100 shares of ABC Corp. common stock at $80 per share at any time prior to the options expiration in July.

The premium is the maximum loss the option holder can ever suffer.

What's the big idea 'ere?

The general idea is, of course, to make money! The flexibility of options provides many ways in which this can be done. One of the simples ideas is (in the case of a call option holder) to buy shares in the future from the option writer at the fixed exercise price and then immediately sell them in the market at a profit, assuming the market price is greater than the exercise price. In the Barclays' example, if the underlying price of the stock were 1200 at expiry in July, the holder would call for his 1000 shares (at a cost of £11 each) and then sell them immediately in the market at £12 each. Call holders therefore want the underlying share price to rise.

Whether or not the option is exercised the writer keeps the premium.

From the point of view of the writer or seller of the option he is obliged, if "called" upon, to sell the 1000 shares in Barclays Bank, and would receive the £11 per share in return. The writer wants to profit from receiving his premium, and not having to have to sell the holder any shares in the future. The call writer therefore does not generally want the market price to rise above the strike price, otherwise he will have to sell to the call holder at a lower price than he could get in the market. In the Barclays' example a call writer would have to sell at £11 under the option, when in the market he could otherwise have received £12. Call writers therefore do not want the underlying share price to rise.

Similarly, a put option provides the holder the right, but not the obligation, for a fixed period of time to sell to the writer a fixed quantity of the underlying security at a fixed price.

Most people trade in traded options. That means they can sell the option contract itself to someone else if they so wish, without ever exercising it.

Strike price

Each common stock will have numerous options with differing strike prices. The strike price for an option is initially set at a price which is reasonably close to the current share price. The exchange introduces other strike prices at fixed intervals from that initial strike price.

Read the press

Premiums for exchange-traded options are often printed in major financial newspapers. Typically the listing may look like Table A2.1 (only calls have been shown):

Option and closing price	Strike price	May	June	July
ABC	105	$7\frac{1}{2}$	$9\frac{1}{4}$	$10\frac{1}{8}$
$112\frac{3}{8}$	110	3	$4\frac{3}{4}$	$6\frac{1}{4}$
$112\frac{3}{8}$	115	$\frac{13}{16}$	$2\frac{1}{8}$	$3\frac{1}{2}$
$112\frac{3}{8}$	120	$\frac{13}{16}$	$\frac{7}{8}$	$1\frac{3}{4}$
$112\frac{3}{8}$	125	$\frac{1}{16}$	no option	$\frac{13}{16}$

Table A2.1 Premiums for exchange-traded options

In this illustration ABC May 115 calls are trading at $\frac{13}{16}$ or $81.25.

How is the option price calculated and how can I profit?

The price at which an option is bought and sold is called the premium. In the Barclays' example, the option premium was 67p. This is a little like a margin payment.

An option's premium has two components, the intrinsic value and the time value.

Intrinsic value

A call option has intrinsic value if the underlying security price is greater than the option's strike price. A put option has intrinsic value if underlying security price is less than the strike price.

(Share price) < (strike price) = put option has intrinsic value

(Share price) > (strike price) = call option has intrinsic value

---

*key points

Intrinsic value

In the money option (an option with intrinsic value)

Out of the money option (an option without intrinsic value)

So, in our example, if the price of Barclays' shares was 1110p then the option's intrinsic value would be 10p. That is, if you exercised the call you could buy Barclays' shares from the writer at 1100p (strike price) and sell them in the market at 1110p (underlying security price). That is also why an option can never be worth less than its intrinsic value.

A call option would have no intrinsic value, and so only time value, if the underlying price was lower than the strike price. If an option has intrinsic value it is in the money. If an option has no intrinsic value it is out of the money. An option whose strike price is nearest to the underlying price is at the money.

(Share price) < (strike price) = in the money put / out of the money call

(Share price) > (strike price) = out of the money put / in the money call

Time value

The second component of option premium is time value. It is the difference between the option premium and its intrinsic value.

$$\text{Time value} = \text{premium} - \text{intrinsic value}$$

See Fig A2.1 for a diagrammatic representation of these two values.

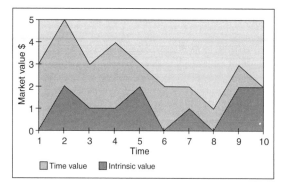

Fig A2.1 Time value and intrinsic value compared

So, in our Barclays' example time value would total 57p. Time value essentially represents the price the holder pays the writer for the uncertainty. It is the cost of risk which the writer faces. Time value erodes as expiry approaches. Therefore an option is a wasting asset in the hands of the holder.

Time value can be calculated using complex mathematical option-pricing models such as the Cox-Rubenstein Model. The variables are risk-free interest rates, strike price, underlying security volatility, and underlying security price, any dividends which would be paid if the underlying security were held (see Table A2.2).

Interest rates	Higher interest rates tend to result in higher call premiums and lower put premiums
Dividends	Higher cash dividends imply lower call premiums and higher put premiums
Volatility	Volatility of the underlying stock places a greater risk on the writer that the stock will expire in the money and so volatility raises premium

Table A2.2 Factors affecting time value

From this then, it follows that at expiry (when time value equals zero) an out of the money option is worthless and an in the money option is worth its intrinsic value. Note than since an option cannot have negative intrinsic or time value the most an option holder can lose (and the most a writer can make) is the premium, no matter how much the underlying price changes.

Relationship between option price and price of the underlying security

The most important thing to remember is that the price of a call tends to rise as the underlying security price rises and the price of a call tends to fall as the underlying security price falls. The price of a put tends to rise as the underlying security price falls and the price of a put tends to fall as the underlying security price rises.

So, why buy an option and not the security? Because an option is leveraged. This means that, for a given percentage change in the underlying price, the option price can change by a greater percentage. You get a bigger bang for your buck.

Going back to our previous example: If the price of Barclays moved from 1110p to 1150p the option price may move from 67p to 97p. That means there would have been a 3.6 percent change in the underlying price and a 44.7 percent change in the option price. You could then decide to sell the option or, as before, exercise it. There would be more money to be made from selling it.

The price of an option rarely has a 1:1 correlation with the underlying security price. The delta is the rate of change of the option price to the rate of change of the underlying price. So, for example, a delta of 0.5 means that if the underlying price rises by, say, 10 cents then the option price will change by 5 cents. Obviously the greater the delta then the greater the bang for your buck. However, the delta is greatest for in the money options, i.e. those with the most intrinsic value and, therefore, the most costly options. Consequently, a balance has to be drawn when calculating potential returns between the delta and the price of the option.

An example will clarify the situation.

---

example

Barclays' shares are trading at 1110p.

July 1100 calls are 51p; July 1200 calls are 16p.

If tomorrow, the price of Barclays' shares were to be 1200p then it may be that the July 1100 calls trade at 123p (average delta of 0.8) and the July 1200 calls trade at 22.5p (average delta of 0.25).

The return from the July 1100s is 141 percent and from the cheaper 1200s is only 41 percent. Of course in this example we have only estimated deltas and have ignored costs and bid ask spreads. Nevertheless it gives you some idea of the balances that need to be drawn. For modest moves one is likely to profit most from just in the money options.

Example of leverage

To own 100 shares of a stock trading at $30 per share would cost $30 000. By the same token, to own a $5 option with a strike price of $30 would give you the right to buy 100 shares for $30 at any time up to expiry. The option would only cost $500 ($5 × 100 shares).

If, one month after the option is purchased, the stock price has risen to $33, then the gain on the stock investment is $300, or 10 percent. However, for the same stock increase the option may have increased to $7, for a return of $200 or 40 percent.

Leverage has parallel downside implications, of course. If in our last example the stock fell to $27, the loss on the stock investment would be $300 or 10 percent. For this $3 fall the option may now be worth $3 itself, i.e. a 40 percent loss.

Vive la différence

Options are in many respects similar to stocks for the purposes of trading for profit (see Table A2.3).

Similarities	Differences
Orders to buy and sell are handled by brokers	Options have a limited life
Trading is conducted on regulated exchanges	There are fewer options than stocks
Pricing mechanisms are open and transparent	Option owners have no rights over a company, they are not shareholders
Investors have the opportunity to follow price movements second by second if they so wish	Option holders receive no dividends

Table A2.3 Vive la différence

Strategies

Although there are only two types of options, calls and puts, there are a lot of option strategies. With options you can protect your stock holdings from a price decline, you can prepare to buy a stock at a lower price, you can increase income on your current stock holdings, you can participate in a large market move, even if you are unsure beforehand which way the market is going to move, and of course you can participate in a stock rise or fall.

Kids' stuff

The simplest strategy is to go long a call or a put. That means you buy to open a call or put. If you go short (write the option) then you sell to open a call or put. In the latter case, you have to post margin since your losses are potentially unlimited. It is a lot safer for the lay investor to be long puts than short calls even though on both you profit from falling prices. A common options strategy already discussed is to purchase calls to participate in an upward price movement.

Locking in a price

Another popular use of calls is to lock in an attractive stock purchase price. Imagine that ABC is trading at $55 and you believe it is about to increase in value, but you do not have the funds to buy 100 shares. You know you will have the funds in six months, but you are afraid that if you wait that long the shares will have already increased in value.

You see that the option expiring eight months hence at the strike price of $55 costs $3, i.e. $300. If you buy one contract and then in six months the price of the stock is $70, you could exercise your option and buy the stock for $5500 + $300. Whereas if you did not have the option and had to buy the option in the open market, it would have cost you $7000. So you just made a saving of $1200.

Puts to protect unrealized profit in a stock position

Imagine you bought ABC stock at $50 and it is now trading at $70. You fear there may be a short-term fall in the price but do not want to sell your holding on the hunch. By buying an ABC put option with a strike of $70 for $2 you are assured of being able to sell you stock at $70 no matter what happens to the stock price. If the price does not collapse, then you will have lost the premium $2 x 100 = $200. Consider it an insurance premium.

But if the stock had fallen to, say, $55, you could have sold it at $70 per share, less $2 per share for the option premium. That means you would have earned an extra $13 per share with the option than if you had not taken out the insurance policy.

Option strategies are beyond the scope of this book but I will mention a few to give you some idea of what the professionals and experienced non-professional can do with options.

Hedge
A hedge is a position where one position profits if the other position loses. So a hedge can be thought of as an insurance against being wrong. For example, a hedge against a long call, one could sell short a different call or go long a put.

Straddle
Buy to open an at the money call and buy to open an at the money put. You profit by increased volatility in the underlying price irrespective of direction. The strategy is a guts if the options are both in the money and a strangle if they are both out of the money.

Bull call spread
Long in the money call and short out of the money call. Profit from upward price movement. This becomes a bull call calendar spread if the short call is nearer month than the long call.

Bear put spread
Long in the money put and short out of the money put. Profit from downward price movement. This becomes a bear put calendar spread if the short put is nearer month than the long put.

Various other strategies exist depending on one's views as to volatility, direction, and extent of risk one wishes to take. These strategies have some unusual names, e.g. butterfly, condor, iron butterfly (buy a straddle and sell a strangle because you expect a limited size move), combo, ladder, box, conversion, and reversal.

See the further reading section if you want to investigate options further.

key terms

Leverage

In the money

Out of the money

Time value

Intrinsic value

Call and put

Exercise period

Writer

Premium

Volatility

Strike price or exercise price

Summary

The essential things to remember about options are that they are leveraged; decrease in value the longer they are held; calls increase in value with the underlying asset, and puts do the opposite.

Minimum essential hardware and software to get you going

Online trader problem

- What gear do I need to get up and running as an online trader?

In this appendix

You can't sky dive without a plane and you can't trade online unless you are online. In this appendix, we look at the minimum hardware a trader needs for trading. You could, of course, go higher spec, that's up to you.

Hardware

Computer

A PC and not a Mac is recommended

For reasons best known to Bill Gates and Steve Jobs, most trading software is not Mac compatible. It makes far more sense therefore for you to stick with a PC (which are always Windows compatible) than buy a Mac and be disappointed.

For trading, a classic Pentium processor 100 MHz is sufficient

Although there are as many new processors produced each year as sex allegations against Bill Clinton, it remains the fact that old is best (when it comes to processors, at least). Newer, faster processors are great for games, but not necessary for trading.

It is not necessary to buy the latest PC

It will go out of date and you will be paying a premium. Instead, buy a cheaper PC and upgrade later.

32Mb RAM is minimum requirement

RAM is the temporary memory in which your computer runs programs; a little like room to play. The more room the computer has, the quicker it can get things done. However, 32Mb is more than enough. If want you can buy more, but you do not strictly need it for your trading.

3 Gb hard drive or larger is best

The hard drive is where all the programs and other things you save are stored. Storage space is useful as over the years we all tend to collect clutter, such as bric-a-brac, spouses, etc. 3 Gb would probably last most traders until they decide to upgrade their computers (and their spouses).

Windows 98 operating system is recommended

When it comes to programming trading software, most programmers use the latest version of Windows.

CD drive useful, x16 or faster

Most programs and much data are provided on compact disks. A 16-speed one is more than adequate although many computers now come with nothing slower than 32 speed. DVD players not needed as yet.

Soundcard and speakers

Soundcard and speakers can be useful for online news broadcasts, and more trading software, such as metastocks using videos of advisors. However it is not essential.

Many internet sites provide live broadcasts, and a soundcard and speakers will add even more value to the internet. Fortunately, these are often thrown in with new computers, or are available pretty cheaply.

Modem

Internal or external modem, it makes little difference

It does not matter from a trading point of view whether the modem is some electronic wizardry inside the computer, or a separate attachment outside it. The latter option may be better if you are not keen on opening up the computer.

At least a 56k modem is recommended

You do not want to be waiting all day to receive trading news and information. The speed of your modem is important to ensure you can have an outside life, too.

Consider ISDN or ASDL if you can afford it

This is digital connection that is faster than a normal modem. It is lightning fast, but can be expensive.

Monitor

15" minimum required

Beyond 15" and monitors start getting very pricey. Less than 15" and you start needing a magnifying glass. With 17" screens becoming standard, you could even go to 19".

Anti-glare and anti-radiation filter essential

The radiation emitted from the trading screen that is on all day may cause you to grow a second head, but there is no evidence that two brains would improve your trading performance. So buy a filter, and keep your uni-head good looks.

Printer

Laser printer most expensive but best for drawing charts

These printers have dropped dramatically in price and are best when it comes to printing out all those trading charts and for reading text.

Inkjet minimum requirement

If the purse strings are tight an inkjet is likely to be adequate for printing charts and text.

Internet service providers

ISPs provide access to the internet

ISPs not only provide access to the internet but they also have their own member-only content, rather like an online magazine. Many organize events like online special guest stars.

IAPs or internet access providers

Unlike internet service providers, these do not have their own content, but only provide internet access. However, they are cheaper than ISPs and are sufficient for trading purposes.

An unlimited online time plan is required

ISPs and IAPs usually have different charging plans, many charging by the number of hours spent using their services. Since we traders may spend a lot of time online, the cheapest pricing option is almost always the "unlimited" time plan since there is only a monthly flat fee for access.

Take a free trial of internet service providers

Try before you buy is the advice here. Almost all ISPs and IAPs permit a one-month free trial, and it is best to use this to test their reliability.

Compare access providers

The web-site www.consumeratings.com ranks internet access providers according to numerous variables. It can be a good pointer for narrowing down the providers you would like to test before subscribing.

Browsers

Software

Browser software turns data into pictures and so lets you view sites in graphics, sound, and video. They are a great and essential part of trading, as important to trading as the remote control is to television viewing.

The latest versions of Internet Explorer or Netscape Navigator are recommended

If you are looking for a browser then you want the most sophisticated one and one catered for by almost all internet sites. So Internet Explorer and Netscape Navigator are highly recommended. They are available free from cover CDs of most internet magazines.

Bookmarks

It is essential to familiarize yourself with bookmarks in Netscape Navigator or Favorites in Internet Explorer for the purposes of managing information.

PC TV

If you are trading from home, then you could have a TV playing in a small section of your monitor, such as CNBC or Bloomberg, to keep you up to date with the markets. Not essential, but I like it, also great for watching the Simpsons while you write books – only kidding, you, the reader, have my undivided attenti . . .

Summary

This chapter covered the basics for those already familiar with computers and the internet. Most entry-level PCs will cover all the aspects mentioned here and you will not have much to worry about. People with older systems may need to upgrade, however.

Orders: Your order is my command – sometimes

Online trader problems

- Too much slippage – i.e. the difference between the price on the screen and the price you eventually end up paying to buy and receiving for a sell.
- Not knowing if there are better ways to place an order in the market.

In this appendix

Since we are trading short time frames, the price we get for our orders is particularly important, because we are relying on small price movement for our profits. So, it is especially important we fully understand order types and use them to our advantage. One of the many problems online traders have is the lack of knowledge about order types. So, in spite of having a good system their profits, in reality, often fail to reproduce what their system said should happen in theory.

There are many different ways to place an order to enter or exit a trade. In this appendix we examine some of them. However, you do not need to memorize them all since some are more useful than others and indeed many firms only permit the most popular ones.

First some jargon . . . before more jargon

You are "long" the market when you own a product, e.g. I am long 3 March S&P 500s. There are several terms that all mean the same thing to describe your sale of this long position: "liquidating," "covering," "closing out," "offsetting." After that you would be "flat." If you never had a long position and then made the sale you would be "short" that product.

All or none order

An order to "fill" either the entire order, or none of it.

example Buy 500 McDonald's at 59½ all or none.

When used

When you want to buy all 500 shares at the specified price, but not less, or want to average out at the price.

Day order or good for day order

If the order cannot be executed before the end of the day, it is canceled.

example Buy 500 McDonald's at 59½ good for day. If the current price is 60–60⅛ and the bid price fails to reach 59½, then the order will not be executed.

When used

If you want to enter at a specific price, but only for the day in question, because the next day you may revise the order.

Good till canceled order or open order

This order stands until the customer cancels it or it is executed.

example Buy 500 McDonald's at 59½ good till canceled. If the current price is 60–60⅛ and the bid price fails to reach 59½, then the order will not be executed until the price reaches 59½ or the order is canceled by the customer.

When used

As with the good for the day order except the customer wants to keep the order open until he cancels it.

Limit order

An order to buy or sell at a specific price or a better price.

> **example** Buy 500 McDonald's at 59½ limit. This means the broker can pay a maximum of 59½. You may get "filled" at a better price if you are lucky.

When used

Where the buyer or seller wants to place a limit on the price he wants to buy or sell at. Often this order is used for when a position is to be opened at the market opening when the price could gap. The order ensures the trader is not "blackmailed" by the market by having to accept whatever price the market dictates.

Market order

The order to buy or sell at the best price available in the market, immediately. This is the most popular type of order, but can be disastrous for the day trader as he is at the whim of the market. In a way he is asking the market to charge him what it wants. Would you go to a second-hand car dealer and say, "Charge me whatever you like"?

> **example** Buy 500 Yahoo! at market.

When used

When the buyer or seller wants to buy or sell as soon as possible.

Market on open order

A market order to execute during the "opening," usually the first minute of the session.

> **example** Buy 50 Amazon market on open.

When used

Just as the order says, to enter the market as soon as it opens. There is a substantial danger of getting a very poor price.

Stop order

An order that becomes a market order as soon as the price is reached. Can be buy stop or sell stop orders.

example   Buy 500 McDonald's at 59 stop.

When used

When the buyer or seller wants the order executed at market price only after a certain price level has been reached. For instance, if you are long 100 Cisco at 80 and don't want to risk a loss greater than $5 per share, then the order would be to sell 100 Cisco at 75 on a stop. This is a sell stop.

Another way to use stop orders is to enter markets. For instance, if you were looking to buy some AOL shares, believing that if they move above $100 and they are presently trading at $90, then you would place an order to buy 50 AOL at 100 stop. Once the price of AOL reached 100, your order would become a market order.

Summary

Although many types of orders have been examined, most traders only ever find the need for one or two types, these usually being market and limit orders.

Recommended reading

Online trading

Trading Online ***
Alpesh B Patel
FT Prentice Hall 2000

New and revised version of the best-seller covering all the steps to trading from getting set up to monitoring positions.

The Complete Idiot's Guide to Online Investing *
D Gerlach
Que 1999

Que are known for their computer books and this venture appears to be a bandwagon thing. But the *Complete Idiot's* guides can be clear and more comprehensible if you are, um, well, a complete idiot.

Investing Online ***

S Eckett

FT Pitman 1997

Encyclopaedic in coverage and an excellent reference tool with a focus on global investing.

Short-term trading

Long-term Secrets to Short-term Trading ***

L Williams

Wiley 1999

Larry Williams is a proven trader. An excellent title, because he clearly knows his stuff and trades off it.

Day trading

How to Get Started in Electronic Day Trading ***

David S Nassar

McGraw-Hill 1999

Nassar owns a day trading firm, and this book is written from the perspective of a man who know his business.

Electronic Day Traders' Secrets **

M Friedfertig and G West

McGraw-Hill 1999

This book has a series of interviews with day traders from Friedfertig's own brokerage company. A lot of trading psychology here, but light on strategies.

Day Trade Online *

C Farrell

J Wiley 1999

Farrell is a young man who trades for a living. Some good content in here, but lay-out, design and substance lacking in other respects.

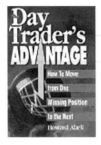

The Day Trader's Advantage *
H Abell
Dearborn Financial 1996

A little dated from the ubiquitous Abell, who seems to be a full-time author producing what feels like one book per month. Focusses on the trading psychology aspects of day trading.

The Electronic Day Trader ***
M Friedfertig and G West
McGraw-Hill 1999

A very popular title indeed for day traders from a day trading brokerage owner.

The 22 Rules of Day Trading Online **
D Nassar
McGraw-Hill 1999

After the success of his earlier day trading book, David Nassar returns with a different format.

The Compleat Day Trader *
J Bernstein
McGraw-Hill 1999

A very good seller, with an unusual title. Covers not only day trading but also risk management.

High Impact Day Trading **
Robert Barnes
Irwin 1996

This book highlights the author's Mountain Valley system, going for longer moves and ignoring shorter ones. It has proved a very popular title.

Trading psychology

The Bhagavad Gita ***
Various editions

Although written more than 2000 years ago, and not directly about trading, I found it to be one of the most useful "trading" books I have ever read. It largely discusses discipline – how and why – and the benefits of discipline. Since a lack of mental discipline is one of the major downfalls of traders, this is likely to be a very profitable read.

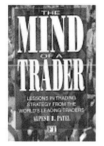

The Mind of a Trader ***
Alpesh B Patel
FT Pitman 1997

Advice on becoming a better trader from the world's leading traders, including Pat Arbor, Chairman of the Chicago Board of Trade, and Bill Lipschutz, former Global Head of Forex at Salomon Brothers who made on average $250 000 each and every trading day he was there, for eight years!

The Disciplined Trader **
Mark Douglas
Prentice Hall 1990

An extremely good book. Written in a very intelligent fashion and gets away from Mickey Mouse fashion psychology. Deserves a far higher profile than it has to date received.

The Inner Game of Trading **
Robert Koppel and Howard Abell
Irwin Professional 1997

Includes interviews with some leading traders, but its value comes from the analysis of psychological difficulties traders are likely to encounter. Definitely recommended.

Classics

Reminiscences of a Stock Operator ***
Edwin Le Fevre
Wiley 1994 (reprint edition)

An undoubted classic. The fictionalized trading biography of Jesse Livermore, one of the greatest speculators ever seen. While dated (it was written in 1923), it nevertheless provides some insight into the difficulties encountered by traders. A very enjoyable read.

Extraordinary Popular Delusions and the Madness of Crowds and Confusion de Confusiones **
Charles Mackay and Joseph de la Vega
Wiley 1995

Explores crowd psychology and how that affects market movement. While its examinations are 300 years old, it is highly relevant today. Short and interesting.

The Art of Speculation **
Philip L Carret
Wiley 1997

Apparently highly regarded by Victor Niederhoffer. However, in spite of that, I would recommend it as a good read.

Manias, Panics and Crashes **
Charles Kindleberger
Wiley 1996

Why do the economists, statisticians and government nerds always get it wrong? This book does not provide any answers, but it does provide some insights.

Stocks

Getting Started in Stocks **
Alvin D Hall
Wiley 1997 (3rd edition)

A very good primer for stocks. Hall has a clear style and injects humor now and again to alleviate the rigor.

Winning on Wall Street *
Martin Zweig
Warner Books 1997 (revised edition)

Zweig is famous for his market reports and for being one of Schwager's market wizards. I found a copy of this book for $11.99 – you can't go wrong.

Futures

Getting Started in Futures **
Todd Lofton
Wiley 1997 (3rd edition)

Very clear and easy to understand as well as giving lots of information for delving deeper.

A Complete Guide to the Futures Markets ***

Jack Schwager

Wiley 1984

This book covers fundamental analysis and technical analysis as well as spreads and options. Characteristic of Schwager's books, it is very thorough.

Commodities trading

Mastering Commodity Futures and Options **

George Kleinman

FT Pitman 1997

This book is very well-presented indeed. A little like a textbook in style, but covers the ground very well for both beginner and intermediate user.

The CRB Commodity Yearbook **

Knight-Ridder

Knight-Ridder annual

A very useful reference guide to commodities. Filled with data, charts, tables, and articles on trends and strategies. If you are serious about commodities you should have this.

Soybean Trading and Hedging **
Wheat Trading and Hedging **
Corn Trading and Hedging **
Investing in Wheat, Soybeans, Corn **

William Grandmill

Irwin Professional 1988, 1989, 1990, 1991 (respectively)

A series of books by the appropriately named Grandmill for commodity traders. Grandmill provides details of the commodities, and his own systems for picking entry and exit points. If you think it is best to become an expert in one area of commodity trading then books such as these should be a good starting point to developing your skills and understanding.

Options

Traded Options **
Peter Temple
Rushmere Wynne 1995

For those trading options on LIFFE. Thorough and explains all the basics, from what options are to buying software.

Getting Started in Options ***
Michael Thomsett
Wiley 1993

Again, very clear and easy to understand. An excellent start for beginners.

McMillan on Options ***
Lawrence McMillan
Wiley 1996

Brands itself as the "Bible" of the options markets. Why do publishers refer to their books as the "Bible" of something? I wonder if they mean only a minority of people will ever read the book but more are supposed to and it competes with equivalent books for the rest. Anyway, that aside, McMillan goes beyond explaining the basics about options and actually applies a degree of critique. Should consider if you are a beginner.

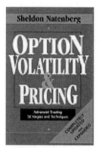

Option Volatility & Pricing Strategies *
Sheldon Natenberg
Probus (1994 edition)

Natenberg is a leader in this field. This book is definitely for the more advanced trader wanting to dig into option mechanics.

The Options Markets *
John Cox and Mark Rubinstein
Prentice Hall 1985

This is a classic text on options. The book is about valuing options – these authors, of course, created the famous Cox-Rubinstein option pricing model.

All About Options **
Russell Wasendorf and Thomas McCafferty
Probus 1993

The good thing about this book is that it covers both strategies as well as some of the background mechanics behind options, such as what happens on the trading floor.

Advanced Options Trading **
Robert Daigler
Probus 1993

This book moves beyond basics and discusses some strategies generally used only by the professionals. That does not mean a private investor using them will have hit upon some sector – so beware. But if you are interested in knowing more than just the basics, this book is better than most.

Trading Options on Futures *
John Labuszewski
Wiley 1998

This covers treasuries, currencies, and commodities. I think if you are trading options on futures there is more to it than understanding options and understanding futures. The whole is greater than the sum of the parts, and therefore a book such as this is added value in being exclusively written for one trading sector.

Make Money with S&P Options *
How to Make Money with Corn Options *
Make Money with Soybean Options *
William Grandmill
Irwin 1989, 1990, 1990 (respectively)

If you are concentrating on one of these areas and feeling like you need something specifically addressing your trading needs, then these books were written with you in mind. Grandmill is a prolific writer and knows what he is talking about.

Trading and Investing in Bond Options *
M Anthony Wong
Wiley 1991

This title covers strategies, pricing models and details the peculiarities of trading this market using options.

Options on Foreign Exchanges *
David DeRosa
Probus 1992

Not to leave out the currency option boys and girls, this market specialist covers valuation of options, pricing of currencies, as well as how the various markets work. Probably useful for the beginner and intermediate level trader in forex options.

Commodity Options **
Larry Spears
Marketplace Books 1985

This one is for beginners who may not have settled on a particular commodity and want an overview.

Technical analysis

Technical Analysis Explained **
Martin Pring
McGraw-Hill 1991

The first half of this book is more relevant than the second. While a little disappointing, nevertheless provides insights not available elsewhere.

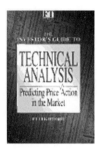

The Investors Guide to Technical Analysis **
Elli Gifford
FT Pitman 1995

While the book uses UK companies to illustrate points, it is nevertheless useful to traders in any country. Thorough, comprehensive, and easy to read and understand. Good as a starter and for more advanced study; however, it is not mathematical.

Technical Analysis from A to Z **
Steven B Achelis
Probus 1995

A good introductory guide which is comprehensive. Lot of pics of indicators.

The Visual Investor **
John Murphy
Wiley 1996

Former CNBC presenter provides a good primer on technical analysis. He draws on one of the key aspects of technical analysis – it is visual.

Encyclopedia of Technical Market Indicators **
R Colby and T Meyers
Business One Irwin 1988

As would expect of a book claiming to be an encyclopedia this is an exhaustive study. It will be most useful if you want a good overview before settling down on a few chosen indicators.

Martin Pring on Market Momentum *
Martin Pring
McGraw-Hill 1993

Aimed at the user who has chosen momentum as one technical indicator from his arsenal and wants to learn more, this book is typical Pring; clear and useful. Unfortunately Pring maintains his habit of stylized artificial charts instead of giving more real market illustrations to make his points.

Momentum Direction and Divergence *
William Blau
Wiley 1995

Definitely for the advanced user. If, after learning about oscillators, you want to take things further and uncover some mathematics to better understand their weaknesses then this is a good book.

Stock Market Trading Systems **
Gerald Appel and Fred Hitschler
Dow Jones Irwin 1980

This is a classic and discusses the price ROC and moving average trading systems among others. It is always best to go to the original source to gain insights which later secondary texts are likely to miss.

The Moving Average Convergence-Divergence Method ***
Gerald Appel
Signalert 1979

Appel is the creator of this highly popular trading method, and this book explains it straight from the source's mouth. Useful if you plan to place large weight on this indicator in your own trading.

Volume Cycles in the Stock Market **
Richard Arms
Equis 1994

Arms is a well-known technical analyst and this book delves in depth into volume. If volume analysis is something you intend using then this a very good source of information.

How to Use the Three-Point Reversal Method of Point and Figure Stock Market Trading **

A.W. Cohen

Chartcraft 1984

Despite the cumbersome title this is a useful book on this popular method of drawing charts.

Understanding Fibonacci Numbers **

Edward Dobson

Traders Press 1984

Not too difficult to understand if Fibonacci fascinates.

New Strategy of Daily Stock Market Timing for Maximum Profit **

Joseph Granville

Prentice Hall 1976

Another one of the technical analysis gods. This book discusses on balance volume in particular. Granville created that indicator, so who better to learn more about it from?

Japanese Candlestick Charting Techniques ***

Steven Nison

New York Institute of Finance 1991

Steve Nison is regarded as the expert on Japanese Candlesticks. This book is very clear and very easy to understand. Nison uses actual charts and not stylized fictional ones. He also focusses on how and when the chart indications fail. The book helps an understanding the rationale behind technical analysis, and why it works, and why it does not. Excellent.

New Concepts in Technical Trading Systems **

Welles J Wilder

Trend Research 1978

Wilder is very highly regarded in the technical analysis world. Here he explains and interprets numerous indicators, including RSI.

Fibonacci Applications and Strategies for Traders *
Robert Fischer
Wiley 1993

Taking Fibonacci study further with this book. While you do not necessarily need such detailed knowledge, if you are going to use it, you may as well know all there is.

Volume and Open Interest **
Kenneth Shaleen
Irwin 1996

A good starter to investigating these two popular statistics in technical analysis. Probably unavoidable if you are trading futures.

Point and Figure Charting **
Carroll Aby
Traders Press 1996

Both a beginners' guide and a reference book for this method of plotting prices.

Traders' profiles

The Mind of a Trader ***
Alpesh B Patel
FT Pitman 1997

As noted at the beginning of this appendix, the world's leading traders share their insights, not merely in a question and answer format but in an easy-to-understand category-based layout. You can see at any point what exactly is being discussed and, with a summary at the end plus author comment, the conclusions are made clear.

Market Wizards
New Market Wizards ***
Jack Schwager
Harper Business 1993, Wiley 1995 (respectively)

An absolute must. Fascinating, although since it's in a question and answer format you are left to draw many of your own conclusions.

100 Minds that Made the Market *
Kenneth Fisher
Business Classics 1991

Biographical in nature and the profiles are somewhat short, but nevertheless a good bedtime or holiday read.

The Super Traders *
Alan Rubenfeld
Irwin 1992

Nine profiles of traders from diverse backgrounds. While a little bit too biographical, nevertheless makes for a good read.

Floor trading insights

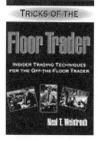

Tricks of the Floor Trader ***
Neal Weintraub
Irwin 1996

One of the few books of its kind. Gives the outsider a view of what the insider does. Provides knowledge which is useful to know.

The Trader's Edge **
Grant Noble
Probus 1995

Some very useful insights into what they do on the floor. A good insider's view and useful pointers on some of the advantages.

Trading Rules **
William Eng
FT Pitman 1995

While some of the rules will be familiar, others provide valuable enough information to justify buying this easy-to-understand book.

Smug traders' glossary

Speak the jargon and be smug

It may not be enough just to trade well and make money to be smug; occasionally you may not be able to flash your wad of cash and have to fall back on the following lingo to maintain that air of smugness – so, go ahead: read, learn, and be smug.

Abandoned option   Where an option is neither sold nor exercised but allowed to lapse at expiry.

Accumulation A technical analysis term describing a stock whose price is moving sideways.

Acid test ratio A measure of financial strength. Also known as the quick ratio. Cash plus short-term investments plus accounts receivable divided by current liabilities for the same period. All other things being equal, a relatively high figure may indicate a healthy company.

Active channels A feature of Internet Explorer 4. Internet sites that are selected as channels provide special IE4 content. Gates wants to lead internet TV – hence the term channels.

Active market Securities trading with a relatively high degree of liquidity, the major benefit of which is narrow spreads. A term of art rather then precision.

Aftermarket Also known as "secondary market," refering to the trading in a security after its initial public offering.

All or none Order instructing the broker to buy or sell the entire amount of the order in one transaction or not at all.

American depositary receipt (ADR) Effectively like owning in dollars stocks of non-US-listed companies. A popular form of owning shares of foreign companies.

American option An option that is exerciseable at any time within its life. Can be traded outside Europe and are.

American Stock Exchange (AMEX) Located in New York, this is the third-largest US stock exchange. Shares trade in the same "auction" manner used by the larger New York Stock Exchange unlike the Nasdaq's "market-making" methods.

Arbitrage The purchase in one market of an instrument and the sale in another market of it or a closely linked instrument in order to profit from the small price differentials between the products in the two markets. Arbitrage profits usually only exist for a small time because someone usually scoops on them since they are "locked in."

Arbitrageur A trader engaged in arbitrage. They seek to make a lot of small, quick profits.

Ask The lowest price at which a dealer or market maker will sell a security (also, "bid," "offer").

Assign To oblige a call option writer to sell shares to the option holder, or to oblige a put option writer to buy shares from a put option holder.

At the close Order instructing to be filled as close as possible to the, um, close of a particular security, or to be canceled otherwise.

At the market An order to buy or sell at the best price obtainable in the market.

At the open Order instructing the transaction to be filled in one of the first trades for a particular security, or to be canceled otherwise.

Averaging Where a price moves against a trader and he trades more of the stock to enlarge his position but to lower his overall entry price. It will mean he will have a lower exit price at which he can make a profit.

Away from the market Trade orders that cannot be executed because they are above or below the current bid or ask. For example, a limit order to buy 50 shares of AOL at $105 when the best offer is $109 will not be filled and is said to be "away from the market."

Backbone A high-speed connection within a network that connects all the other circuits. Another name for a "hub." A central connection from which "spokes" or connections radiate.

Bandwidth The capacity of a network to carry data. If your pipes are clogged (low bandwidth) then things take forever to load. It's an issue not of length but of width.

Basis point Used to calculate differences in interest rate yields, e.g. the difference between 5.25 percent and 6.00 percent is 75 basis points.

BBS A bulletin board system. A little like an electronic notice board. You "post" messages to the board and everyone who subscribes to the board can view them.

Bear(ish) An individual who thinks prices will fall.

Bear market A market in which prices are falling.

Bear spread An option position where it is intended to profit from a falling market. Usually the position involves the purchase of a put at one strike price and the sale of a put at a lower strike price.

Beta This measure the stock's volatility to the market as a whole. A beta value greater than 1.0 represents greater volatility than the general market; less than 1.0 represents less volatility than the general market.

Bid An offer to purchase at a specific price.

Big Board Nickname for the New York Stock Exchange. Greatly adds to your smugability if you only ever refer to the NYSE as the Big Board. The ignorant will instantly fall admiringly at your feet. That a person of flesh and blood could know so much!?

Black-Scholes Pricing Modelability A mathematical model used to calculate the price in theory of an option. The main input variables are: the risk-free interest rate, volatility, dividends, time to expiry, the strike price, underlying price.

Block As in "the sale of a block of shares." A transaction involving a large number of shares or other security. Often blocks are bought or sold at a discount to the current market as an accepted cost of trading a large number of shares.

Boiler room Derogatory term to describe a brokerage firm where investors are aggressively solicited over the telephone with high-pressure telephone sales tactics. Smug traders, stay well clear.

Bounce What happens to mail which for some reason (e.g. wrong e-mail address) cannot be delivered.

Breadth Comparison of issues traded on a stock exchange on a given day to the total number of issues listed for trading. The broader a market move the more significant it is.

Break A sudden fall in price.

Breakout When the price moves out of its recent range. Sometimes signals further moves in the direction of the breakout.

Broker An individual who executes customers' orders.

Bucket shop Slang term for a disreputable brokerage firm that regularly engages in illegal practices, such as selling customers stock it may own at a higher than market price without disclosing the fact.

Bull(ish) An individual who believes prices will rise.

Bull market A market in which prices are rising.

Bull spread An option position where it is intended to profit from a rising market. Usually the position involves the purchase of a call at one strike price and the sale of a call at a higher strike price.

Buy in A person having to buy a security because of an inability to deliver the shares from a previous sale of said shares. Often associated with short sellers.

Call option (calls) The right, but not the obligation, existing only for a fixed period of time, to purchase a fixed quantity of stock at a fixed price.

Cash flow per share The trailing 12-month cash flow divided by the 12-month average shares outstanding. All other things being equal, a relatively high figure, growing steadily, is sign of a growing and healthy company and may indicate a rising share price.

Churning Illegal practice by a broker to cause excessive transactions in a client's account to benefit the broker through increased transaction fees.

Clerk An employee of an exchange's member firm, who is registered to work on the exchange floor.

Closed When referring to a position this means one has made an equal and opposite trade to one already held and so has no more exposure to the market on that trade.

Co-mingling Illegal act of combining client assets with those of the brokerage to boost the fiduciary's financial standing.

Contrarian An individual who generally believes it is usually better not to do what the majority is doing, because the majority does not make money.

Cookie According to conspiracy theorists, a cookie is a small piece of software that is downloaded from a web-site to your computer's hard drive that tells the web-master all your hidden and deepest secrets. According to everyone else, a cookie is a small piece of software that is downloaded from a web-site to your computer's hard drive that tells the web-master your username, password, viewing preference, and one or two other things. It means you do not have to enter the same information over and over again.

Crossed market The highest bid is greater than the lowest offer due to buyer and seller imbalance. Usually only lasts a few seconds until the market "sorts itself out."

Current ratio The ratio of total current assets divided by the total current liabilities for the same period. A measure of financial strength. All other things being equal, a relatively high figure would indicate a healthy company.

Cyberspace William Gibson's name in his fantasy novel *Neuromancer* (William Gibson, 1994) to describe what is now known as the internet.

Daisy chain Creating the illusion of trading activity in a stock through collusion of a number of brokers. Yes, it is illegal.

Day trade(r) A position that is closed the same day it was opened.

Deep discount Often, internet brokers that charges commissions far less than full service or discount brokers; as cheap as you can get.

Delta The change of the options price for a change in the underlying price. A delta of 0.5 means a 10-point move in the underlying causes a five-point move in the option.

Depreciation Not a measure of spousal dissatisfaction. An accounting measure used to reduce the value of capital expenditure for the purposes of reclaiming tax.

Diversification Reducing risk by spreading investments among different interments. Not putting all your eggs in a few baskets.

Dividend ex-date This is the date from which a purchaser of the stock will not be entitled to receive the last announced dividend. Appropriately, when a stock goes ex-dividend its price falls by approximately the value of the dividend.

Dividend growth rate A measure of corporate growth. The annual positive change in dividend paid to stockholders. All other things being equal, an increase should indicate a growing company and should be reflected in rising share price.

Dividend rate This is the total expected dividends for the forthcoming 12 months. It is usually the value of the most recent dividend figure multiplied by the number of times dividends are paid in a year, plus any extra dividend payments.

Dividend yield This is calculated by dividing the annual dividend by the current price and expressing the figure as a percentage.

Domain Part of a web or e-mail address. Separated from the rest of the address by dots.

Dotted quad A set of four numbers separated by dots that constitutes an internet address, e.g. 123.32.433.234.

Down tick A trade in a security that was executed at a lower price than the previous trade; same as "minus tick."

Drawdown The reduction in trading capital as a result of losses.

Dynamic HTML This makes web designers very excited. It means bits of web pages can be made to do things like change color when you point to them. These bits are therefore dynamic and not static (unlike their designers, who are definitely not dynamic).

Encryption These scramble data and so keep them private from those who want to sneak a peek or drop an eave (eavesdroppers).

EPS Earnings per share. A measure of corporate growth. The value of corporate earning divided by the number of shares outstanding. All other things being equal, a growing figure reflects a healthy growing company and should be reflected in the share price.

European option An option that is only exercisable at expiry.

Exercise Where the holder of an option uses his right to buy or sell the underlying security. Also means to workout.

Expiry The date up to which a trader can exercise his option.

Flame An e-mail that is abusive or argumentative. Usually includes the words "You are a . . ." somewhere in the message.

Flamefest The same as a flame orgy.

Flat (1) A market where the price of a stock and/or its volume have not changed significantly over a period of time; (2) to no longer hold a position in a particular security or account.

Floor broker A member who executes orders for clearing members.

Floor trader An individual who trades on the floor of an exchange either for himself or a company.

Free speech An issue relating to the internet about which the US Congress spends inordinate quantities of time. Essentially, the concern is to give rights to those who would deny them to others, including those who granted them.

Freeriding Rapid buying and selling of a security by a broker without putting up funds for the purchase. Yup, it is illegal.

Front running Buying or selling securities ahead of a large order so as to benefit from the subsequent price move.

FTP (file transfer protocol) The protocol for sending files through the internet.

Fundamental analysis Forecasting prices by using economic or accounting data. For example, one might base a decision to buy a stock on its yield.

Futures A standardized contract for the future delivery of goods, at a pre-arranged date, location, price.

Gap Where a price opens and trades higher than its previous close.

Geek Also known as a net nerd. They were the kids everyone hated at school, who wore thick black-rimmed spectacles and were extremely uncool. They would also get sand kicked in their faces and were so unpopular no one would be seen dead with them – sometimes not even their parents. Now the sand has settled, and it has become clear that because they were unpopular they spent all their time studying, and can now be considered some of the wealthiest people on the planet, with the fastest flashiest cars. They definitely had the last laugh.

Gross margin A measure of company profitability. The previous 12-month total revenue less cost of goods sold divided by the total revenue. All other things being equal, a decrease in gross margins could indicate troubled times ahead.

Hedge Protection against current or anticipated risk exposure, usually through the purchase of a derivative. For example, if you hold DM and fear that the price will decline in relation to the dollar you may go long dollar. You would then make some profit on your long position to offset your losses in holding DM.

Hit the bid When a seller places market orders with the intention of selling to the highest bidder, regardless of price.

Implied volatility Future price volatility as calculated from actual, not theoretical, options prices. The volatility is implied in the prices.

In and out Term for day trading in a security.

Income per employee The income after taxes divided by the number of employees. A measure of corporate efficiency. All other things being equal, a greater the figure, or a growing figure, indicates a more efficient company and should be reflected in a rising share price.

Initial margin requirement Amount of cash and securities a customer must have in his/her account before trading on margin.

Initial public offering (IPO) First sale of stock by a company to the public.

Insider Person such as a corporate officer or director with access to privileged company information.

Insider share purchases The number of shares in the company purchased by its insiders – officers and directors – over a stated period of time. All other things being equal, a relatively large move may indicate a forthcoming upward move in the stock price.

INSTINET A "fourth stock market" allowing members to display bid and ask quotes and bypass brokers in securities transactions. Owned by Reuters.

Institutional net shares purchased This is the difference between institutional share purchases less institutional share sales in the company over a stated period of time. All other things being equal, a relatively large move may indicate a forthcoming upward move in the stock price.

Institutional percent owned This is the percentage of shares owned by all the institutions taken together. It is a percentage of the total shares outstanding. All other things being equal, a relatively large move may indicate a forthcoming upward move in the stock price.

Intranet This is a collection of computers connected to one another and usually located in a company or other organization. Unlike the internet, the network is private and not principally intended for the public.

Java An island or a coffee bean or a programming language developed by Sun Microsystems. It allows users to do lots of clever things with web pages.

LAN (local area network) A network of computers operating up to a few thousand meters from each other.

Level I quotes Basic service of the Nasdaq stock market that displays current bid and ask quotes.

Level II quotes Service of the Nasdaq stock market that displays current bid and ask quotes and the bids and asks from all market makers in a particular stock.

Level III quotes Service of the Nasdaq stock market that allows a market maker or registered broker–dealer to enter a bid or ask on the electronic trading system.

Limit The maximum permitted price move up or down for any given day, under exchange rules.

Liquid market A market which permits relatively easy entry and exit of large orders because there are so many buyers and sellers. Usually a characteristic of a popular market.

Long A position, opened but not yet closed, with a buy order.

Long-term debt to total equity A measure of financial strength. The long-term debt of the company divided by the total shareholder equity for the same period. All other things being equal, a relatively high figure may indicate an unhealthy company.

Margin A sum placed with a broker by a trader to cover against possible losses.

Margin call A demand for cash to maintain margin requirements.

Mark to market Daily calculation of paper gains and losses using closing market prices. Also used to calculate any necessary margin that may be payable.

Market capitalization This is the product of the number of shares outstanding and the current price.

Market order *See* At the market

MIME Multi-purpose internet mail extensions. This enables you to attach files to e-mail.

Momentum An indicator used by traders to buy or sell. It is based on the theory that the faster and further prices move in a particular direction, the more likely they are to slow and turn.

Moving average A system used by traders to determine when to buy and sell. An average (simple, exponential, or other) is taken of the closing (or opening, or other) prices over a specific number of previous days. A plot is made based on the average. As each day progresses, the moving average has to be recalculated to take account of the latest data and remove the oldest data.

Net After expenses, or short for the internet.

Net profit margin A measure of profitability. Income after taxes divided by the total revenue for the same period. All other things being equal, downward pressure on the net profit margin could provide advance warning of impending share price decline.

Netiquette Proper net behavior. For instance, swearing is neither appropriate etiquette nor is it netiquette.

Network A group of computers connected to each other so that their users can access each others' machines.

Offer A price at which a seller is willing to sell.

Off-line browser A browser that permits viewing of sites previously downloaded without being connected to the net.

Open position A position that has not yet been closed and therefore the trader is exposed to market movements.

Overbought/oversold A term used to mean, broadly, that a stock is likely not to advance further and may decline (overbought) or advance (oversold).

Position Trades which result in exposure to market movements.

Price, 52-week high This is the highest price the stock traded in the last 52 weeks. It may not necessarily be a closing high, it could be an intra-day high.

Price, 52-week low This is the lowest price the stock traded in the past 52 weeks. Could be an intra-day low price.

Price to book ratio The current price divided by the latest quarterly book value per share. All other things being equal, a relatively low figure may indicate the stock is undervalued.

Price to cash flow ratio The current price divided by the cash flow per share for the trailing 12 months. All other things being equal, a relatively low figure may indicate the stock is undervalued.

Price to earnings ratio The current share price divided by earnings per share before extraordinary items, usually taken over the previous 12 months. All other things being equal, a relatively low figure may indicate the stock is undervalued.

Protocols A set of rules with which two computers must comply in order to communicate.

Push technology The internet can be quite a passive experience, needing the user to log onto a site to determine if changes have occurred, or to download information. With push technology, the browser can be set to automatically download data from a set site.

Put option A right, but not the obligation, existing for a specified period of time, to sell a specific quantity of stock or other instrument at a specified price.

Pyramiding The increase in size of an existing position by opening further positions, usually in decreasing increments.

Quick ratio A measure of financial strength. Cash plus short-term investments plus accounts receivable divided by current liabilities for the same period. All other things being equal, a relatively high figure may indicate a healthy company. *See also* Acid test ratio.

Return on assets A measure of management effectiveness. Income after taxes divided by the total assets. All other things being equal, a relatively high or growing figure may indicate a company doing well.

Return on equity A measure of management effectiveness. Income available to shareholders divided by the total common equity. All other things being equal, a relatively high or growing figure may indicate a company doing well.

Return on investments A measure of management effectiveness. Income after taxes divided by the average total assets long-term debt. All other things being equal, a relatively high or growing figure may indicate a company doing well.

Revenue percent change year on year A measure of growth. The revenue of the most recent period less the revenue of the previous period divided by the revenue of the previous period. All other things being equal, a growing figure indicates a growing company and should be reflected in a rising share price.

Sales per employee A measure of company efficiency. The total sales divided by the total number of full-time employees. All other things being equal, the greater this figure the more efficient the company.

Sales percent change A measure of corporate growth. The value of sales for the current period less the value of sales for the preceding period divided by the value of sales for the preceding period, expressed as a percentage. All other things being equal, a growing figure indicates a growing company and should be reflected in a rising share price.

Scalper A trader also seeks to enter and exit the market very quickly and thereby make a lot of small profits.

Seat Exchange membership that permits floor trading.

Server A computer that shares its resources with others. The resources may be disk space, or files, or something else.

Shares outstanding The number of shares issued less those held in treasury.

Short An open position created by a sell order, in the expectation of a price decline and so the opportunity to profit by purchasing the instrument (so "closing out") at a lower price.

Short-term debt The value of debt due in the next 12 months.

SMTP (simple mail transfer protocol) The standard set of rules for transferring e-mail messages from one computer to another.

Speculator An individual who purchases financial instruments in order to profit. Often used to refer to a non-professional. Sometimes used derogatorily.

Spread The simultaneous purchase of one contract and the sale of a similar, but not identical, contract. Depending on the exact combination, a profit can be made from either a rising or falling market.

Stop order (stop-loss orders) An order left with a broker instructing him to close out an existing position if the market price reaches a certain level. Can be used to take profits or stop losses.

TCP/IP (transmission control protocol/internet protocol) A set of rules used to connect to other computers.

Technical analysis Method used to forecast future prices using the price data alone (for example, by plotting them on a chart and noting direction) or using the price as an input in mathematical formulae and plotting the results. *See also* Fundamental analysis.

Technical rally or decline A price movement resulting from factors unrelated to fundamentals or supply and demand.

Tick The smallest possible price move.

Total debt to equity ratio A measure of financial strength. The total debt divided by total shareholder equity for the same period. All other things being equal, a relatively low figure is a sign of a healthy company.

Total operating expenses A measure of the cost of running the company. All other things being equal, a lower figure is preferable to a higher one.

Trendline A line on a price chart indicating market price direction. The line connects at least three price points which touch the line, with no prices breaking the line.

Volatility A statistical indication of probable future price movement size (but not direction) within a period of time. For example 66 percent probability of a 15 pence move in three months.

Webcasting This is the internet trying to be older – like TV or radio. Instead of viewing pages, you view a stream of data in the form of radio or video. Unfortunately, the infrastructure is lacking to make this a popular alternative to TV and radio.

Whipsaw A price move first in one direction, and, shortly thereafter, in another direction thereby catching traders wrong-footed. Such markets may be termed "choppy." Such effects often give rise to false buy and sell signals, leading to losses.

Index